OPENINGS

OPENINGS

A Guide to
Psychic Living in the Real World

JOAN PANCOE

Modern Mystic
New York

Printed in the United States of America

FIRST EDITION

Library of Congress Cataloging-in-Publication Data

Pancoe, Joan, 1953–
     Openings: a guide to psychic living in the real world / by Joan
Pancoe.
     ISBN 0-9644936-0-8
     1. Channeling (Spiritualism)   2. New age movement.   3. Mental
healing.   4. Pancoe, Joan, 1953–   . I. Title.
     BF1286.P36   1995   133.9'3—dc20   95-3846

Design by Laura Hammond Hough

Modern Mystic
P.O. Box 1748
New York, NY 10009

10 9 8 7 6 5 4 3 2 1

Dedicated to all the Senders and Receivers
who made this book possible

If a tree falls in the forest
and no one is there but me,
does it make a sound?

Acknowledgments

I owe a debt of gratitude to the readings of Edgar Cayce and to the Seth books of Jane Roberts, which I read in 1972. Through them, I became familiar with trance channeling just as my own psychic development was beginning. They aided me immeasurably, paving the way for me to travel my own path with much less fear.

The Zen meditation technique of mindfulness has been my daily mainstay for well over the last decade, helping me maintain serenity and peace of mind and keeping me in the moment. Practicing chi gong and Taoist meditation for the past two years has allowed me to maintain and channel increasingly greater amounts of life force, or *chi*, without burning out. I am deeply grateful to my teachers, Bruce Kumar Frantzis and Susan Rabinowitz, of the Taoist Arts Center in New York, for their guidance.

The universal readings could not have been done without the energy and support of many people close to my heart. My unending thanks go out to Jim Rush, Gene Hardesty, Dagmar Williams, Suzanne Mauer, Lynn Philo, Irene Politis, Cathy Nicklaus, Wendy McLoud, Harold and Phyllis Davis, Lynne Wood Block and Lawrence Block, Jerrold Mundis, and Luna.

I owe a special thanks to all those who have supported my

work through the years and to those who have allowed me to use excerpts from their personal readings. I would like to express my gratitude to my family, especially my mother, Gari Swygert, for their love and unconditional support.

I would also like to acknowledge and express my appreciation to Chuck Thompson, Bonnie Levy, and Rick Pracher for helping make the production process for *Openings* relatively painless, easy, and fun. And, of course, this book would not have been possible in its present form without the expertise, patience, humor, and unique perspective of my editor, Joan Arnold.

Contents

Part VII. READINGS FOR THE COMING AGE 277

Appendix 311

Author's Preface

This book is the outgrowth of my spiritual and psychic journey. Through time, I have developed the ability to channel information from higher energy sources into the physical plane for those who want personal readings. I am also a channel for readings of a universal nature, and these make up the core of the book. I hope that they will be an aid to those who are seeking a life of greater depth and purpose.

Most of these readings were originally recorded on tape. The rest were done earlier, by automatic writing or dictation. For the purposes of clarity and continuity, I have transcribed and edited them, using punctuation to emphasize the theme and tone of each. In most of the personal readings, names have been changed to protect privacy. Words in brackets are my additions and were not in the original. Other pertinent information is included at each reading's beginning or end.

For each session, I have included the date, the names of those present, the procedure for inducting the trance, and the statement of focus for the reading's direction, which was read aloud by whoever was present. For the reader to get the most out of the readings, each chapter needs to be read and absorbed as a multidimensional capsule, so that the reader can digest the layers of depth within the vibrational language of the reading on all levels of the being—not just the mental.

I have no doubt that these readings are catalysts that will stimulate shocks of awareness in those who are ready to move. Even now, through the process of rereading and editing them, I am continually reminded of levels of awareness that I tend to forget, within the daily challenges of being human. The readings ignite and inspire me with a clarity of consciousness to remember why I am here in the physical plane. They are openings for expanded dimensions of beingness in the "real" world, for anyone who wants more from living here and now.

I know from my own experience that it is possible to live comfortably in the physical plane as a psychic being, with faith in one's inner voice and trust in one's intuition. The expanded consciousness that has come to me from living this way has enriched my humanness, expanded my focus and freedom, and enhanced my sense of responsibility with an enlivening sense of humor. I know that it is the birthright of each of us to live this way as part of the ongoing evolution of consciousness. And, as my personal readings always remind me: "There is no time like the present to begin."

Joan Pancoe
New York City
October 1994

Editor's Introduction

When I first met Joan Pancoe, I was in despair. Like many who seek the unconventional help of a psychic, I felt backed into my own tiny corner and yearned for a larger perspective. Years of psychotherapy had produced many satisfying changes, but my knottiest problem—with intimacy—had resisted professional help, my own earnest efforts, and the compassion and advice of good friends. At the end of another lousy relationship, I was frustrated and crashingly depressed. I came because a friend had told me this particular psychic was no lightweight who would divine a tall dark stranger in my future. More out to educate than mystify, she could guide me through a rich process of self-discovery.

To enter Joan's storefront in New York's East Village, one goes down a few steps from the throbbing city sidewalk, into a front room she uses as a painting studio. Tubes and brushes stand on the windowsill; drawn green and blue blinds give the room a cool, underwater quality. A painting in progress leans on the large professional easel. You take off your shoes before stepping into a cozy warren that serves as both living quarters and work space. Once the door to the outside world closes, there is a sense of utter privacy.

The stuccoed walls are hung with her paintings—a forest

scene inhabited by a woman surrounded by a surreal glow, a face that suggests images of aliens—colorful, beneficent, dream-like. Scattered around the room are candles, fossils, and small Olmec, Hopi, and Balinese statues. Under a framed photo of the Sphinx is a stereo and tape recorder, a microphone ready, the power on.

I came in August 1992 for a reading, to decide whether to embark on the ten-session series she had developed, called psychic therapy. True to form, she had tuned in to me before I arrived and could sense the depth of my pain. We talked, and she explained the session's protocol and asked me to write down my questions. I realized that the environment and her presence worked together to shift me into a slightly altered state. She placed the microphone near her, turned on the tape recorder, lay down on the floor in the dimly lit room, and went into trance. In that slightly flat, remote tone that seems to mark a channel's vocal style, her words zeroed in on the essence of my issues—fear of a loss of self.

In a relevant, hopeful reading, the way was laid out: commit to a spiritual path, and the partner I had always yearned for would follow, from a "willingness to open the heart as an act of love and commitment to the higher self. For, having gone through it before, hasn't the personality always come out the other side, risen from the ashes? So it will be again, at a higher level still, and from this the purposes in this incarnation will be fulfilled and the experience transmitted to others in the life and through the work."

As a movement teacher for over twenty years, I have led students on journeys into the unknown to help them tap their own deeper resources. So I knew what to look for when seeking a teacher for myself. Joan's subject matter may be ethereal, but like any good educator, she promotes independence. Once she's taught clients how to do a reading, she will no longer do readings for them and will only guide them through their own. While one part of me yearned to surrender to someone who offered a way out, another watched vigilantly for signs of muddleheadedness in a realm that easily tends toward the vague or flaky. Joan's clarity, professionalism, and sense of structure made me decide to take this strange new walk under her guidance.

Oscillation between the logical and the suprarational is a thread that runs through Joan Pancoe's work and life. Born in Chicago in 1953 of Jewish parents, she first came to New York at age seventeen to attend Barnard College. She was headed toward a career in law, but her freshman-year affair with an older man—then thirty-four-year-old Jim Rush—led her away from the profession she had been groomed for by her stepfather, a federal appellate court chief judge. "Jim tried to get me to read Seth and Edgar Cayce," she recalls, "but I was an atheist, a hedonist, a pothead hippie. My mother named me after Joan of Arc, who heard voices, but there was no way I was going to get into the psychic arena."

An LSD trip in February 1973 changed all that. Jim and Joan were visiting a friend in Kutztown, Pennsylvania, when Joan took LSD for the first time. "At one point in the trip," she says, "we were sitting at a table with friends, eating spaghetti and meatballs. I looked at Jim, and the universe cracked open." Jim remembers a "sudden popping sound—like a cannon— and we were in seven different places simultaneously. In each of them, we recognized one another totally, in a different relationship each time."

It was Joan's spiritual awakening. "I did my first reading," she recalls, "saying, 'We're on the seventh plane now.' I didn't even know what that meant at the time, but I know now it's the highest plane where separate entities are still manifest, before we become one with the Godhead. 'I don't know how long I'll be able to maintain this level of communication, but it is for us to acknowledge our eternal connection and our eternal nature. That is all this experience is for, to remember what we already know.' Since that moment twenty years ago, the crack in my perception of the universe has never closed; I have never had one iota of doubt about the eternal nature of all souls."

From there, Joan's psychic development was slow and

steady. The pair traveled to Virginia Beach, where they stayed for nine months. During that time, Joan began to realize that her psychic shift had changed her perceptions. Among those she met, she could see "the energy within everyone's face move. That changed their features so I could actually see different aspects of their souls, like flipping cards. I learned how to freeze the faces, look at them, and read their past lives. Whole scenes would open up behind them—throne rooms, battlefields." Jim suggested that she draw these images in a sketchbook, which she did. Realizing that she could channel her psychic vision through her art, Joan returned to New York to study drawing and painting at the Art Students League and the New School. In 1975, Jim decided to take his own psychic ability seriously and began working with Gene Hardesty, a clairvoyant who conducted weekly gatherings. This little spiritual group had a Christian bent. "We met in the Ansonia Hotel in a rented room," says Joan, "and sang hymns." At age twenty-two, Joan was beginning to get a sense of her gift. "At that point," says Jim, "I had been around the field much longer than she had. When I met her, my own development accelerated radically. But hers seemed to emerge almost intact at once." Hardesty did her astrological chart and saw, from a grouping of planets in the eighth house, Joan's natural psychic ability.

Curious about her talent, Hardesty decided to test her. "After the group," recalls Joan, "we used to go to Howard Johnson's in Times Square and have a bite to eat." In this unlikely environment, she remembers, "Hardesty said, 'You're a natural psychic. I want you to do a reading.' I said, 'I can't do a reading. I don't know what you're talking about.' He said, 'I have the keys of a friend of mine. I want you to hold them in your hand and close your eyes.' " In this technique, called psychometry, the vibrations of an object can tell a psychic about its owner. "So I took the keys, closed my eyes, and for ten or fifteen minutes described what I saw. They were symbolic images, like a movie." When she opened her eyes, she saw Gene's amazement at their accuracy.

On one evening in 1976, Joan and Jim decided to experiment with a Ouija board. But what emerged was garble. Frustrated, Joan picked up a pen and tried automatic writing. On the page these words appeared: "Each and every one of us has something to deliver. I am Joseph. Tonight we will start." Readings from this phase (see Part V, Chapter 1) directed them to form psychic study groups. Jim began to lead astrology classes and Joan to lead a weekly group with exercises she improvised for healing, dream, and energy work. Though she sometimes channeled for those who sought her out, the responsibility of dealing with so much human pain was too much for her twenty-four-year-old psyche.

In 1978, she dropped psychic pursuits and traveled to Europe to paint and study art in Salzburg. She and Donovan, a man she had met in New York, spent one romantic year living in a Portuguese fishing village. She painted, and he composed music. But the idyll was marred by her periodic migraine headaches—what she has since come to realize was a symptom of her blocked psychic energy.

When they returned together to New York, her relationship with Jim ended. Extrasensory adventures had been intertwined with their romance, and, always dependent on Jim as her generator and anchor, she felt shaky channeling without him. But the relationship with Donovan—headed for a conventional future out of sync with who she really was—didn't feel right either, and it ended in September 1980.

Now, for the first time in her twenty-seven years, she was completely alone, and she went through a dark time of heavy drinking, drugs, and acting out. Waiting tables had always been her financial mainstay, but when she was fired from a lucrative waitressing job for stealing, she realized she had hit bottom. A friend helped her see her frayed physical and emotional state and get sober—which she has been since January 1981.

That same year, while waitressing at the Carnegie Tavern, she met another struggling artist, Suzanne Mauer. The two became friends. "She was having problems with her mother," says Joan, "and I guess my heart went out to her. So I started doing readings for her—not professionally, just as a friend. We would sit in my den and she would tell me what was troubling her. I would close my eyes and channel past-life information about whatever she was working on with her mother. It was as if I'd never taken a two-year break."

Though interested in the metaphysical, Suzanne says, "I had never really done past-life work before I met Joan. What came out in her back room just rang true." It was Suzanne who first suggested that Joan do the more general universal readings that compose the heart of this book. Taking dictation as Joan spoke, Suzanne ultimately "got tired of writing in the dark, by the light of a candle." It took the channels coming through in the reading to figure out that it was better to use a tape recorder. "It was such a relief," says Joan, "to just let the words come out."

But these were the only readings Joan was doing. "Jim wasn't talking to me," she says, "and professional psychic work was on the shelf."

In the winter of 1982, Joan developed a frightening physical symptom: her left leg became numb and so swollen she could barely stand. Her livelihood was threatened, and a doctor recommended surgery—a route she preferred to avoid. So Suzanne suggested doing a reading about it. "Basically," recalls Joan, "the reading said, 'You're a very stubborn girl, and this is the only way we could get your attention. But if you make a commitment to do psychic work, we guarantee that all earthly needs will be met.' When I decided to go for it, my brother told me about a small family trust that could help me." In the summer of 1982, Joan stopped waitressing, dedicated herself to her new profession, and began to see clients for readings.

Something as mundane as an apartment lease sparked a reunion with Jim, and their relationship evolved into its present form—a psychic partnership that continues to nourish each of them.

Not content with channeling for those who sought her out, she has since evolved psychic therapy—her ten-session format combining psychodynamic and spiritual techniques with past-life regression work. What she has developed does not replace psychotherapy's step-by-step process of exposing the assumptions from the past that drive our behavior. But for veterans of therapy who have bumped into its lack of a spiritual context, it is a fascinating synthesis that can access memories hidden in the body and, through the imagination, explore new levels of perception. For me, it catalyzed an opening. By gaining access to a crucial childhood memory, I saw one underpinning of my fear of closeness. I returned to psychotherapy to continue the process, and—for the first time—opened myself to a loving relationship.

Editing this material, with its odd, impersonal voice and many repetitions, presented a unique challenge. The most important task was to preserve the meaning of each reading, yet make elusive concepts accessible. Also important was keeping the rhythmic repetitions that allow the reader to savor and deeply understand sometimes complex, sometimes deceptively simple ideas.

Though the spiritual realm interests me and informs my work as a writer and teacher of the Alexander Technique, I don't read channeled material as a matter of course. But as I worked on the book, it also worked on me, reminding me that "there is more going on in the play of daily life than is physically manifest." It also changed my understanding of the voices that come through in readings—away from the idea of superior, separate deities in the sky, toward seeing them as higher aspects of ourselves. As Joan's growth has proceeded, she perceives her sources as less fixed and more fluid, stations on the psychic band that emanate from a single origin, one whole of which we are a part.

Whatever these presences are that she channels, they represent a supremely compassionate perspective that can touch that part in each of us, guide our perceptions, and inform our choices. The daily madness and crushing conflicts we experience take on meaning as part of a learning process. Readings can give a tough-minded nudge toward a truer path, with a refreshing generosity that can inspire us in our inevitable struggles. From them we have the benefit of the infinite view: that we are here to learn, to grow, to evolve, and to return to our Source.

Joan Arnold
Brooklyn, New York
April 1994

Part I

DEALING WITH
REALITY

1

THE NATURE OF TIME

"To the degree that one is willing to accept the moment fully, to this degree will one's perceptions flower and live in the eternal."

Commentary

The channel giving this reading—the Sympathetic Bridge Recorder—while acknowledging time as simultaneous and infinite, articulates the reason for the sequential perception of time as a tool for human development.

The reading I originally channeled on this topic two weeks earlier—October 22—was not recorded because I failed to press the record button on my tape recorder. I was afraid the material was lost. But this reading reassured me that nothing universal is ever lost. It is just recorded again, in a slightly altered form, in its proper time.

November 5, 1983
Sophia present

"I'm going to count from 1 to 10, where you will please focus through the eyes of the Sympathetic Bridge Recorder and do a reading on the nature of time and how it affects physical focus."

▼

There is no time like the present to do this reading.

Let us say, as the channel well knows on the deepest levels, that the essential nature of our interaction is open-ended. In doing individual readings for personalities who come to her, in terms of concept and receptivity, timing is everything. But for universal readings, always remember that the concepts are universal, and the language that expresses them may alter slightly due to seasonal vibrations. The key here is the clear receptivity of this channel system.

Time is a sequence mechanism that allows souls to explore physical focus in physical form. The nature of all time is simultaneous in its universal manifestation. The sequence mechanism of time came into being as the optimum tool possible for souls to experience being in three-dimensional form and to move through this space to its fullest range and depth. A finite series of moments—passing consecutively and never to be experienced physically again—allows growth that would not be possible if the true nature of the eternal moment was perceived. Outside the physical plane, there is no past and no future in terms of memory or focus. But there is the past present moment and the future present moment, all of which can be perceived when not in physical form, beyond the vibrational limitations of space or gravity.

From our perspective, all historical periods are going on *now*. Just as there are cycles of exploration and development along the reincarnational line, the karmic line, the sexual line, and in the development of the ego and spiritual perception, there is also a line of development involving the physical focus. Expanding range in the plane allows the personality to develop to the most finite focus within the physical moment, and then to expand the line: to appreciate the simultaneous nature of all time.

Time is also a mechanism through which a human being can learn, while experiencing the life of the personality one is presently in. So time allows the race to fully develop within the given moment. This is necessary until the point where the personality can perceive and fully appreciate each moment, regardless of whether that moment is finite or infinite. The paradox is that within physical existence, it is *both*. Within the physical focus, it is both finite and infinite.

The optimum development of the use of time is to allow the blinkers of perception to expand, to perceive the eternal moment in any given moment and, with this recognition intact in the cells of consciousness, to utilize the eternal moment as unique, one that will never come again. One of the human race's great experiments is to explore the full range of time in physical form. Space is another, and matter within space, and learning to deal with finite space and, as in the finite moment, to utilize it fully. Then perception can expand within matter to infinite space.

To the degree that one focuses fully in the moment, in the space one is in—as the only time and the only space—to this degree of absolute perceptual acceptance and intensity can the clarity of this process be fully experienced in its universal and eternal sense.

In closing, we will say that for those personalities who are interested and willing to grow in time, space, and the physical form, to the degree that one is willing to accept the moment fully, to this degree will one's perceptions flower and live in the eternal.

One of the true joys is to experience the infinite while in the physical form. While those not incarnate are able to have the expanded perception of simultaneous time and space at all times, the experiencing of such while in the physical form is really one of the keys to the experiment now in progress and en masse to the evolution of consciousness.

▲ ▲ ▲

2

ACCEPTING WHAT IS

"Accept what is as the hook for the eternal."

Commentary

The source for this reading identified itself only as "souls with strong and fond ties to the reincarnational process."

At the time of this reading, I was moving along my path, yet wondering what the point of it all was. All I could see was that many people I knew seemed more focused on external striving than inner growth. This judgmental view not only distanced me from others and slowed my own development but also manifested physically as pressure on the left side of my head and a feeling of being split in two.

Since 1976, I have periodically felt pain and pressure in the head that is connected with my psychic process. I have learned from experience that these sensations are due to a block of energy—one of a psychic's occupational hazards. I did this reading to help clear one such blockage. The act of channeling releases this pressure, as the reading's energy and information flow in. What I didn't know before this was that this blocked energy was also a blocked perception of others. That knowledge helped me get back on a clearer track. Not only did I stop feeling a pressurized split in my head, but I also realized unconditional acceptance could be a potential way of life.

Now, when I can grasp the concept in a given moment (not

every moment, mind you) that "this is it—this is all there is," I really do experience an expanded perception within the moment that is eternal . . . and the direct knowledge that the key to feeling eternal is accepting what is.

This reading is both personal and universal. Using my development as a springboard, the reading's information—like many of these personal readings—can apply to all who want to use it.

June 14, 1984
Sophia present

"I'm going to count from 1 to 10, where you will please focus on the channel now waiting and do a reading on a topic of the channel's choice."

▼

There are many different ways to view the earth plane based upon the vibratory nature and the quality of the perceptor's development.

It is in line with the channel Joan's current development to view the levels of perception generally available to those now incarnated. And to recognize that from our view—as souls with strong and fond ties to the reincarnational process—we view this process as a means to generate power in other realms that benefits the Creative Forces.

Let us say that we, here, view the present situation on earth as an accomplished fact. There are certain pieces of the puzzle on the earth plane that we must choose to work with as they are, accepting and recognizing their shape and size in proportion to the puzzle as it is, and to change them based on that acceptance.

As the channel Joan moves through the plane, she can recognize that each personality in the plane is a piece of the puzzle—*as is*. From our level, we work with those in the plane, accepting them as they are. The channel now views those in the plane with a certain, shall we say, loving intolerance for her role as a piece in the puzzle. There is a split along the left side of the being, particularly facial, as this is the soul side, the eternal side. [The right side is the personality side in me, although it's not the same for everyone.] As the levels of perception change, a split is now occurring in how the channel views the earth plane and her own role.

The regenerative process of the Creative Forces of All That Is is ongoing. It has been so from before entry into the plane and will continue to regenerate on other levels and in the plane—no matter what direction the experiment now in progress takes—along which line the human race is now evolving.

For a new level of perception, it is important first to see and accept what *is*, and from this recognize that the personality who sees clearly what is can also view the full range of the puzzle from a higher development, as we are viewing now.

The primary function of this reading is to guide the channel and others who utilize this information to realize that the regenerative forces of All That Is move into the plane and work through personalities in whatever way possible.

The ability to be a catalyst for optimum change is keyed to the finite perception of what is as an absolute reality, and then the acceptance that *this is it*. From this, all veils will fall. With this acceptance, there is also the strong suggestion that one keep one's sense of humor as this new level of perception balances. For the channel Joan, it will be a process of two or three months.

In the past week, a disconnection on certain levels has been experienced. But from our level, we see that perceptions are shifting and that the ego is still clinging tightly to the view that there is no point to striving for quality transcendental states when, as far as the eye can see, everyone else is scurrying around in their pieces of the puzzle. It is also important to recognize that the channel is both a piece in the puzzle and *not* in the puzzle, as is every other personality. The only qualifying difference is the level of perception.

In dealing with those one comes in contact with daily, the acceptance of an equal level of what is will fuel the recognition that there is so much more to matter than the physical state can reveal—a perception that comes from the regenerative forces. Regeneration can only occur through those personalities who accept and deal with the reality of what is, and from this channel fuel in the higher vibrations of perception. But this is the hook: to get the attention of those whose blinkers of ego consciousness have allowed them to see only the physical focus in this particular lifetime.

Accepting that the channel of physical seeing is valid (because even on this level the regenerative forces do move through, though mostly in the subconscious and dream states) triggers the conscious widening of perception, but not if there is a split within the being, expressed through intolerance for those who cannot yet see.

This is the key right now: to accept that eternal perception can be reached by understanding that this is all there is; for the channel Joan to accept the moment to leap from the perception that now splits her. For through this acceptance, personally and in dealing with others, the eternal nature of any moment will flow in. It is time to allow the eternal side of the being to flow into the ego personality on all levels, waking and sleeping, for this bridge, which is causing the fear, to be accepted with grace, as the next step in the ongoing process. We may take questions.

"Are there any other suggestions for the channel?"

The suggestion is—from this day, from this hour, from this minute—to accept what is as the hook for the eternal.

▲ ▲ ▲

3

ENLARGING PERCEPTION WITHIN THE MOMENT

"Fueled by the Creative Forces, the way is now open. There is no excuse for any personality who is ready to move, in terms of the past or of past debts. The given moment will unravel all."

June 29, 1983
Sophia present

"I'm going to count from 1 to 10, where you will please focus on the channel now waiting and do a reading on a topic of the channel's choice."

▼

For most personalities in the plane at any time, the prevalent nonchalance for taking responsibility for personal reality is an expression of madness or contempt. On the deepest level, there is always a fear of returning to the source and of the need to continually evolve until reality is seen and acted upon with clear vision. This will not be as a mirroring for others, and not solely, as in the Eastern philosophies, of karmic return. It is a recognition that the race will continue to be connected to the earth plane until individual souls can see that the only way to free themselves from the reincarnational cycle is in the present moment. To see in the dealings, and in the seeing, and in the thinking on a daily basis that here are the fruits reaped for all past, all present, and all future repercussions.

If the veil were lifted so that each personality could see clearly the vast effect of each thought, dream, or movement in daily life as it reverberates through time and space, from the core out to all those close to them in this lifetime, to their past and future reincarnational lives, they would connect thinking and feeling first within the being, so that these are not different disconnected vibrations, but flow together. So the view of compassion combines with the practical aspects of the mind/ego. This integration will make it possible for any personality in any lifetime to cut through all past reverberations in the present moment.

So what we suggest here is that personalities who wish to move to a new level of awareness first attune the mind with the heart, with the emotions, so that one can communicate and see clearly and rationally with a compassionate view. New perception is possible only from this stance, making it possible for the Creative Forces to move into the plane. Some will be able to perceive, on the subconscious level, that there is a way out— without pushing, without trying to communicate rationally in words—but only through compassionate vibrations. Blockages of communication will clear, speeding the growth process—not just internally, but with all those one comes in contact with.

We are dealing, of course, primarily vibrationally at this point. But remember that to establish a core network of fellow travelers in which to enlarge the scope of human existence, the vibrational level is the place to start.

In manifesting this compassionate view, that this moment is the clearinghouse connected to past and future, the perception can be enlarged. One need not verbalize this with those one meets, but only pulse it out and be aware of it at all times. It is in acting on this awareness in any situation that the unwinding of the blocks and knots within one's physical being can be done. It is not necessary to unwind them with the original partners in the karmic dance. For those who choose to take responsibility for their reality at any point, in any lifetime, it is a way to speed up the reincarnational process.

Fueled by the Creative Forces, the way is now open. There is no excuse for any personality who is ready to move, in terms of the past or of past debts. The given moment will unravel all.

We will just reiterate, in closing, that it is now possible to vibrationally communicate this to others: that for those on the line of upward mobility of the reincarnational cycle, to speed the process, the Creative Forces are fueling in enough compassionate light energy, through those who are receptors for it, to channel in the vibration that, taking responsibility for one's feelings and one's thoughts with others in any given moment, the unwinding karmic process can be unraveled in any lifetime.

▲ ▲ ▲

Commentary

Like many of universal readings, this one made no sense to me when I returned from trance. That's because while channeling, I am so detached from my personality that my usual physically focused mental capacities are bypassed. But in this reading there were new concepts for me that are, like any new idea, disturbing on the rational level.

From the creative process I've learned that if I paint something new in a light trance state, without thinking, the results at first are disturbing. Then I get excited. Now I know, whether painting or channeling, that when it doesn't make sense visually or rationally, I'm onto something. It may, in its newness, disturb or inspire, but it can strike universal chords that expand perception.

4

EXPRESSING INNER GROWTH OUTWARD

"One who sees clearly and expresses one's vision vibrationally changes the nature of the vibration of the encounters one moves through."

December 26, 1982
Suzanne present

"I'm going to count from 1 to 10, where you will please read from the channel now waiting on the potentials for manifesting inner growth outward as physical reality."

▼

We are here to tell you that the essence of expressing inner growth outward is in the quality of the vibrations of the daily communications. By raising consciousness to a level where with every movement of the dance, whatever is undertaken or done, the consciousness acknowledges growth in the being by communicating to others through the vibratory structure of the interactions that there is more going on in the play of daily life than is physically manifest. In this recognition, encounters will take on more depth.

While others may not be aware of the development of consciousness in the individual who is expressing this depth, they will experience it on other levels. If one is in a room full of people, all there for various reasons, and one sees clearly the group reality, the combined energy in the room, all the plays being

acted out there, it only takes one seeing clearly for it to be recorded on the ethers as a manifest physical reality in terms of
the historical nature of the Akashic Records. One who sees
clearly records in all its depths. One who sees clearly and expresses one's vision vibrationally changes the nature of the vibration of the encounters one moves through. This is truly the
highest expression of inner growth outward: through the seeing, and through the expressing and acting appropriately based
on the seeing.

Just as the inner growth process is constantly flowering,
changing, and flowing through the seasons of the being, so too
is one's view changed by the inner growth as well as by the seasonal climate of all those one encounters. In clear attunement
with the center of one's growth process can one see clearly the
layers of interaction in physical existence. From the center out
into the *vision* of physical reality will the actions taken be available with the optimum layers of depth, enhancing and enlarging the vibratory repertoire of the soul consciousness in
physical reality.

There is a clear parallel between how willing one is to
deal with one's growth and how clearly one will be able to
see the world around. The internal blinkers to the self are equivalent to the outward blinkers. So if one is unwilling to see
clearly the processes of letting go or one's own pain, one
will also not see clearly in the world the processes that could
alleviate or help, but only those that seem to enhance or reinforce the process one is in. There is a direct parallel between the personal view of physical reality and the view of
one's growth process. The bottom line in this endeavor—
expressing inner growth outward—is to see clearly at what
point the self is in the process of self-discovery and growth
on any given day, hour, or minute. If one can see this, then
the vision outward to the plane will also be clear. Layers of
illusion, levels of depth, the combined reality of all those one is
dealing with will be seen and cut through. All the layers of
reality will blend. That gestalt can only be seen by the con-

sciousness, the physical being who sees clearly his own point of development.

Souls who are not now incarnate can have an overall view of the gestalt nature of physical reality. But only one who is here with the soul consciousness can have this unique view of the growth process within the being, this crystal-clear gaze that scans the panorama of the physical repertoire with a loving eye inward and outward, seeing clearly when to stop, when to go, when to take the next step in the dance. The individual whose gaze is crystal clear upon himself hears the play's music very clearly and knows and sees without doubt in which direction and how to take the next step in the personal dance. We may take questions.

"Do you feel that, in taking note of what one views outwardly, one can assess what one sees inwardly?"

There is a mirror reflection here. However, assessing in the rational sense is not the optimum means to perceiving inner growth manifested outward. Rather, if all is well, viewing the physical reality manifest around one, one may assume or assess that all is well within, and this is good. For most individuals, only when things go awry do they consider assessing the situation from an inner developmental level.

What we suggest is a new mode of operation for those souls on the path of self-discovery, in the process of conscious inner growth. Rather than looking at the effects and then mirroring back to see the cause, start with the inner workings and reflect them outward. They are the image, and physical reality is the mirror.

"So that in the discovery is the focus?"

In the discovery is the primary focus one carries: it is a multifaceted focus in the physical world. As one moves through the world, this focus is projected outward. When this focus is centered within the being, it can be projected outward.

It is the main line. In its optimum nature, it is flowing in and out, a clear connection, as if it were a battery continually recharging. Rather than being charged by the external, the charge comes from the inner core of being, from the Creative Forces, and then flows on to physical reality. Do you see?

"Yes, I do. Thank you."

Anything else, more personal?

"Is the fear I experience a rational response to the newness? Is this fear from not knowing, as opposed to the excitement of knowing through intuition?"

Fear, in its essence, is not rational. Rather, it is a polarity between the pulse of the Creative Forces from whence we came—that we are all right, full, connected in every moment—and fear. The fear we all feel in physical reality is from being disconnected from our source energy.

The reason for this fear is to discover, within each ego consciousness, how to reconnect. With this reconnection, there is never any rational reason for fear. It is opposite to the intuitional knowledge that whatever step we take, we know that we are still connected, that we are all right.

Fear comes too from the feeling that if we move further into the development of the ego through acquisition—relationships, power, material things—we will lose our connection. This, in the spiritually developed soul, is karmic in the case of Suzanne. But we would suggest that you recognize that as you move through your dance, as long as you carry within the consciousness of the inner growth process, you will always be connected. Your source battery will always flow into you from the core outward. From your primary focus, which goes both inner and outer, recognize that whatever experiences or challenges you may encounter are part of your inner growth process—

clearly along your mainline vibrational tract manifested out-ward—for you to develop more strongly.

Blessings to the scribe Suzanne.

"Blessings to the channel Joan."

▲ ▲ ▲

5

EXCERPTS FROM PERSONAL READINGS

TIME

February 16, 1983
Leo, age: early 40s

▼

This message from your higher self is to remember the wings of time. You have all the time in the world . . . and no time. And for you to see clearly through all the levels of your perception, that you have reached a point at which there is a choice to be made in this lifetime. So you have all the time in the world and no time, in terms of affecting from the present moment your past lives and your future. The power to change the whole line of the vibration within the plane is within your grasp now. In making your choices on a daily basis, you can now perceive very clearly the span of action available to you, within your soul's vibration.

▲ ▲ ▲

CLEARING THE VISION

September 24, 1983
Joan

▼

At this time in development, it is suggested that the channel Joan, while at most times utilizing full clarity of vision, needs to acquire a vibration of more stillness and receptivity. Stillness and objective receptivity. This will lead to the next stage of the entity's integration with the present personality: to infuse the personal vibration with the clarity of vision inherent within the entity, but not yet within the personal structure. So in viewing oneself, in daily interactions and in the world around, stillness and objective receptivity, so the internal and the external can align in a new balance of clear seeing.

▲ ▲ ▲

FLOWERING OF INDIVIDUALITY

May 1983
Sharon, age: 40s

Sharon requested this reading while she was recuperating from knee surgery after a tennis accident. She was accustomed to a high degree of physical activity and was afraid she would never be active in the same way again. Over the last decade, since the reading, some of her fears were realized, and she has never returned to the same activity level. But the limitation has forced her to turn more of her physical energy inward.

▼

The primary purpose behind the physical problem of the last year, set up by the entity through the personality Sharon, was to allow the focus to gently swing toward the inner crises, to the inherent potentials not yet explored in this lifetime.

On the emotional and spiritual levels, development is not negative, but rather undeveloped and childlike, which is a throwback to the reincarnational cycle now being played out. We see that the two daughters, the mate, and, in earlier years, the nuclear family all fed the being's focus—functional, stable, external. And, this is—or was, until this year—a safe existence that does not allow for fulfillment on the being's deeper, untapped levels.

If the personality chooses to focus on spiritual and emotional development in the coming year, it is probable that the external or physical situations will naturally align themselves. That can occur if the personality chooses to think, feel, read, and meditate on inner development, to get in touch with who Sharon is and how she, from her center, connects to All That Is, to nature and her personal relationships. This will form the basis for a new life of contentment within the same physical existence, a second life changing not the externals but the inner focus.

Consciously exploring emotional and spiritual connections in the second half of this existence will make possible a flowering of the personality, in terms of calm, contentment, flowing connection to professional work with colleagues, students, with the spouse. As you, the personality Sharon, see yourself in a new, larger light, so it will also be necessary for your mate to see you in a larger light. The knee slows you down just enough to question what else is there.

When one's scope enlarges by connecting to the inner self, then outer connections will be as if born anew, with a new depth of perception. It is a time to connect the inner workings of the personality, and the knee was the trigger. We will open it up for questions now.

Sharon: "Do you see any differences in my dealings with colleagues or the people I work with?"

By October, after the external changes and inner connections are formed, you will find that you see people differently.

Your perceptions of the human beings who flow in and out of your life will be much less threatening, with more flowing and detached experiences on all levels. Once the inner connections are made, you will find that you will not be thrown off your center so easily, that your perceptions of those who once threw you off can be transcended to mild amusement—no drama, only light farce. Next question.

Sharon: "How about my relationship with my husband and our future together?"

There will be quite a few adjustments in the coming year in how he views you, as your view of yourself enlarges. At times he will resist your focus on the inner. Practice patience with him. Communicate what you need as you enlarge the self, and that this does not diminish love. It will enlarge the channels for the relationship to grow along more equal lines in terms of personal validity. He will gradually accept this, but patience will be necessary, as he may feel diminished briefly as you enlarge. Nurture his growth also, but not so that it impinges on yours. It will not be painful if you communicate with love and nurture his validity as you work on your inner self.

It will not be in your hands to control his reactions to this. The timing of his acceptance will come when his own growth reaches a point of acceptance of himself and his developmental limitations in this life.

Sharon: "Will I also develop more calm in my ability to deal with people on an emotional level? Will it seem that I won't be so hurt emotionally in dealing with people as I develop this inner connection?"

That is correct. You will not so easily be pushed off your center. There will be more flowing communication and connection with those around you and you will be able to reciprocate or take action from your base, not from the push or shove of others.

The hurt comes from not having the resource of inner connections. From this nurturing of the inner self, the strength will come to take action based on others' actions, rather than just reacting and feeling incapable of acting on one's own will and feelings. The inner self will fuel the ability to stand one's ground emotionally, having the strength to deal with whatever comes your way with no fear. It will be very pleasant.

We will close with saying that there is a good external framework here in the view of the self from children and spouse, a firm base of love for you to start nurturing your inner growth. Recognize and give yourself credit for establishing this firm external emotional base. We send blessings for your new endeavor.

▲ ▲ ▲

INNER VALIDITY VERSUS EXTERNAL BAGGAGE
May 30, 1983
Sarah, age 21

When Sarah requested this reading, she had just graduated from college and was wondering whether to marry the man with whom she was living.

▼

Viewing how the present personality, Sarah, is now dealing with the energies available to her, we see that she has acquired many external skills, through training and upbringing, that are necessary and expected of her. In terms of the optimum mainline development available to this personality, they are accumulations that we perceive as baggage. Much of it is held on to as security, behind the lines of the conscious mind, a continuation of messages received subconsciously from the mother about the importance of external security.

There is a probability that will allow the personality to keep the security of the indoctrinated baggage. Now is a crossroads, a time to look back before one steps forward, to see that if certain assumptions about reality are unwound and released, there is the probability of a leap into a broader vision of why the personality is here.

It is an acceptance of initiative and responsibility based on inner security: the recognition that the personality has her own unique perspective, and that her view is valid. From this comes a new belief structure that allows letting go of the need to hold on to material baggage and the relationship (with the boy-friend). Of course many of these messages—falling back on se-curity—are latent and subconscious, in case the personality is not valid enough for herself—on her own—at this time.

In the coming year, we see the personality moving into growth that will accelerate and build on the personal core for the entity vibration not before experienced in this lifetime. It will bring with it exhilaration and longing to experience per-sonal freedom. Also, as with any acceleration of personal growth, will come feelings of vulnerability and nostalgia, sad-ness for the baggage left behind.

Recognize that there is an equation that will be operative in the personality's life for some time as this acceleration stabi-lizes over the next ten years: as willing as the personality is to let go of the baggage of emotional and material security, the faster she will be able to develop, the clearer and wider her vi-sion will be, and the more she will have the freedom to choose and the ability to initiate action. Letting go equals lightness and mobility within the physical plane, mobility of vision in a light-ened consciousness.

It will be a process for this personality to achieve the light-ness that she is here to attain, enlarging her scope in ways not presently imagined by the personality. Letting the baggage go before the vision enlarges is a leap of faith in her own validity.

▲ ▲ ▲

FOCUS AND FREEDOM

September 7, 1983
Gordon, age 33

Gordon, a very talented composer and musician, came for a reading because of a conflict between his own personal path and what he saw as society's expectations. As many others do, he came seeking outer confirmation of his deepest desires.

"I'm going to count from 1 to 10, where you will please focus and do a reading for the personality present, Gordon, through the eyes of the Sympathetic Bridge Recorder on the purposes for which he chose to live this life at this time and the nature of the soul's vibration which is his source."

▼

The personality Gordon is working from a line of five previous reincarnation experiences in which certain skills, disciplines, strengths, and structures were developed within the personality.

In viewing these five lives—the primary causal chain to the present existence—we see several recurrent patterns or themes. While the strengths, structures, and skills developed are within the present potential, there has been a lack of focus on the integration of these into the personality as expressed through enjoyment of daily life.

Sometimes, in viewing such lines of development, we see that it becomes an increasing challenge to shift the focus from the formation of skills and disciplines toward enjoyment of the small pleasures that daily interactions hold, in and of themselves. There can be a more compassionate view of the self as a human being who is here, in this personality at this time, to integrate the layers of past experience with present potential, through music and in dealing with people. Recognize that having a strongly developed inner structure and discipline needs a view of the self that is more relaxed, joyful, and compassionate.

We see music and daily interactions as the outlet. At this

point, the personality has reached a dead end in that the development of the ego's discipline has closed down the openness and childlike spontaneity that, for balance, now needs expression. The ego armor is so tight that very little light from the world is coming in, and very little light from the soul can shine through the heart and mind, giving the personality more compassion for himself.

The structures for dealing with physical reality have become a barrier to fresh experiences and other personalities. At this point, even creativity is stagnating because of the armor of belief about skill earned through hard work and suffering. Recognize that this trap in the belief system is causing emotional and spiritual despair.

So we are going to move now to the personality Gordon's higher self for more direct communication on how to break through this armor and to alter and expand the personal focus so that more light can come in—both inner and outer. There is the possibility here, if the personality acknowledges at the deepest level that it is time to open up the personal vibration so that the personality's core can better reflect the compassionate light of the source from whence he springs. One to five, please.

We are now sending in light and source energy to expand within the physical being and rejuvenate the knowledge of beingness on the cellular level. Also we send the inner knowledge that this light and this feeling of comfort are possible in the physical plane and can be attained by inner, not outer, events.

But in this case, because of stagnation in the belief structure, we see that a change in the external environment may help expedite the change in focus toward a lighter, more compassionate view about what this life's purpose is. It is an integration of all the creative and interpersonal skills with a vibration of spontaneous joy and openness that is comfortable to live with daily, with a more open connection to emotions in relationships that run along deeper currents than presently possible.

We see a period of three to six months to change the focus

of the physical being and the perception of the personality. The sense of not feeling free to move is an old belief structure that the personality has set up to whip the self. It is time to let this one go. The personality can be as free and as open as he chooses.

The key here is that openness—inner and outer—equals the feeling of freedom. Openness allows more light in, from others and from the inner source in connection to the Source. On a more spiritual path, a spiritual connection can be experienced so that the being will know and feel at all times the eternal nature of this experiment now in progress on the earth plane.

In this case, the change in the physical environs will work only if the personality acknowledges that there will be a new deep breath of freedom—if he chooses to open himself to it. Otherwise, wherever he travels, he will carry the prison of his ego armor with him.

So then, the need now is to acknowledge that it is time to change focus toward more openness. Blessings to the personality present. In closing, remember that every step in your personal dance of development has led you to the present moment and was necessary to get you here. Recognizing this, you can free yourself to focus and open completely in the present, with no past repercussions.

▲ ▲ ▲

THE PERSONAL BECOMES UNIVERSAL

Commentary

The remaining excerpts in this section were channeled for my friend Sophia over the period of a year, but it took her about six years to integrate them consciously into her life. They explore in depth her process of self-discovery and renewal. At the time she was a stylist, but unfulfilled in her work. It was suggested that she go back to school and become a therapist—an idea that was quite a stretch for her. But she did begin her training in 1988, and by 1990 she had become a therapist and loved her new profession. When I ran into her years later, she didn't remember that, years before, the readings had encouraged these changes.

All of the personal readings (including mine) are meant to stretch the individual and plant catalytic seeds to help growth on all levels. After almost twenty years of feedback from those who have received personal readings, I have learned that with the probabilities come time frames—usually the shortest possible in which developments can occur. This is because my channels perceive the speed of human development as if there were no ego resistance to spiritual evolution. And, of course, there almost always is. But in the last year I have noticed that several clients have actually evolved faster than their readings predicted. I can only account for this by the acceleration of planetary energies as we enter the New Age; anyone now willing to move faster is being carried by the speedup in the natural universal flow.

Some are ready to follow a reading's suggestions almost immediately, usually because they are in enough pain to get the message that a course correction is indicated. Others ask about potential mates or career paths, and even if the reading suggests that their ego desires would not be optimum for their spiritual growth, they pursue that path anyway. Others kick and scream because the route suggested will take so much time, effort, and discipline but eventually surrender when they exhaust the limitations of doing it the easy way. And some choose not to change at all.

LETTING GO OF THE VIEW OF SELF

June 29, 1983

▼

In some ways, the personality is experiencing the joy of childhood, viewing herself, relationships, and the world in a refreshingly new way. It is good to keep in mind that, in the process of letting go of past views of the self and relationship to others, the self can potentially begin a new cycle.

It is suggested to continue pulsing out from the core vibration to let go of all views of the self, both inner and outer, that are based on past entanglements. Utilize instead the pulse of the core vibration in daily dealings. Then slowly form the new view of the self based on the core vibration, as if being reborn. With the mind attuned to a compassionate view and to the emotions, with outward actions based on this perception, a new self-image will gradually grow.

On many levels, it will be like a flowering process not experienced in the original childhood, a process that can bring much joy in being.

▲ ▲ ▲

RECEPTIVITY TO NEW SOURCES

July 23, 1983

▼

We see that while the personality deals with daily energies, on some level there is a calling out for new sources of aid within the being. This calling out is not being manifested in daily life. In this way, it allows the personality to appear to the daily network that all is, in the interchanges, moving along. But we see by the calling out, while very natural and lyrical and with a sense of humor, that there is unmistakably a calling out for other sources of aid.

It is perfectly all right to do it this way, but recognize that there will be energy and aid coming in through the subconscious, from sources other than physical, through guides and the personality's Higher Power. There will be then a period of integration into the personality, and then outward into the world.

Recognize that the process will be threefold: receptivity to new sources other than physical, integration into the being, and manifestation out into daily dealings. The process will change the personality's view of itself. In meditative and dream states, as in external dealings, be receptive for this new energy to come in.

▲ ▲ ▲

GETTING OFF THE BUMPY RIDE
November 5, 1983

▼

What we see now is that on one hand, the personality is attempting to try on different hats, so to speak. On the other hand, we see that the personality feels that the ride she is on is so bumpy that perhaps it is best just to hold on to one's hat so that it doesn't fall off.

The optimum suggestion now is to recognize that the bumpy ride is really a mechanism that the personality has fueled through various periods in her life, based on feelings of past inadequacies. The bumpy ride starts with these feelings, so in a practical way the personality chooses not to try on different hats, but holds on to what she has.

The key to getting off this ride once and for all is just to change hats, without waiting for the perfect hat to appear, without analyzing the proper one for the season, but rather trying on one that is available and comfortable for now. Utilize this as a mechanism to change the ride into one that is controlled more by the personality than by unseen internal forces.

▲ ▲ ▲

SEEING CLEARLY

November 17, 1983

▼

It is time now for the personality to open her eyes wider still and to see clearly where she really is. The levels have shifted, the vibrations have altered, the quality of daily existence has changed to a much lighter, clearer, higher vibrational tone. But the personality does not yet see that she is part of this tone. It is as if she is trying to weigh herself down with the past image of self. Yet all around her there is evidence that the lighter vibrational tone is being generated by sources around her, her own higher sources. They are surrounding her, from many directions. She is actually sitting on a higher plateau of being, and yet is still feeling and acting as if she is weighed down by a personal image from the past.

As we see it, holding on to this heavier impression of the self blocks the light from coming in. The self-image is now the only obstacle to living in a lighter, freer, and more rarefied atmosphere on all levels. As we see it now, it is all there, surrounding the personality.

▲ ▲ ▲

COMFORT

November 30, 1983

▼

There is a strong message here from the entity of the personality present: conscious examination is now indicated of the feelings of self for self, in terms of comfort, as part of the ongoing process of loosening and letting go of the barriers that separate the self from others.

The key here is: as comfortably close on the conscious level as you feel the self becoming with the self, that will be the key to minimizing the distance that you allow in interchanges with others on the energy and vibrational levels.

So the degree of comfort that can be developed with self for self will indicate the next step in the integration process between the self and others. It is a probability that you will choose to maintain established distances here. But there is also the free will present and the energy channeling in for you to consider choosing a more open system of interchange. It would certainly allow the second part of this incarnation to be more comforting.

▲ ▲ ▲

THE PROTECTIVE COCOON

March 5, 1984

▼

There is no doubt that the personality present, Sophia, is now undergoing the first major shift in aligning the personal core energy with the entity's higher purposes. What we are seeing now is that as the personal energy alters in intensity, speed of interaction, and lightness of tone, the personality has been experiencing some new twists in her personal interactions, specifically with the self, and these are reverberating outward.

It is the beginning of a new ballgame. The personality has recognized now on deeper levels that as the core energy aligns with a lighter tone, for several months interactions will not be as smooth or reciprocal as in the past. The personality has chosen to wrap herself in a protective cocoon tied to her with the ropes of the current structural regimes. While she is hopping around in this cocoon, a conscious recognition is needed that the cocoon is to protect and nurture the new vibration within.

The energy interactions that have been operative until recently and have become, shall we say, not completely aligned with the new direction. When the new core vibration is comfortably aligned and centered, the personality will untie herself and leap over those boundaries. Beyond the boundaries of her present dealings will be new interactions. After the inner nurturing period, the quality of vibrational intensity possible will be of magic.

In closing, we will say that the specific change involved here is primarily raising the level of energy interactions, lightening the tone and developing self-confidence in the ability. But that ability is not just to affect and change through communication. It is also the inner knowledge that the personality can affect change and growth on electromagnetic levels that will seem, in rational terms, like magic.

It is time now to cleanse physically so that the ability to be a catalyst now latent will be on much higher vibratory levels, aligned with this incarnation's primary purposes. Fulfillment will come in being a center for electromagnetically charging and recharging from sources higher than the self to sources that are ready to move. We will open it up now.

Sophia: "One question on daily focus. Aside from working on the internal, how much should I focus on work and worrying about finances?" [Sophia was then freelancing in her field.]

At this point, the major focus can only be on nurturing the self for the leap over the established boundaries, as old ways of dealing are no longer personally fulfilling. The priority here is to be open enough to interaction on the material level that it flows easily to the personality through the end of May. At that time, we see that the personality will start to untie some of the ropes holding the cocoon. Then there will be several months of enjoying the new internal energies available. By fall, the alignment for new dealings on the material level will be clearer and easily accessible.

So focus on nurturing the self and recognize that this is the step necessary to change the way the personality fulfills the self.

▲ ▲ ▲

DEALING DIRECTLY

July 19, 1984

▼

What we are seeing is that the mechanisms the personality has used to deal with external reality are no longer operative for the vibratory direction in which she is moving.

There needs to be a letting go of the past tools and mechanisms for dealing with external reality. A more direct interchange of energies between the personality and the world will involve some adjustments through the next three months, in the capacity to digest energies without using mechanisms outside the self. Rather, absorb the energies moving directly toward her on a daily basis, being open without being vulnerable. There will be a lapse here before the ingestion, digestion, and ability to transmute these energies outward again will occur. But then the personality will truly be able to generate and synthesize energies on the heart level and from the lower chakras.

The sense of humor needs to be maintained, for, as with any major personal development or endeavor, one never really knows what one needs for the trip until one is on it. In this case, the inner vibration has changed to a lighter tone. Now the means of operating with the world's energies needs to become more direct.

It will be a period of experiencing the newness of the vibratory tone, first by becoming receptive and comfortable with fewer boundaries between the self and the world. Then the ability will develop to regenerate and transmute these energies outward, with the personal vibratory stamp on them.

It is a new level of development for this personality in this lifetime, and an interesting one in that it will mean getting in touch, on the deepest levels, with what kind of energy—through action—the personality desires to infuse the personal world.

▲ ▲ ▲

Part II

RELATIONSHIPS . . . THEIR
TIMELESS NATURE

1

THE ESSENTIAL NATURE OF HUMAN INTERACTION

"The entity can experience through the physical plane the full-ness of an actor who has mastered the whole potential repertoire of physical existence."

Commentary

Since February 1972, when Jim and I first met, our roles have naturally shifted. At various times we have been lovers, best friends, psychic partners, father and daughter, mother and son, brother and sister, teacher and student, opposites, and soul mates—to name a few. The readings refer to the idea that Jim and I originally came from the same soul that split into two— one definition of soul mates.

A strong element in our relationship was, and still is, in-tensity—in all roles, on all levels. This intensity has allowed me to vibrationally experience some of Jim's journey in this life in ways that have expanded my own repertoire of being and have given me a greater capacity to interchange energy and a range of emotions and empathy in other relationships. We're so close that I can absorb a lesson through his experience without neces-sarily going through it myself. Now, when I listen to the experi-ences of others, I can get the lessons, empathetically.

December 13, 1982
1:00 A.M.
Suzanne present

"I am going to count from 1 to 10, where you will please focus through the visor in your funnel cap [at the time, this seemed pretty funny] and do a reading from the channel now waiting on the essential nature of human interaction in the evolution of consciousness." (Please refer to Part V, Chapter 7, for the funnel cap story.)

▼

In a given lifetime, every personality in the plane has a repertoire of parts of being to express with other parts of the greater self from which he springs. There are dramas to be played out, tragedies and comedies, and sometimes many different levels of the stage in any given interaction of groups of personalities playing out parts of self with self.* From a reincarnational perspective, the roles played out individually and in groups are interchangeable. All potentially contain all the roles.

One plays out various roles in the repertoire of being with other vibrations, as they play out theirs. In this way, one sees mirrored through others the essence of the core of the Creative Forces, expressed through the linking in time of any two beings as they exchange energies in their roles on the stage, which is the physical plane.

Even the greatest, most powerfully skilled creative actor could not possibly act out alone, at one time, all the dramatic variations and roles available among all vibrations of being. So that he may express all aspects of his potential, he takes his turn playing out parts that every person has in his repertoire. This is where the process of reincarnation comes in: to develop certain roles in the repertoire. As one role is strengthened, others are

---

*This means that we are all part of one greater self or Godhead—cells in the body of God.

naturally latent. Through different lifetimes, different roles can be developed to round out a personality's inherent repertoire so that the entity can experience through the physical plane the fullness of an actor who has mastered the whole potential repertoire of physical existence.

We use this analogy of the stage as the physical plane so that one may easily see that as one moves through life, one is moving across the stage of the drama, of the comedy, of the tragedy, with the humor of it all. As one interacts in daily life with those one meets briefly or becomes involved with, one recognizes that, though some are more developed than others, each person contains the full repertoire of being.

With those one becomes close to, one can play out more of that repertoire. More roles can be interchanged and a deeper level developed based on, in many cases, reincarnational triggers. When two personalities interact on many levels, playing out many roles in the repertoire together, they are combined into one larger being, making a whole.

The entity would view one personality in the plane in one time-space sequence, then another reincarnational personality, and then link these two to get the same vibrations possible in an interaction between two different entities. In this way, both entities gain from the interaction between the two personalities in the plane, and there is more intensity between different unique personal vibrations. Being in the same slot rather than in different reincarnational periods increases the intensity.

For example, if the channel Joan were to experience the kind of existence in another lifetime that part of her entity, Jim, is experiencing in this lifetime, these would combine to the source self and enhance its repertoire. But when these two personalities meet in one lifetime, the intensity of the source self's repertoire multiplies because the roles are interchanged on a vibratory level, rather than experienced separately through different personalities. A relationship in which the repertoire is played out eliminates the necessity for lifetimes of energy in developing the repertoire. If the intensity of the interaction is maintained at a level of playing out as many roles as one can in a relationship, it is developed all within one lifetime. One moment.

[A new channel from a higher vibration moved in.] There is incredible prism-like funnel energy coming in now from higher sources.

Now then, from our perspective, there are always unique angles and developments in the fullness of the repertoire. Whereas you could say that every role played is an old one—in terms of the uniqueness of the intensity of the personal vibration—it has also never been played out quite as it is in a given personality, who sees clearly the role they are in as they are doing it.

In terms of the evolution of consciousness, this is the key: to see the role in its fullness. As one moves through the play, as one perceives its dimensions and interactions, the key is to recognize that, in the fullness of being, the repertoire contains both infinite variations of roles and in essence, the core being—no role, just being. So when one has experienced all the variations of roles available in the play of physical existence, then one transcends into just being. For once one has played them all, one can just be—in the play or not in the play.

We have a suggestion for the channel, to be recorded for the psychic work: that three to four times a week, in the early morning, the channel allows herself to go into an altered state of consciousness to develop further the heightening pyramids of energy. Go into the altered states of consciousness and just *be* and receive. That is all.*

▲ ▲ ▲

---

*I have gradually incorporated this meditative exercise into my daily routine.

2

REINCARNATION

"Reincarnation is the schooling—through time, in the physical plane—for the development and growth of the soul."

Jerry was a musician and jewelry designer. Right before Christmas and shortly after this reading, he was mugged and had all his jewelry stolen. After that, he moved upstate and was hospitalized with a clinical suicidal depression. He emerged from that traumatic period and returned to school to become certified as an alcoholism counselor in a homeless shelter.

September 12, 1984
Jerry present
"I'm going to count from 1 to 10, where you will please focus through the eyes of the Sympathetic Bridge Recorder and do a reading on the universal nature of reincarnation, using the personalities present as examples."

▼

To begin with, let us say that *nothing* in the universe happens without a purpose.

In essence, in the beginning of souls' immersion in the earth plane, All That Is and the Creative Forces of the universe gave to souls the ability to create matter and man, based on certain divine patterns. After the initial immersion, in which bonds to this plane were formed through free will and the souls' ability to co-create, the Creative Forces sent souls to the earth plane and said, basically: "Take this show on the road and do what you will with it. But remember that wherever you travel, however immersed in matter you may become, I am always with you. And also remember, be it ever so humble, there's no place like home." And with this divine humor, planted as a seed at the beginnings of the reincarnational process, souls began their journey as human beings through the physical plane.

Societies and civilizations were formed, which are the schools of learning for humankind, just as reincarnation is the personal school of the soul. Each life that a soul chooses to lead is like a course of study—in a different time, a different place, a different focus, for a different purpose.

One could see the process of reincarnation as a school for the growth of the soul. But how are choices made as to what life, for what purpose, in what sex, in what time? Although the soul exercises free will to a certain point, some of the criteria for these choices correspond with the degree of the soul's immersion in the physical plane's early stages. Some souls delved very deeply into the ethers of the material vibration and became stuck in heavier vibrations, as in some sort of quicksand. The more these souls struggled to free themselves, the more firmly immersed they became.

One of the keys to the reincarnational process, so aptly developed in Zen and Taoism, is the ability to experience physical reality and unconditionally accept all its paradoxes, with no struggle or desire to be elsewhere. This is one of the keys to graduating from the reincarnational cycle: to be clear in the physical plane on all levels to allow for reconnection with one's original sources.

There is also another matter here: through lives, through the learning process, various actions are taken that incur karma, or the law of return upon the doer. In another life, another personality, as part of the balancing process, the soul will be given the opportunity to balance out the karma incurred, within the universal law. Karma does not have to be unwound with the same souls originally involved, although this is often the way chosen by those in a karmic bond or debt. For the purposes of certain lives, souls choose to be reincarnated with other souls with whom there is karma to work out. This is one choice involved.

It is necessary for each soul to experience the full wheel of existence through roles in the physical plane—various degrees of vibration from the civilized to the primitive, from the mental to the natural, from strongly male to strongly female, and all points between. From a different focus, vocation, and spiritual discipline, from having no belief to having absolute faith, and all points between. So a soul, through various lives, chooses circumstances in which to learn, to connect karmically with old friends and old enemies, to develop the capacity to be a balanced, whole being through various lives. These experiences also feed the soul.

There is always a two-way connection between the reincarnated personality and the entity—the part of the soul focused on reincarnation. While the entity of the soul is focused primarily on the reincarnational cycle, the soul is also involved in many other spheres of creative endeavor on higher levels than the physical plane, involving other planetary systems and other gestalts of energy. While one part of the soul—the entity—is focused on the physical, on reincarnational development through the subconscious, dreams, creative and spiritual states, the soul, as co-creator, also feeds the Creative Forces. One moment.

[Deep breath.] We will now scan the panorama of the reincarnational development of Jerry, the personality present, as an example of the growth process of reincarnation. One moment.

First, let us say that the personality present comes from a soul family with several sources whose primary purposes through the ages have been healing, service, and creative communication.

This personality is now working off a cycle, or period of

schooling, in which there are several lives connected to the present one. We see a life in the early Atlantean civilization in which the entity experienced physical and mental disturbances, a life of much suffering. Through that life, chosen by the entity, the seed was planted for the development of a deep core of compassion. In that life, the entity was male, although very close to neuter because of the physical problem.

We next have two parallel lives, one as a male in Egypt and one as a female in the early Mayan civilization. While at different times chronologically, both were experienced simultaneously by the entity as a balancing point on many levels—an interesting choice.

Before we delve into these, let us say that before the Atlantean, there was also a connection to the Lemurian civilization in terms of early consciousness of the immersion of the race into the plane. The entity was not one of those who immersed, full of curiosity, and got stuck by accident, but came in after the initial immersion. The entity chose to enter in order to help.

The Egyptian life was as a healer, involving the hands, therapeutic massage, chanting, using stones for vibratory purposes and healing amulets—a speciality very similar to certain connections in the present life. The entity then knew the channel Joan.

Again, in the Mayan civilization, the personality there was female—involved in the healing arts but not so positively, for uses of personal power. Also developed in that life was a distance from the personality's powerful female side, which was very devouring in some of its vibratory actions.

Another connection to the present is with a life as a male in the Far East, in which musical skills were developed and also a certain, shall we say, slyness that is being unwound in this life.

So, taking the strands or vibrations of this entity's experiences in this cycle—only one of many cycles of this soul in the physical plane—the five mentioned here are directly connected to the present personality, in terms of growth, vibratory feed-ins, communication, connections, and karmic unwinding. At various times in this life, other reincarnational lives will be more prominent than the ones mentioned, based on the focus of the present personality and those with whom he interacts.

Let us just say that the purposes of the entity in this life are primarily ones of highly evolved integration along the sexual, emotional, spiritual, and creative communication tract. The karma can be unwound within the self. It is not necessary to do so with specific entities. The karma involves certain character defects of the personality that are being seen clearly, dealt with, and unwound in this life.

The purposes, then, of this reincarnational cycle are for the entity to grow and see clearly, to integrate these and have knowledge of that integration. On the vibratory levels—from which this personality is a member of the soul families of healing, creative communication, and service—the purpose through this life is to align more strongly with the entity and to connect to the sources from which the personality springs.

We will open it up now for any questions from the personality present.

"Is there any message for Jerry?"

We will say, to reiterate, that if the personality keeps in mind service, healing, and creative communication, in whatever forms feel comfortable, then the purpose in this lifetime will be fulfilled on the deepest level and, in time, consciously felt. Another question.

"Is there any message for Joan?"

We have not gone into a detailed reincarnational cycle description in this reading for the personality Joan, for she knows it well through her own meditations.

To connect this reading with the present moment, let us say that the channel system developed by the entity of the personality Joan is a culmination of several cycles of growth experience involving many lives with a focus on the mental; on the creative; on healing through the mental, creative, and psychic; and on balancing through the vibrational sexual lines.

While working on inner and outer as a balance beam on which to experience her beingness, the personality in this life, through psychic and creative work, is not just experiencing a culmination of several reincarnational cycles that have allowed this development to occur, but is also beginning a new cycle. The channel is developing as a catalytic guide, metaphysical teacher, mystic, seer, etc., as new role models with appropriate vibrations for the coming age.

As is always the case with new variations of roles based on ancient models, she feels some alienation from the society she moves in. But not to worry, not to fear: all manifestations of external disturbances, physical pressures, etc., are transitory, as long as the channel knows and feels on a daily basis that the being is centered on a clear path, so that the higher forces can move through.

▲ ▲ ▲

3

KARMIC BONDS

"The role of karmic bonds is to develop grace in responding to whatever music one encounters in the flow of life."

Commentary

When I did this reading in 1983, both my relationships—with my lover Paul as well as with Jim—were virtually nonexistent on the physical plane, though I still felt a strong karmic connection to them.

By 1990, Paul was very much in my life as a lover and mate. Just as the reading intimated, it became a far more enjoyable relationship, without so much karmic bondage dragging us down. This evolution took place over almost eleven years: one year on, eight months off, one year on, three years off, and, finally, five continuous years—lighter and freer of karmic bondage.

As it unwound in our first three years together, I had a passionate, obsessive desire to be with Paul, yet I felt suffocated when with him for very long. When I felt that I no longer owed him anything karmically—an oppressive burden in our early years together—I felt I could give freely to him, emotionally and energetically, without feeling stifled.

In April 1992, as Paul and I were both dealing with our power potentials, the relationship became stagnant and we agreed to end it. The theme of our karmic dance has been power, and the glue that held us together was a strong, primal bond. According to a recent reading, neither of us can fully develop our soul potentials in this life if we stay together. Our karmic bond will continue to unwind on deeper and deeper levels as we come into power separately and maintain separate paths. For me, the karmic healing will come through accepting this unwinding with grace, for the highest good of both our souls.

Since this reading, my relationship with Jim has evolved to a working psychic partnership: we meet to stretch each other psychically and do readings, with Jim as conductor, on universal topics. As this reading predicted, we did begin in 1988 to operate on a higher level, primarily involving energy, with much more clarity and ease.

August 6, 1983
Sophia present

"I'm going to count from 1 to 10, where you will please focus through the eyes of the Sympathetic Bridge Recorder in the Hall of Records and do a reading on the essential nature of karmic bonds, with a special focus on their unwinding, using as examples the personalities present."

▼

The essential nature of karmic bonds is seen most clearly in the metaphor of the dance. One develops through different kinds of music, tempos, different styles, themes, different vibrations of the music, of the dance, of the variations explored.

The purpose behind the dance is primarily to develop grace that does not depend on the type of music or the partners or the setting. Rather, a grace of movement within the dancer, a grace developed through experience, the wisdom of flexibility, muscular control, and a finely tuned ear.

There are ways in which the dancer can explore his potentials on his own, by choosing types of music that he wishes to learn from before the dance begins and once it is in progress. By viewing the self and seeing the movements in the mirror, as in a dance class, one sees the reflection on a one-to-one basis. This reflection can be seen most clearly in the selection of one partner for a particular dance, using this partner; or in some cases by the polarity of reactions, as the mirror for the dance and its progression through time-space.

A solo dancer, while able to see progress through the mirror, can only on the stage experience the true depth and intensity of the play through the dance, when the dancer is interchanging movements and energy to the music with others, in group dances and duets.

So before we move on to a more refined focus on this subject, let us say that the role of karmic bonds is to develop grace in responding to whatever music one encounters in the flow of life. This is the natural state of souls before the preliminary explorations in the physical plane, and it is to achieve this state again that souls in the plane are moving toward. This enterprise has existed from the beginning of souls dwelling within matter—to achieve the grace of movement within matter that is inherent in souls who are not encased.

Using such examples as the Buddha and the Christ, the experiment has shown that grace in the dance comes from allowing the music to flow through one, with ultimately no reactions, just becoming part of the music. The karmic dances we engage in, through the various reincarnational cycles, are to explore aspects of energy available in the plane for combining and interacting. In exploring these variations, the vibrations within the being become qualitatively concentrated to a point, at the central core, where grace is the natural state.

In terms of unwinding karmic bonds, it is, shall we say, the final set of the dance that is in progress. It is in its most natural state unwound where one feels the state of grace descend within the dance of the bond. And, of course, there is always the longing to start the dance again because one knows it once one has done it. It is comfortable to play the same music with a slight variation, to do an encore rather than to explore new bonds, new works, new variations on new themes.

In essence, one can move through interactions and do a complete dance with someone without incurring any karma to be unwound at another time.

In this case, we will focus now on some yet unfinished dances. One moment.

In the dance we are viewing between the personality present Sophia and the personality Leslie, there is, at this point, an unwillingness on Leslie's part to resolve the dance in its third unwinding act. On the deepest level, this is based on a desire to maintain the connection at whatever cost, because the personality does not feel strong enough to accept a resolution with grace. So, as we can see through this lifetime, there is a clinging desire to prolong the dance indefinitely.

We do see the desire on the part of the personality Sophia to develop the readiness to unwind the karmic dance. But the other partner is unwilling to unwind, due to a fear of standing alone and a deep inner knowledge that if the dance were unwound, the loss of strength from this interaction would be deeply felt. The personality Sophia can choose to accept with grace that the personality Leslie will not unwind willingly or with grace in this lifetime. So the choice is to move on to new music and new dances, and in this case the karmic bond can be unwound with grace, if love and strength are imparted with every thought, every act. In this way, the energies will be assimilated and integrated within the being and then utilized in a new interaction in which the partners will make a stronger and more equal duet. One moment.

We see that if the personality Sophia chooses not to continue unwinding the third part of this dance, there will be more knots in the karmic bond for the personality and the entity to carry into future probabilities—the entity's choice. Personalities always have the free will to choose to carry as much weight for as long as they choose—in or out of the dance. In terms of the potential for soul expansion, the weight of karmic bonds accumulated in the dance equals the weight carried when not incarnate. It is the entity's choice, always. One moment.*

For the channel Joan, we see the potential for a new cycle now coming into line with the entity Redada, personality Jim. This potential is released through the unwinding of the karmic bond with Atar, personality Paul. That karmic bond is unwound, but the dance is not yet off the stage. It will be a question of grace and time for both to clearly acknowledge that the karmic debt is paid. Any future interactions will be a focused energy exchange with no karmic repercussions.

For the personality Joan, recognize that the choice is always hers, but stand the ground gained through the unwinding of the karmic dance. Stand the ground, for the music will be played again. With grace and love and time, there will be enjoyable future interactions with Atar, as long as the personality stands the ground gained. No more karmic bondage here.

With the personality Jim, we see that it will be five more years before there will be again, in the truest sense, a working relationship. In the meantime, stand the ground here also, and recognize that both personalities in this case are standing ground gained—coming out of the tunnel of this long karmic dance in an individual light, to very personal music.† And to recombine on a new level, there will first be the recognition of the ground gained, the distance acquired, and the different strains of the music now. When these two again combine, it will be on a much higher level, primarily involving energy, not personalities. With patience and grace, it will take five years until the relationship will be possible on a new level of clarity.

---

*For more detailed information on the two "acts" connected to this third unwinding, see Part II, p. 87, "Cleaning the Slate."
†Reincarnationally speaking, one of Jim's high points was a life in Egypt in which he, as a high priest, trained me as a priestess. A past-life connection is mentioned on page 89, where Sophia was a male in the ruling family and Joan was a priestess in the Temple Beautiful. Jim is there referred to as Redada, head priest of the temple.

We send blessings to the personality Sophia and a message: the unwinding of the dance mentioned is primarily an internal, emotional process. It signifies cutting the emotional bonds, not all manifest physical bonds. You may explore this also in the dream state.

▲ ▲ ▲

4

LOVE

"It is the primary emotion from which all others spring."

September 4, 1983
Sophia present
Lee, MA

"I'm going to count from 1 to 10, where you will please focus on the highest available channel and do a reading on the nature of love, in its universal and present manifestations."*

▼

The quality of love is best expressed in the primary burst of creation. When All That Is created separate parts from its infinite energy, all souls were endowed with the potential to be co-creators with the whole, with the potential to burst as they grew, to create new parts of themselves based on this primary blueprint of expansion. In this primary burst, the impetus and the vibration for this genesis can best be described as love.

Love is the vibratory bond that connects all souls to their essence and their source. It is expressed as the vibration im-

---

*Although a specific channel was not requested for this reading, it is clear from the tone and language that the Compassionate Hot Wire (see Part VII, Chapter 1) was the channel for this information.

parted from one aspect of All That Is to another, whether in the plane or not in the plane—between souls, between groups of souls, between gestalts of energy, between entities, and between personalities. It is the burst of creation. Then, along with this creation, it is sending out the desire to reconnect with the Source, sending out this vibration of love with the desire that those one sends it to fulfill their highest potential to become co-creators and unite with the Source that created them.

This is the universal blueprint for the vibration of love—the primary circuitry that wires the Creative Forces with compassionate consciousness. It is the primary circuitry that connects personalities in the plane to each other and to All That Is. In its essence, it is the primary emotion from which all others spring. All other emotions in the plane have developed to deal with the circuitry of love, which is optimally expressed in the sender's desire for the receiver to fully develop his or her potential as co-creator.

In the plane, the circuitry is, in its latent state, intact in every being who becomes part of the reincarnational process. The circuitry is latently intact. But if the desire is there, then there is the need to recharge this circuitry from sources beyond the physical, so that through its manifestation in the plane, it can rise to a vibratory level consummate with its potential, based on the universal blueprint.

To generalize, as we view civilization in the probability now unwinding, in many cases the circuitry has been subdivided and rechanneled, sidelined by the personality's ego to express love only as it is mirrored back, only as it can be understood through its material manifestations. The sending of this vibration along the circuitry does not deal with the potentials for the sender to be without a self-fulfilling role.

In many cases, the ego has rechanneled the vibration of the circuitry through the heart chakra so that it is not sent as freely as possible, except by those souls on the spiritual path who see clearly how we in the physical plane all mirror each other. In this recognition and acknowledgment, love is sent freely to others based on nothing more self-fulfilling than the recognition that love, by its nature, can only be expressed according to the universal blueprint if it is given freely—with no expectations, no strings, and with joy in the sending. The energy sent is infinite, constantly expanding within the being as it is freely given.

In this constantly expanding state is the expression of the universal manifestation, and one of the keys to shifting the probabilities in the coming century. This is an ever-expanding experiment in creation, and the fuel for this creative process is universal energy. The vibration of this energy is wired with a circuitry called love.

▲ ▲ ▲

5

THE NATURE OF SEXUALITY

"As the race evolves, coming generations will slowly become more androgynous, combining optimum male and female vibrations, accepted in the plane within one being."

October 20, 1982
Winston present

"I'm going to count from 1 to 10, where you will please focus on the highest available channel to do a reading on the nature of sexuality, using as a reference the personality present, Winston, and the channel's reincarnational development."

▼

Yes. Concerning the origins of the innate qualities of sexuality, our perception is that in early experimentations in the material plane, the splitting of the Creative Forces into positive and negative polarities was originally conceived of for the separated parts of All That Is to more closely interact, as a necessity for their continuance in the plane.

First, we see that through the development of creatures that birthed themselves by splitting parts of being, cells enlarged and split into smaller entities, who then developed personalities. By necessity, it was conceived that there would not be total self-sufficiency. This would develop an overdependence on personal power rather than the interdependency now perceived by the human race. To continue the process, the sexes need to combine their energies. As souls split off from the Creative Forces in the beginning, there was no sex. And on the highest levels of soul consciousness and development there is still none.

Through time spent developing in the plane, there has been, because of the soul vibration along the grid, formation toward one sex or the other. Coming out of oversouls, entities have developed that combine all the positive and negative attributes of the Creative Forces.

For example, we see that—in terms of moving consciousness back toward the gestalt soul and toward the consciousness of All That Is—any particular entity as it develops through various personalities will try to choose, before entering the plane, to balance positive and negative energies along a bell-shaped curve—male toward androgyny and then toward femininity—so that through time the full range of positive and negative polarities is experienced and absorbed into the personal vibration. This is one of many variables of soul development.

For example, we see in the personality present, Winston, a strong development in his entity toward the left, the female. This primarily involves the Venusian side—the sexual, aesthetic side of the present personality. So in terms of the present life, this development balances out the positive and negative vibrations of the entity's overall vibration.

We perceive that the receptive qualities of the intuitive feminine side are, through the present development, overbalanced slightly to the left. We see the present line coming from three or four male developments to rectify this overbalance, incorporating the intuitive Venusian aspect almost intact in the present personality, with the ability to take action based on the aesthetic and the intuitive.

Just as this personality is an expression of the entity, and the entity is oriented from its oversoul toward androgyny, in expressing its oversoul this personality is striving now for the balancing of the male and the female. Through male development, the capsule of female development is carried intact to achieve a balance in this lifetime of the exterior male vibrations with the female intuitive, utilizing this development appropriately for taking external action.

We see that much of the enjoyment of hedonistic pleasure in the physical plane has been experienced as a female. In the male development, there has been the warrior, the power manipulator. We see these vibrations combined in this life on a more gentle path, a synthesis of these extremes with compassion, viewing self and others in different stages of their sexual development. This will allow optimum balance in the present.

Symbolized by the channel Joan, we see what the race is striving for in its evolution: to develop within a single sex the balancing of the male intact within the female—the ability to take action within the velvet glove of intuition. As its opposite number, we perceive male entities in the race developing the abilities to take external action with the compassionate vibration of the intuitive feminine. As the race evolves, coming generations will slowly become more androgynous, combining optimum male and female vibrations, accepted in the plane within one being.

This is the next step for expression of God consciousness within each being, which, in its innate form, contains All, contains Every, contains both and either in one movement, in every movement, the positive and negative in every step of the dance. Souls, to express themselves in the plane as material beings, use physical bodies as vessels for the Spirit as they acknowledge their connections to All That Is. This drive—to express the balance they feel out of the plane in the plane—is worked out through the reincarnational cycle.

Let us just say, as further reference for the channel, that this particular source energy which she is reading from is along the line of the spirit of the joy of Santos. Our primary purposes from this way station of influence have always been to encourage and utilize the consciousness of All That Is by seeding the cells of consciousness in the physical, before entry into the plane, and in the dream state. That is all.

Blessings to the personality present and blessings to the channel.

"Blessings to the source."

▲ ▲ ▲

6

THE ART OF MAKING LOVE

*"The optimum nature of the sexual union between two beings in
physical form is the joy of celebration of oneness with the universe."*

June 16, 1984
Lynn present
"I'm going to count from 1 to 10, where you will please focus
through the eyes of the spirit of Santos and do a reading on
the optimum human development of our sexual natures on all
levels."

▼

The Universal Forces contain All, contain either, contain
none, becoming One. The optimum human development along
the sexual path is to become vibrationally attuned to the Universal Forces: containing both, containing either, containing
none, becoming as One.

At whatever point in sexual development, reincarnationally, at whatever point in the polarity (positive/negative,
male/female, yang/yin), the combining of vibrational energies
is the human interpretation of the symbolic union of souls as
they dance as co-creators with All That Is.

In terms of sexual energy, the combining of two souls—as
they are manifested in the physical plane in the human form in
the sexual act—is a combining of energies to make a vibrational

whole, regardless of physical sex. The key here is to combine two beings' vibrations to—on one end of the spectrum—make a whole for the purposes of creation through conception, or to combine energies to reconnect like polar magnets in a spiritual dance—a momentary reminder of sources beyond and within, birthing and born again. The optimum nature of the sexual union between two beings in physical form is the joy of celebration of oneness with the universe. The inherent physical pleasures are at one end of a spectrum, rising vibrationally toward the Universal Forces. They are, shall we say, the inspirational catalyst beyond instinct to the spiritual level to return to oneness through combining polar energies.

When two people connect in an embrace with a loving regard for each other's humanness—kissing, holding, with heart chakras melding—and combine in sexual intercourse *all* levels of the chakra system, they combine and interchange energies, infusing the beings to the degree of their compassionate openness.

If the sexual act is involved only with the genitals, with nothing else open—whether through emotional blockage or choice—to this degree will the optimum energy interchange of the union be limited. This optimum interchange raises the two beings involved to a state—momentary perhaps, yet eternal—akin to the bliss felt as souls, floating in space, completely open, combine with each other and All That Is.

On one hand, it is the symbolic representation of the male and female's need for each other for completion and survival of the race. It is, on the other end of the spectrum, recognizing the interconnectedness of all beings through union with All That Is. Ideally, this act is an expression of love, of one's humanness, of one's connection to the earth, and of a longing to reunite with the source from which one springs—through the creation of a whole vibrationally with another being.

It is not possible to make love with another human being without there being love present, if all levels of the chakra system are open. If one's personal and emotional energy is blocked, then love is inhibited. And if the person chooses to close down and deal from the lower chakra levels, it is not possible for loving intent to be expressed in its universal nature.

So the key to the optimum expression of sexuality in human development is to work on being open on all levels—to self, from self, and as a channel for the Creative Forces. To the degree that one is open to All That Is, to others in the world (through the art of making love, through the combining of the polar energies to create a whole) to this degree can the sexual nature and the expression of universal love and union be expressed through the human vessel.

Openness is the key here. For if one is truly open, there is no doubt and no fear in combining energies on the sexual level. But if there is any need to close down, then [whispered] the optimum expressions are not possible.

The equation is this: The degree of openness will equate with the degree of wholeness felt through the love act.

The art of making love, as it has been expressed in other civilizations in times past, is still part of human development today. It is an expression of the being's ability to be flexible within the vibratory nature, within self on the positive/negative polarity, to be open and accessible to a wider range of beings through sharing on all levels. The development of openness of the vibratory tone in the sexual area is an art that can evolve toward its spiritual nature as long as the vibrational tone is maintained and open on the heart level, combining clear vision with compassion.

There is an acknowledgment here of one's humanness and one's spiritual nature optimally combined into a whole. It is a healing art. It is a dance of gratitude. And it is a blessing for those who are open and are comfortable staying open.

▲ ▲ ▲

7

WEALTH AND SCARCITY

"To the degree one chooses to see inner wealth clearly, the re-
sources of the physical plane are available to be utilized."

October 8, 1983
Sophia present
"I'm going to count from 1 to 10, where you will please focus on
the channel now waiting and do a reading on the nature of
wealth and scarcity, as it is expressed in the physical plane."

▼

Anyone in the plane can get off the elevator of accumulation of material wealth at any stop, once it is absorbed into the
cells of consciousness that material and external resources are
not where it's at, in terms of personal and soul fulfillment. Of
course there are those who amass wealth, choosing to take the
elevator all the way down, to experience what they consider
taking the elevator to the top. After becoming millionaires or
billionaires, or whatever the top seems to them at the time, they
experience a moment of clear-seeing, awakening, a realization
that this ride goes nowhere except outward. The inner self is
never touched by this external accumulating, even if the amassing reaches a point where the personality needs to bottom out
on becoming rich.

Just as some personalities need to ride the elevator of accumulation all the way, so too do some personalities, to round

63

out their soul development, need to ride the elevator of material deprivation. Here, too, the entity involved can get off this ride at any stop, once the lessons to be learned have been absorbed into the cells of consciousness. As we view personalities on their various rides of accumulation and deprivation, a sense of humor and a strong sense of compassion are necessary to clearly see the rides one and one's fellows are on, if one is on any. Compassion and humor.

As in the rounding out of the bell curve of sexuality, there is also feeling and clear-seeing in the plane on these rides of wealth and scarcity that souls of those personalities are experiencing to enlarge the depth of being.

The key here is for the personality to completely comprehend and understand the state he is in, to clearly see and absorb it, down to the cells of consciousness, for the particular ride to be no longer necessary. In working with those who are on fast-moving elevators, it is helpful to point it out, with humor and compassion, and to question the riders as to how long and how far this particular trip is going to be necessary. "How far do you plan to go before you choose to take responsibility for the ride?" And as they answer where they are willing to draw the line on deprivation or accumulation, then that is the line they have chosen at which they will see clearly.

So each personality can decide the line, the floor, at which they can get off into the light. Once this line is established, it becomes harder to change. As the personality develops in other areas, sometimes the level of accumulation is no longer aligned with the fulfillment of potential. In such cases, if personal fulfillment, inner flowering, internal wealth is amassing at a rate far exceeding the rate of the elevator of external accumulation, in these cases it is possible to tilt the balance of perception so that the personality can stop the ride of material accumulation and see that the wealth has always been there—treasure houses of uniquely vibrational personal gold, to be utilized from the inner sources from All That Is—uniquely tuned to any personality's inner flowering.

Once grasped, this true wealth can allow the personality to

let go the hold on the external need for accumulation. In this recognition, all external resources will come into balance to the degree and the vibratory quality of the inner flowering, inner wealth. There will be an equal balancing. For those working on amassing the inner wealth of self-knowledge and self-fulfill-ment, the external balance is the next ride. And it is as smooth, as swift, and as joyful as the personal inner flowering process is.

We see this equation now operating everywhere in the plane: To the degree one chooses to see inner wealth clearly, the resources of the physical plane are available to be utilized.

▲ ▲ ▲

8

HUMOR

"Recognize that the dealer who dealt the cards you now hold is yourself. By recognizing this at all times, it is not hard to recognize the cosmic humor in each step in the dance of physical existence."

October 15, 1983
Sophia present

"I'm going to count from 1 to 10, where you will please focus on the appropriate channel now waiting and do a reading on the nature of humor in its universal essence and in its earthly manifestations."

▼

While viewing events within the earth plane, there is much more that we find humorous from our outside perspective than personalities in the plane can possibly experience. The angle of perspective is different. The perception of events in physical focus is, by the nature of physical existence, tighter and more narrow. Also, in most cases there is less freedom to perceive the humor in almost any given situation. This includes those that involve serious dramas, such as the Christ drama, or in the realities of war or poverty or political torture.

It is very hard, in the midst of one of these tragedies—whether political, economic, or religious—to perceive within the moment of the experience the broader nature of the humor. But in any one of these seemingly humorless situations, all roles are played out or at least comprehended fully through time by all the participants. Not only are the roles in the plane inter-changed at various times, but also the parts are agreed upon and taken responsibility for before the performance even begins.

The purpose is to enlarge the depth of the entity vibration through experience in the plane. These humorless experiences are dealt out, and the dealer is the entity—the source self from which springs the personality experiencing these events.

So from our perspective, as entities now primarily focused in teacher or guide realms, or even from the perspective of enti-ties between incarnations, we see that when personalities choose to develop in a particular way, they set up before entry certain coincidences or synchronous events in which—meeting those with whom karmic bonds are being played out—much humor is allowed in.

We find that the degree to which the entity has developed his repertoire of emotional depth through the reincarnational cycle is one of the keys to how much humor is allowed in. So we find that with those entities in whom there has been much earth plane experience as well as development in other realms, there is a great deal of humor allowed into the experience or the per-ception of the personality in the plane. This is, in its cosmic in-tensity, similar to what we experience here. [A chuckle.]

Recognize that the dealer who dealt the cards you now hold is yourself. By recognizing this at all times, it is not hard to recognize the cosmic humor in each step in the dance of physi-cal existence.

One of the keys to fully experiencing the cosmic humor of the Creative Forces in All That Is and the gift of that humor is to experience the catharsis from the well of being—to cry, the tears flowing uncontrollably for self, for others, for circum-stances or events or inner changes. A trigger or catalyst is possi-ble within each being, supplied by the entity, in which this catharsis of crying can be turned, within the structures of time and space, into the momentary lapsing of the blinkers of human existence, in which the cosmic humor of the moment can also be experienced as the full catharsis it is.

So we see that it is possible to reach a point in development where the wellsprings of consciousness, from the heart on the emotional level, are tuned to see the place one is in and the places one's fellows are in with great compassion. Also it is possible to perceive that humor in the plane, based on its universal essence, is in allowing the blinkers of perception to enlarge with the unique feeling tone of each individual, so that it may encompass the feeling tone of the cycle of the entity the personality is in. Recognize that, in every moment in the dance [said very slowly], all emotions are from the same wellspring of love. In the repertoire of emotions, humor and laughter are the spice that allows each experience to be tasted with its full flavor. This enlarges and develops the range of depth in physical existence.

In other probabilities, more developed along the lines of Eastern philosophy, contentedly laughing at it all is considered the highest spiritual development possible in the plane. Along the present probabilities of this race, it is a sideline probability at this time.

The key to the continuation of the experiment now in progress is, first, for the race to develop the depth in the emotional range of compassion before the development of humor can be explored.

In closing, let us say that in planning and working, creating and playing, in the dream state and between lives, humor is what makes all the development and work on enlarging the repertoire flow. It is a quality and a gift that all souls possess when not in the plane.

However [said tongue-in-cheek, as other energies began influencing the reading], physical existence does seem [a little throat-clearing here] to make some entities extremely serious, and this narrows the range of the repertoire outside the plane also. We recognize this too. So, without getting into the various factions or vibrations along this line, we will close this reading.

Blessings to all those present.

▲ ▲ ▲

Commentary

It appears that my compassionate, humorous channel for this reading got vibrationally crossed at the end by some Saturnian energies or entities. When this happens, which is quite rare, the initial or primary channel usually closes the reading so that there will be no sustained conflict within me, and no heavy-handed influence on the information.

9

EXCERPTS FROM PERSONAL READINGS

UNCONDITIONAL LOVE

February 5, 1983
Adelaide present

Leo and Adelaide, who requested the following two personal readings as gifts for each other, were married in the fall of 1983.

▼

We will view now the panorama of the reincarnational relationship between the personality Adelaide and the entity she is involved with on several levels—the personality called Leo in this life.

As we view the primary motivating factors now operating in this phase of the relationship, we see first that there is some karmic guilt the personality holds involving past dealings with the personality Leo. As we view the panorama of this development, we see that, in another time and place—before the birth of Christ in the Fertile Crescent, in an area more recently known as Persia—the personality was a member of the royal class or family. Through that lifetime, the personality Leo was in many respects a guide, a teacher of many things not physically manifest to the personality present. He worshiped her throughout the lifetime. But because of the class structure, the love was not returned (though she felt it subconsciously), partly because she did not believe it was possible, due to external factors.

Bringing it forward to the present, you could say that there is a very interesting positive formation of emotions now occurring in the personality Adelaide. On one hand, with the karmic memory intact in the subconscious, she recognizes that the love she is receiving is unconditional. Also, there is much to learn here. There is guilt for the incapacity to love before and a block based on karmic conditioning that she is learning to overcome slowly. The important thing to emphasize in this relationship is that it is not necessary for you to pay a karmic debt of love directly to the personality from whom it was withheld at another point. The karmic debt is to yourself. The choice is within you as to when you will unwind the chain you are in, to let go and love unconditionally. The choice of whom is up to you. You have a situation available now where it is possible for you to choose to play it out. Another may come several years hence. But it is possible to unwind this chain within yourself now. Unwinding the binding chain around your heart and loving unconditionally unwinds within the self in many directions: toward the self and toward all those one comes in contact with.

For the development of the soul consciousness within the present personality, you are in a situation that has been lined up for you with, of course, hope on the part of the other personality involved. But the primary focus here is on the soul level— the communication of souls with unconditional love.

In terms of projections for the future, it is not necessary in this case. For if the decision is made by the personality present to open the chains around the heart with this personality Leo, that flowing will be eternal. It will also untie the emotions unexpressed in the past incarnation, because these energies flow backward and forward in time.

With this relationship as a catalyst, we emphasize the opening of the heart chakra because we are receiving very strong indications from the entity, or source self, of this personality that it is now time to start allowing the energies of compassion and love to flow—first allowing them in, from the compassionate sources we are all connected to, to flow into the being with a loving regard for self, with a compassion and forgiveness for self. As the being starts to feel full of compassionate energy for self, it will naturally flow outward to others.

We have a final message to you from your higher self—who has been sitting in and guiding in this reading, using us as a midpoint in the communications. The message is: The reason you are here receiving this information on the part of the personality [Leo] who arranged this for you is that, on the deepest level, he only wishes for you to love yourself more. Blessings to the personality present.

▲ ▲ ▲

COMMITMENT ON THE SOUL LEVEL
February 16, 1983
Leo present

▼

Leo: "Can you tell me something about my relationship with Adelaide?"

There is a chance for you to break the shell of the self-image in this relationship. This would greatly benefit both personalities involved in giving love where it is much needed and not looking for any response in loss of image, loss of respect, loss of the shell. Recognize that giving love is an eternal act of commitment. In this case, recognizing that is all that is necessary. There are no bonds on you in the physical plane. On the eternal, yes. This is the level on which it is suggested the breaking of the shell be viewed.

The level on which you have been trying to maintain this relationship is harmful to you both, in terms of growth as a relationship and in terms of intimacy. Adelaide, from past karmic ties, will extend herself to please you, as she feels much guilt from past incarnations when she was not able to extend herself to you because of demands placed on her by society and by her own fear. But on the deepest level she is looking for confirmation and acceptance from you, validation of her personal vibration based on the recognition that her development has equal validity to yours. Now is a time where you can easily break the karmic pattern you are in because your feelings are true to your soul vibration for growth. You just need to break the shell and let them out. There is no alteration, no change of direction necessary in this case—just cracking the shell. Do you see?

Leo: "Yes. I think so. I want to marry Adelaide. Is that something that can happen for us?"

Slowly on this, slowly, for there are certain vibrations here that it is suggested be worked out, some to let go and others to move in, before this commitment on the physical level can be exchanged.

There is time now for a merging through the hearts, through touching and through the eyes, to communicate emotional commitment. We see at least eight more months of the interchange of emotional commitment—through the eyes, through touching, and through the heart.

You have already started to allow her to see you clearly without the shell, but because of her love for you, you have many defenses up. There is a need for you to slowly, with trust, let those defenses down. It is suggested that the commitment be made on these levels first. The physical act of making a marital commitment will not change the level of defenses still up now. More questions?

Leo: "What can I do to let go of those defenses, to continue that process? I sense that the process is already in operation, and I wonder what positive action I can take toward that end."

Again, between you and the personality Adelaide, we see on the deepest intimate level a communication that is not verbal. That is through the eyes, a knowing of souls from one to the other and an acceptance of all the variations, all the potentials within each of you. What you have to give each other is a balancing of these vibrations. You both have very unique repertoires that can balance each other. By recognizing what she has to give you, through seeing and inner knowledge, defenses will let go because you will see that, on the soul level, it is truly an equal commitment.

For you to let down your karmic pattern of power and control through the mental, it is needed to develop on other levels—the intuitive soul knowledge that the partnership is equal.

▲ ▲ ▲

SEXUAL LOVE VERSUS SEXUAL SPORT

▼

Leo: "Do I have any health problems that I should be concerned about?"

One stress is overactivity in the sexual area. It is suggested that there be a more calming influence in the sexual vibration, involving more feeling and less emphasis on strenuous sexual sport. Anything else?

Leo: "Yes. Adelaide and I have been having sexual activities involving other people as well. Is that useful or dangerous for us. Can we safely pursue this?"

You can pursue it, as long as your shell holds. She can pursue it for you as long as her love holds, in spite of your shell. That is the answer.

Leo: "By pursuing that, will I hasten or impede the cracking of the shell?"

Pursuing what?

Leo: "Sexual relations with . . . group sex."

Through emotional communications with Adelaide, you will reach a point where there will be a split clearly seen in the personal vibration. At that point you will choose.

▲ ▲ ▲

▼

Adelaide: "Is the sexual path that Leo and I are on recommended or not?"

We see that there is a block or split here. In terms of the primitive animal magnetism to be found in certain sexual energy linkups, we would say at this point that is not the case in the present relationship. However, there is a block here based on the personality's limiting view of how to express love through sexuality.

We suggest to open this block or split in the desires of both. They seem to be on different levels. Try to find a middle ground in which the operating force is one of stroking and caressing with a loving regard, with the eyes connecting. If there is to be a catalyst on a new level, this is the vibration suggested to work on.

▲ ▲ ▲

REAL FAMILY DETACHMENT

May 22, 1983
Sharon present

▼

Sharon: "Can you see anything regarding relationships with my family that I came from, with brothers and sisters?"

What would you like to know?

Sharon: "My relationship with my family during the last few years has not been good, but I have found a certain amount of peace in not being involved with them. I don't really want to be, but I was wondering what the future might hold for any kind of relationship."

If the willingness is not there, we do not see it necessary for you to communicate this year. Regarding thoughts or feelings connected to this grouping from whence you came, we would say that the karmic connections along this line are not deep. It is very important for the spiritual development, in feeling and thinking of the family, to send compassion and forgiveness and detachment along the mental and heart levels—compassion and forgiveness. If this is the vibration, communication is not necessary in the next year while the personal, inner processes are developing.

It is sometimes the case that one is born into a line without karmic connections. For positive development, we would suggest detachment at this time.

▲ ▲ ▲

THE CAPACITY FOR INTIMACY

May 4, 1983
Jacob present

▼

Jacob: "Will my relationships with women change?"

They will change if you are willing to change. It is here that the personality, in previous incarnations, has developed powerfully in the female vibration and has misused power. Mistrust and fear has carried over from the karmic line into this lifetime and is projected onto women, being vulnerable in intimacy based on the inner knowledge that the female of the species, as you have personally experienced, can be dangerous. In developing the male vibration in this lifetime, you are seeing in many women this threatening aspect as a projection from past knowledge of the self.

As the view of self changes, the view of relationships with women will be more centered, more open, and much less threatening. An inside alteration of vision is necessary to accept where the self is right now—a closed bud that needs much light of compassion from the Creative Forces to flow into the self and then out to others. In this process of allowing the light in—not holding it, but allowing it to flow out to others—will develop, through acceptance and love of self, the ability to love a woman in a relationship without the need always to hide and to protect the self. We see that it will take five to six years to move to a plateau of acceptance and centering, to the willingness and ability to give love outward. We can take more questions.

Jacob: "Am I on the right path being in 'the work'?"*

At this point, we see as positive any positive group activity that brings you out of isolation to communicate with other human beings. As you flower, you will enlarge your connections and possibly move into other realms of spiritual work. But for now, it is suggested that in "the work," or in any other area in which you feel positive communication is possible and comfortable, to go with this inner comfort.

▲ ▲ ▲

*Jacob was involved with a Gurdjieff study group.

A LIFE OF ATTAINING BALANCE

August 13, 1984
Cynthia, age: early 30s

Cynthia came for this reading to confirm and clarify her spiritual path. Already very successful in her career as a model, actress, singer, and dancer, she was consciously committed to her soul growth and emanated a very beautiful essence—both physical and vibrational.

"I'm going to count from 1 to 10, where you will please focus on the optimum source energies available and do a reading for the personality present, Cynthia, on the soul's purposes for this lifetime and the most optimum path to fulfill these purposes."

▼

In self-histories in the Hall of Records, this is what we call the life of attaining balance while in physical focus on a higher level of being.

The personality present comes from several simultaneous lines, which can potentially culminate in the present life. This life is not so much the beginning of a new line of reincarnation. Rather, the entity is at a point in development where all the strands of the various reincarnational cycles, with all the talents developed, align all the energies for culmination at the present point. The potential is now there to integrate all these lives, these cycles, in a balanced physical existence, while maintaining the consciousness at higher levels in every moment.

We see that the personality is coming from one line of male development in which the energies were expressed very strongly, through lives of power and lives of no power, through lives as warrior and vanquished, through lives as physically perfect and through lives as physically far from perfect.

In the present incarnation the personality is putting far too much effort into utilizing personal energy. It is not necessary to put so much into expressing who she is, but rather to allow the energy to stabilize the personality structure as the channel through which beingness will flow. For example, when a powerful discus thrower throws the discus, he spins, shall we say, three times for his best throw. If he spins more than this, he loses his balance and, as he lets the discus go, the momentum is not centered. In daily life, recognize that some actions are necessary for optimum expression of personal energy, but avoid putting too much energy into preparing. Rather see that if balance is maintained and the personality structure stabilizes, then energy can be optimally utilized to flow with more power, more directly into the plane. One moment.

The entity of this personality is the midpoint, the mediator between this personality and that part of the soul whose focus is toward the reincarnational process on the earth plane, rather than development in other spheres. For a strong development of this entity's system, the entity of this personality has chosen many extremes of experience through various lives. So there were lives of great deprivation and suffering and lives in a helping capacity, with great compassion for those who suffered.

We see all the extremes of this entity's various focuses to potentially balance in the present lifetime. To fulfill the balance of these diverse energies, first develop and maintain the personality structure to find a foundation, a secure footing in the plane, so that higher energies can move into consciousness with no fear and no projections of negativity based on the present unsure footing.

The way to establish this structure is from internal sources, not external. While interpersonal relationships and creative pursuits are stabilizing and the personality's image projects out to the world, the inner beingness needs to develop a more solid core. In the lifelong process of attaining and maintaining balance, we suggest as the next step to open the reed: meditate, get in touch with the higher personal sources, the entity from which this personality springs. Get in touch with where she comes from vibrationally and feel within the core being why she is here. We see five to six months if the personality chooses to begin realigning with her higher sources. Then, once this is developed and comfortable with this solid connection in the being, then it will be possible to express in the world without losing balance. One moment.

In other lifetimes, this entity utilized the healing arts to help others, using the five senses with music. In alternate realities, the entity uses various healing chords specifically for beings who are imbalanced. Aligning as the present mainline probability is that once personal balance is maintained, the personality will be able to integrate from past lives and alternate realities and utilize gifts for healing through music—music that soothes, balances, tones, and heals those who listen to it.

We see another probability aligning in which the personality's gift for living with joyous exuberance can be expressed in many ways. The probabilities there are shifting. Some can be combined, others depend for alignment on time, the external world, and the physical balance of this personality. Many probabilities are up in the air, so to speak. One is to express personal balance through home, nature, and family, a more intimate emotional balance in a more natural setting. We see a warmer climate, where more connections with the emotions to the earth are possible.

Another probability is the expression of personal balance through dramatic and communicative abilities, creatively expressing how to attain balance to others who suffer from imbalance. Several options are open in these directions combining communication, therapy, and music therapy. Aligning the suggested work with past lives in which this work was done strikes chords in the being. We will open it up now for questions.

Cynthia: "May I ask about past experiences? I feel a close connection to Atlantis and Lemuria. Is there relevance there to my present life?"

The cycle then as connected to the present involves quite a few lives in Atlantis. We will focus on the primary one connected to the present and, adjoining it, one during the Lemurian civilization, and after the Atlantean, one in the Egyptian. In the Lemurian, the entity had exuberant curiosity about the physical plane and, through exploration, disconnected from the Creative Forces in terms of immersion into matter.

Reincarnated in Atlantis in the middle civilization, the being was a worker, not of the high-born Atlanteans but, shall we say, a mutant with scales on the skin. It was a life to experience deep emotions, pain, disconnection and, at the same time, to develop caring. The entity chose to reincarnate in Egypt and did work in a healing capacity.

Cynthia: "When I was young, about seven years old, I heard a big chord in my head that sounded like a choir or an organ. Can you tell me what that was?"

We pick up a manifestation of chords sounded through the healing arts in Egypt. The key to that memory is that as the entity helped those who suffered in Egypt, there was recognition that when the entity suffered in Atlantis, there was no chord to help him. In Egypt the chord helped others and there was recognition on the deepest levels that, in terms of soul connections, helping others was exactly equivalent to helping himself. The chord is a reminder of the interconnectedness of the brotherhood of mankind.

Cynthia: "May I ask who I am speaking to?"

For the reincarnational information, you were getting energy from the channel's contact in the Hall of Records. For the information on attaining balance, you were aligning directly with your own entity. This channel system is only the channel between you and your higher self, and your higher self now sends you blessings, greetings, more electrical energy, and the higher consciousness now feeding in in the dream state and on a daily basis so that the core will pulse . . . pulse even hotter.

▲ ▲ ▲

MONEY AND INTEGRITY

▼

Cynthia: "In a practical sense, what are the best money-making jobs that also have integrity?"

Again, listen carefully. Key yourself to the vibration we are speaking from. The external manifestations of beingness are of no import if the inner core has integrity. One can meet external material needs through modeling or acting. If the integrity at the core is intact, the personality could shovel shit and feel sublime integrity in every moment. Do you see?

Cynthia: "Yes. So the search starts from within and everything else will fall into place?"

Yes. In fact, the momentum to balance the external from the inner core will be felt within five to six months.

▲ ▲ ▲

SOUL EVOLUTION

September 22, 1982
Winston, age: mid-30s

Winston was taking lithium for manic-depression. He suffered not only from severe mood swings but also from a split within his being between the desire for spiritual growth and his karma-driven desire for power over almost anyone he met. This split in his being meant that it was very difficult for him to sustain any personal or professional relationship for very long without destroying it. He asked about his soul purpose for this incarnation.

▼

We see the present cycle of the entity. It is a most interesting twist in the unraveling of layers in the evolution of this particular soul. In fact, the present personality's vibration remains in many ways similar to that of the past, brought forward intact from the beginning of this reincarnational cycle in the Atlantean Third Civilization. In viewing the line in the plane along the skein of time and space, between that Third Civilization experience and the present similar vibration, we see five layers or lives separating the two.

This entity experimented by experiencing the other five lives in an almost dream-like state, compared to this cycle's intense experience of the first life and the present—or last—life in the seven-life cycle now being experienced.

To bring the entity's full consciousness to the physical, the connecting, dream-like lives between the two intensely experienced ones can be remembered in the present like a dream.

Along the chain now being experienced that triggered the memory linkup to the first, we see a life in a livelihood that used cunning and physical force—piracy, not on the high seas but in small bands at the time of the wanderers during the forming of the Fertile Crescent's early cities. For his acts, this personality was caught and punished severely: blinded with fire to the face.

In the Atlantean life, the entity distributed power crystals to the elite in the controlling circle of the personality's sphere of influence. So, while the personality's power and ability to move matter through the mind and into the crystal was dispersed, not held solely by him, he discriminated, choosing who would lead with this force.

Breaking the pattern started then would require sharing personal power and mental influence in the present, sharing insights gained with others with compassion and yielding the power of mental insight and monetary influence. These power vibrations should be shared, not, as before, distributing power only to those one can control and earning recognition and allegiance as their leader, but sharing the gifts developed through intuition, soul connections, and combining energy vibrations from the heart, with honesty, with those one would like to be with in this life.

Also remember that you will have the chance in this life to come around full circle with the same souls who, in a past life, you overlooked. You are carrying memories from preceding lives of this cycle, with the physical fear and mental torment you have accumulated, from the chain you yourself set up to experience physical pain.

Your higher self has clearly seen the challenges from the first, and, in preceding lives, the intensity of externally inflicted pain was necessary to experience suffering, to balance out, to clear the eyes and see clearly around you that whatever acts you take, whatever energies you share with others, you are, through the mirror of others, only working out your connections to All That Is.

For the cycle now expanding the personal panorama—back to the past, in the present moment, and toward the future—the theme is clearing the vision to see the personal connection, on all levels, to every person with whom you come in contact.

We see that one of the associates from the life of the roving pirate is the father in the present incarnation. In the past life, this associate was filled with fear about your acts of violence and possible retribution directed toward the group you both were in. As the voice of some small measure of conscience, we see that at that time, you eliminated his influence from your small band. His words still grate and annoy, reminding you that he is still filled with fear.

To best resolve this interchange, it is not necessarily up to you to take action at this point because of his own development and sense of powerlessness, his fear. The vibration suggested for communicating now at a distance is to let him know in small ways that you are redirecting your energy toward more humanitarian pursuits. Express to him that he did the best he was capable of with you. This will untie any vibrational obligations at this point. We will open it up now for questions.

Winston asked about his connections to his mother, his ex-girlfriend, and a friend. The questions were inaudible on the tape.

The pertinent one to the present is in the Atlantean incarnation, in the Third Civilization. The mother, then a servant in the household, loved you from a distance but was not in a position to influence your decision-making in any way. She viewed your life at close range, yet you barely acknowledged her. Her fear of the misuse of your power went unexpressed. This fear and the continual inability to express it continue even now.

In a gentle way, it is suggested that this time you acknowledge her existence and the validity of her insights. You don't need to accept them, but recognize that she has as much right to her views and existence as you do. And recognize that you have no control over the pain that comes on her personal path; you cannot help change that. Rather, to untie the bond you have with her, gently along the waves and vibrations and in communications, acknowledge her validity and her existence. Not that she will communicate more with you, but that this will, in some way, ease her burden.

[Your ex-girlfriend] was with you in Atlantis; that is the primary connection to the present. At the time she was your lover, your mistress, and in a position of some influence and power in your household. The pain for her then was that you, as with many others, did not acknowledge her validity as your equal. It was painful because, despite your intimate connection, you disregarded her views, feelings, and advice, causing her much pain at the time. You can now complete the cycle with her by accepting her views and her beliefs as equally valid to yours.

In closing, what is pertinent now is that this cycle is one of many that your greater self has put into the plane through time.

But it is along the present line of development that the metaphysical teacher will emerge. There are many spokes along the great wheel of your higher self. This is the one for you to focus on because it is the one pertinent to your present spiritual development.

We send blessings to you from those of us here.

▲ ▲ ▲

THE KARMIC DANCE OF EQUALITY

August 13, 1983
Sophia present

▼

Sophia: "What is my karmic status with my friend Helen?"

You have betrayed her [said sternly] and you are being punished. You have always been a dutiful friend and a dutiful daughter. In *her* view, by becoming more independent from her, you have betrayed the essential nature of your karmic relationship—by changing your attitudes, by changing your view of her self-image, by not showing her as much respect as she feels is her due. She sees all this as a betrayal. In times past, yours was an unquestioning loyalty, dependence, and respect—whether in the home or in the army, in the fields or on the sea. [In trance, I heard soft marching music in the background.]

The next stage in this karmic dance will be a rocky one for the personality Helen, as the balance is unquestionably shifting. The next stage, without doubt, will be equality. We see as the mainline probability movement toward this new kind of interaction unwinding over the next ten years. We see a new balance being struck and acknowledged on both sides, but perhaps not until the personality Helen is dying.

Part III

THE PHYSICAL BEING
AS A CHANNEL

1

HEALTH AND HEALING

"To negate the gains made through the mind that are part of today's medical practices is to negate one's own civilization. . . . As man evolves toward the spiritual, there will be a balancing with the healing arts."

January 17, 1984
Sophia present
"I'm going to count from 1 to 10, where you will please focus along the line of Santos and do a reading on the nature of health and healing as it is expressed in the plane—now and in its fullest potential."

▼

At issue here is the dichotomy of mind and spirit. From the beginning of the race, there was provided within nature the remedy for any dis-ease or environmentally produced physical lack.

As the mind developed within the physical plane, along with the will, the split has widened between the race's ability to heal itself through natural sources, and the dis-eases of over-development of the mind/ego. This has caused the split with the spirit. Over time, this split has necessitated the development of the chemical technology the West now calls medicine.

The necessity for medicine has developed as the race's mind/ego capacities have developed. The evolution of man's ability to heal himself is at a high point now of imbalance because of the mind/spirit dichotomy, and the only way to balance this is to develop, through the evolution of consciousness, man's remembrance of his spiritual nature. To restore balance on a new level of understanding, everything the race needs will become available—not just from the earth or from natural sources, but through the creations of the mind optimally combined with the spiritual consciousness.

On a more personal level, the key is to strive for a balancing of the belief structures. To negate the gains made through the mind that are part of today's medical practices is to negate one's own civilization. Rather, recognize that medicine, as it is now practiced as a product of the civilization, is not a healing art form but a technology, a science that is from the mind. Generally speaking, it is not connected to the spiritual, except where individual practitioners are connected to spirit and allow this healing energy to infuse the practice of their science.

The next step is to recognize that as man evolves toward the spiritual, there will be a balancing with the healing arts. The holistic and natural will again combine with consciousness and the remembrance of the wholeness possible in an existence where material and spiritual are more balanced.

For those who are now ailing, the key word is balance—between mind and spirit, between medical science and the natural healing arts. For those who are now whole and maintain good health, the key is to refine the balance and allow the consciousness of the interconnectedness of All That Is to permeate right thought and right action. That way, there will be a synthesis on a daily basis within the being, integrating one's spiritual energy with the energies coming at one from the civilization one lives in.

It is a balancing act now to integrate the direction the race is moving in and fuse it into the daily life, and also to deal with the civilization's vibrations without either negating or being poisoned by them. It is a recognition on a conscious level that it is possible through the spiritual nature to acclimate to any conditions through faith.

Much of the evolution of the healing arts will depend on the direction in which the race is moving in the experiment now in progress, as to whether there will be more utilization of technology or a movement toward more holistic natural sources.

As the probabilities now stand, we see as optimum the integration of natural, holistic methods with spiritual consciousness, balanced with the achievements of medical science. This combination will lead to a more enlightened view of healing, a pooling of source energy with each being's God consciousness and, at its core, living as a healing art. Conscious living—balanced between spiritual and material, inner and outer—is truly a healing art that can manifest through personal physical health and be channeled to others by the power of example to others and vibrationally through the ethers as a catalyst.

▲ ▲ ▲

2

THE NATURE OF DISEASE IN THE HUMAN EXPERIENCE

"A person who 'chooses' cancer sees the devouring nature of civilization and absorbs and internalizes this vision. . . . When the recovering alcoholic clearly sees and absorbs the connection to man, to nature, and to his own sources, in that moment he is cured."

Commentary

I chose to do a reading on the nature of disease focused on alcoholism because at that time I observed that this disease is one in which its threefold nature—physical, mental/emotional, and spiritual—is manifested more on the conscious level than most.

Alcoholics Anonymous, a worldwide fellowship whose members number well over two million, was the first organization to address this threefold concept with a spiritual program for recovery.

Since this reading several years ago, more and more diseases are being treated holistically, utilizing this threefold concept of disease, even within our society's mass consciousness. More Western-trained doctors are discovering the benefits of meditation and creative visualization and prescribing them for their parents, to complement more traditional modes of treatment.

At the time of this reading, AIDS had not yet become the most threatening, challenging disease of our time in the mass consciousness. My next book will include readings on this subject.

August 28, 1983
Sophia present

"I'm going to count from 1 to 10, where you will please focus on the channel now waiting and do a reading on the nature of the disease of alcoholism and how it relates to other diseases in the human experience."

▼

In the beginning, there were no diseases. But as the ego developed in the human race, a disharmony with nature evolved. The beginnings of this disharmony were first seen in the inability of antibodies—the cells' natural defense mechanisms—to withstand certain viruses. Keep in mind that there is ultimately a balance in nature's final result. Everything flows into everything else, feeding even as it dissolves.

As the ego developed, the desire to control the environment created a disharmony with the earth plane's vibration. This disharmony allowed a breakdown of the defense mechanisms that protected humans from the onslaughts of nature. The paradox is that as the will of man became stronger, his ability to maintain the delicate nuances of cellular, psychic, and emotional equilibrium in matter began to break down. This breakdown has been going on, most clearly for the last two thousand years.

As mankind has taken more and more control of the environment, he has less and less control on suprarational levels. Here we see the key to the evolution of disease in mankind. It is a sign, an outgrowth of the imbalance caused by man's manipulation of the natural environment. It is not genetically inherent in the race. It is a probability that the race is now playing out, causing great imbalances within the plane.

As to the nature of the abuse of alcohol—alcoholism as a disease—we see that essential substances from the earth fermented into alcohol, such as wine, were within the framework, a natural substance in harmony with the environment for use by mankind. From its misuse, due to man's disharmony with nature, the disease of alcoholism has flowered and, as in all things in the earth plane through time, has developed layers and levels of depth.

As the human condition has become more estranged from nature and more estranged in consciousness from its sources, the abuse of alcohol has become a cry in the wilderness for those who are seeking but lost, who feel, on the deepest levels, cut off from the primeval elements of nature. They cannot find their way back to open communication with the creative sources from which they spring.

In its early stages, the effect of the chemical mood-changer in alcohol is the reconnection—not illusory, but real—with nature, with self, and with a higher consciousness. As with other mood-changing substances that spring from the earth, it is a signal to change within one's daily life, to remind one that there is more possible.

The addiction sets in within those personalities who long for the reconnection—whether to mankind, to nature, or to their creative sources—and seek but cannot find it. On its deepest level, alcoholism has developed in those who long for reconnection to man, to nature, and to God . . . who wander in the desert, thirsty for this reconnection. They do not know how to look within, and they choose the external substance to fill them.

Because of the seemingly incurable nature of this disease, we would classify it as a challenge, to those who have chosen it, as is the case with other diseases that are "incurable," as with the prevalent cancers in this age and others not part of the aging process. With alcoholism, the challenge* is to recognize that when the recovering alcoholic clearly sees and absorbs the connection to man, to nature, and to his own sources, in that moment he is cured.

---

*The challenge being to experience a daily reprieve from the disease based on the maintenance of one's spiritual condition as outlined in the book *Alcoholics Anonymous* (New York: Alcoholics Anonymous World Services, Inc., 1976).

The relapse mechanism is constantly at play as the sight wavers, as it blinks in and out, based on the disconnection and disharmony the recovering alcoholic sees around him with every breath. Therefore, the maintenance program within Alcoholics Anonymous, based on spiritual nature and fellowship, is a constant reminder to keep the sight from wavering.

There is no other disease quite like it in that the nature of the cure is in seeing the connection to All That Is and absorbing this perception down to the cellular level. In other diseases, there are other challenges of the race to reconnect to All That Is. The nature of cancer is also in the sight: a person who "chooses" cancer sees the devouring nature of civilization and absorbs and internalizes this vision. For the devouring nature of cancerous cells to stabilize, there needs to be a revision, a turnaround, in the sight and the absorption of this down to the cellular level.

In closing, it is through the choice of such diseases as these, through the experience of disharmony, that one can experience and maintain a new harmony. A new vision is possible and has been among the probabilities for mankind in the universal blueprint from the beginning.

By experiencing the nature of disease, the destructive nature of disconnection, man can choose to reconnect. Free will is the motivating force behind all of mankind's development. But even with such a motivating force, it has been necessary to create such disharmonies and diseases for man to choose again the upward spiral, to reconnect of his own free will. That is all. We may open it up now.

"Alcoholism is called a disease, but use of other drugs—marijuana, heroin, etc.—is not referred to as a disease. Can you give me the distinction between the two?"

Each one in itself would be a more specific reading. Each one has its own particular form of delusion and disconnection. Marijuana causes more of a psychological disconnection, a psychological disease. Heroin is more physical, in some ways the bottom line on disconnection. It is a question of semantics here. The addiction to the drug is a disease in the mind of the addict.

▲ ▲ ▲

3

USING NATURAL MOOD-ALTERING SUBSTANCES FOR SPIRITUAL AWAKENING

"In most cases . . . there is no tribe or group consciousness through which experiences with mood-altering substances can be integrated into daily life."

September 14, 1983
Sophia present
"I'm going to count from 1 to 10, where you will please focus on the highest available channel and do a reading of the channel's choice."

▼

The spiritual nature of the human race is as ingrained in the universal blueprint as is the physical structure of the human body. Historically, in the development of the mind/ego, the race has disconnected from the universal blueprint and from the genetic potential for physical perfection. The negative vibrations of disease have emerged because of this imbalance with nature. Because of this imbalance, the potential to realize God consciousness in every moment and the ability to co-create is not now being played out on a mass scale.

But just as the vibration of disease is carried within the cells, the proper catalyst can elicit the cellular memory of a perfect physical state. A catalytic change in attitude can spark the spiritual vibrations within the cells of consciousness, toward the remembrance of the divine nature within.

Because man has chosen to deeply explore the material vibration and develop the mind/ego structure to conquer and rule, his spiritual nature in the modern age is latent. It is within each being, in its probable state, a perfect reality. For aligning with the perfect state of divine consciousness, it is necessary, in most cases, for there to be some form of catalytic event, whether in attitude vibrationally or through some major transformation, that can trigger within the cells of consciousness the recognition of the divine spiritual nature as a living experience.

So we see experimentation with various substances used in the ritual ceremonies of so-called primitive peoples—the Indian of Central and South America, those in Africa, Asia, the aborigines in Australia. The use of substances in the group rituals is for the catalytic reforming of the cells of consciousness toward perfect spiritual union with the Creative Forces. These substances, derived from various sources—cactus, peyote, weeds such as marijuana, jimson, and various hallucinogenic mushrooms—have been used in rituals to catalyze that latent capacity for spiritual union. In group ceremonies, such tribes have been able to integrate into daily life the perceptions gained, through their intimate connection with the tribe and with nature. This has been so for the last ten thousand years.

With this in mind, we now look to the experimentation in the present century, primarily in the West, where there has been much use and misuse of these substances. In most cases, there is no tribe or group consciousness through which experiences with mood-altering substances can be integrated into daily life. While the spiritual awakening sparked by hallucinogens can, in some cases, catalyze an alignment with the blueprint of divine consciousness and these individual spiritual experiences may be as intense, deep, and valid as any tribal ritual, because there is no communion of spiritual purpose, most of these endeavors do not integrate into daily life.

However, much can be gained when a group of like-minded souls utilizes these substances as a catalyst for enlightenment. Integrating these experiences into the material world is not easy. In many cases, the spark in these substances has been sought because the personalities involved have become so immersed in matter that only something so catalytic could jar their consciousness and align them with the original blueprint. In most cases, the revelations gained are stored in the cells as memories—as latently available as the original blueprint.

The key here, as we see it, to awakening the cells of consciousness to the spiritual life—on a minute-to-minute basis, as we are viewing civilization now—is to recognize that, while in some cases the substances mentioned can, on a ritual basis and in an enlightened group, help as a catalyst . . . we do find (for the integration) that as long as there is some catalytic event, or change in attitude, the cells of consciousness can be ignited along the original blueprint. In terms of igniting the divine nature within the consciousness and integrating it into the life on a daily basis, we do see that it is essential to integrate the being with nature and with the fellows in a group, both, for the cells of consciousness to be catalyzed on the original blueprint—in nature and in groups.

The spiritual awakening process in this way is, in most cases, a much slower process than with the substances used as catalyst . . . a much slower process. However, in the majority of cases it is of greater enduring nature.

Those who have sought and briefly tasted reconnection through hallucinogenic substances and then, seeking to recapture this taste, abused them are more likely with this remembrance to use them for spiritual awakening once they accept that it is no longer possible to experience and rekindle this connection from the external substances. Once this is accepted from the deepest levels, then it is possible for the reconnection experiences from the substances (latent within the memory of the cells) to be utilized as a catalyst in a chain of developing attitudes toward the spiritual awakening experience as a *process*. They will be more aware that it is possible and natural to feel connected to All That Is. It has been experienced before. With patience and faith, the "high" of the divine nature in the original blueprint is as clearly defined as physical nature itself, perhaps more clearly. The probability of that realization is aligning again within and beyond the race.

The probabilities are perpetually shifting now for the expression of this universal blueprint in the race for the coming millennium. It is like a sea, with constantly rising and falling tides affected by the planets, by the moon, and by all the atmospheric conditions of mankind's consciousness. Whatever path is chosen within and beyond the plane, each individual's choice is affecting the sea of probabilities.

4

THE SPIRITUAL NATURE OF ALCOHOLICS ANONYMOUS—ITS CONNECTION TO THE EVOLUTION OF CONSCIOUSNESS

"The program of Alcoholics Anonymous offers a group vehicle for those who choose to embark together as enlightened travelers on the upwardly mobile cycle of human existence."

August 13, 1983
Sophia present

"I'm going to count from 1 to 10, where you will please focus and do a reading from the channel now waiting on the spiritual nature of Alcoholics Anonymous and connections between the fellowship and the evolving consciousness of mankind."

▼

Have faith in the channel, for the channel is always with you, within you, carrying the seeds of inner knowing contained within all consciousness.

From the beginning of the Creative Forces' explorations, through energy essences known as souls immersed in physical matter, it was known that only by immersing these essences down to the fullest intensity of the cellular makeup, only by experiencing this physical bottom, could the reincarnation chain unwind back to All That Is. Only through this complete winding to the very depths of matter is the path seen and the knowledge known.

With this basic blueprint in mind, it is in the universal consciousness that because of the nature of physical existence, the nature of consciousness freely chooses to evolve from the bottom through cataclysm, crisis, and other manifestations of desperation. At that point, it is seen clearly within physical matter that the only way to go is back up.

In essence then, the spiritual nature of the AA program is based on one of the primary blueprints contained within mankind's consciousness. Only when man reaches a point of desperation or crisis, when there is nowhere to go but up, only then does the personality choose that direction with the clear realization and the free will to see and act based on this blueprint.

Those who reach a mental and spiritual point of desperation and choose not to plunge deeper into the void of self-annihilation but to join with others in a upwardly mobile direction will reach a point where they begin to move back to their Creators, with ramifications and echoes to the entity.

In essence then, what the program of Alcoholics Anonymous offers is a group vehicle for those who choose to embark together as enlightened travelers on the upwardly mobile cycle of human existence.

The question of those who truly "have" the program can be broken down into the nature of the spiritual and mental bottom and the choice of the personality to surrender to the undeniable reality that there is nowhere to go but up. It is not so much the geographic direction but the spiritual vibration of the direction—less immersion in the ego's desires for acquisition, ever more immersed in physical existence.

It is the personality's choice to, step by step, let go of matter until the being in its essence is moving along a lighter, clearer path. Sharing this clarity is within the nature of the organization, and not just with those alcoholics who are still suffering. Rather, as clarity and enlightenment are acquired through the program's steps, the purpose of this movement is to share this letting go of matter for its own sake with all human beings who are suffering from the illusion that physical matter is all there is.

The reverberation of this band of survivors, these enlightened travelers, is to share with the daily world and recognize that all those one meets are suffering from lack of clarity in consciousness. Recognize that those who choose other diseases—whether for karmic reasons or entity challenges—can also be channeled in a similar way, step by step, as long as they reach a spiritual or mental point of bottoming out.

The only limitation we see in this organization is its primary statement of purpose ["to stay sober and to help other alcoholics to achieve sobriety"]. But, without doubt, this statement allows it to work more effectively.

Keeping in mind the spiritual nature of this particular disease, the organization's connection to the evolving consciousness of mankind is the twelfth step. ["Having had a spiritual awakening as a result of these steps, we tried to carry this message to alcoholics, and practice these principles in all our affairs."] The culmination of the unwinding process is to be found in the daily working of the twelfth step. We will open it up now.

"Why was AA founded so late [June 10, 1935]? The problem has been around for a long time. Why now?"

Regarding timing, one could also ask why Christ appeared when he did. At that time, and again at this time, the immersion of the race into physical matter was—and is—at such a low ebb that the seed within the channel, within all of us, was becoming ready for a new light to beckon. Only at times of the deepest chaos and desperation can enlightened beings, such as AA's founders, open the channel wide enough for others to follow. It is the preconditioning of the race for the coming Age of Aquarius, and its timing was as exact as that of the ripe fruit falling to the earth. Before this time, it would have been like crying out in the desert.

▲ ▲ ▲

5

DISEASES OF THE MIND AND MENTAL HEALTH—THE FULL SPECTRUM

"The definition of sanity is the ability to accept unconditionally the way things are, to deal with external reality as a given, and then to utilize personal power to create one's own reality."

March 28, 1984
Sophia present

"I'm going to count from 1 to 10, where you will please focus through the eyes of the Sympathetic Bridge Recorder and do a reading on the various diseases of the mind and mental health, covering the full spectrum."

▼

Through time, various diseases of the race—physical, mental, and spiritual—have been used as manifestations of the conflict between inner and outer realities. Nowhere is this clearer than with diseases of the mind, for the mind is the builder, the mechanism through which the Creative Forces channel energy, through which man creates his physical reality.

The nature of physical reality is formed through the minds of man into a group agreement on how mass reality will be at any given time. On the deepest levels, each individual's consciousness flows, integrates with, and forms the exterior reality.

When a personality chooses not to accept the agreed-upon nature of physical reality, but let's his own personal perception be the only option, then he begins to move between mental disorder and health. There are many degrees on this spectrum.

The definition of sanity is the ability to accept unconditionally the way things are, to deal with external reality as a given, and then to utilize personal power to create one's own reality. When an individual chooses to experience only his personal reality, no matter how it conflicts with group reality, this we would term insanity.

The spectrum between these two depends on the degree to which an individual can balance, in daily life, his personal reality with the group reality. Those who experience episodic attacks of madness, psychosis, or radical swings in personality, such as the schizoid, express the desire to implement personal reality without accepting or giving regard to the mass nature of reality.

In earlier (pre-Atlantean) times, there was less variation in mental disorders, as there was a more direct connection both to inner reality and to All That Is. Through time, as schisms grew between the ego-developed reality and the inner spiritual one, more mental disease has developed and many more variations flowered.

One can often see links in external reality to chemical imbalances, inherited traits, and karmic imbalances. But on the deepest levels, recognize that those who choose to develop in their earth experience through mental disease do so to experience the pain of disconnection between the mental levels of self and All That Is.

In many cases, such as autism, mental disease is a protection against the mass reality, the violence and aggression of this age of the ego-manifested reality, with the power vibration prevalent. As with the full spectrum of disease, there is no judgment implied, but rather the recognition that personalities who experience diseases of the mind, from mild psychotic episodes to chronic madness, experience insanity to balance and absorb the full range of the spectrum between being connected to different degrees internally with All That Is, without the external connection as it is manifested through the group reality.

As is the case with all diseases, it is a schism between the inner and outer in terms of acceptance of the mass reality. The motivating factor, in most cases, is the pain of separation on the external level from All That Is.

In terms of therapeutic help for the New Age, the key is to develop a gentle, nonthreatening bridge between personal reality and external mass reality, as has been done by creating caring communities with retarded or Down's syndrome personalities.

Using massive doses of tranquilizers and other sedative drugs, rather than creating a bridge to integrate them back to All That Is, in most cases (except during violent episodes in psychopaths) only drives those with imbalances further into the inner reality they have created.

▲ ▲ ▲

6

PARENTING

"The optimum development for parents in the coming century is to nurture the whole spirit based on faith, without the fear for survival mentality infiltrating the system."

July 23, 1983
Sophia present
"I'm going to count from 1 to 12, where you will please focus and do a reading on the universal nature of the parenting instinct, especially as it is manifested through the physical plane."

▼

There is no doubt that the parenting instinct was formed in All That Is as the first instinct coming out of the seed of the Creative Forces as it is manifested in the development of souls. The essence of this instinct is a divine desire to create—manifesting through parts of the self, separate from the self, made from the same stuff as the self, and seeing these parts of the self become whole. In its basic nature, this nurturing is based on becoming whole.

This instinct is primarily tuned vibrationally to divine creativity. It is only through the human race's evolution that this instinct has manifested through fear and the instinct for survival, expressed through protecting the young for the continuation of the line. In its essence, this instinct has no fear about the continuation of the line, no fear about the survival of nurtured parts of the self. But rather, it is in the giving of the self to create and nurture a wholeness outside the self. This is the basic nature of the divine maternal/paternal instinct.

It is the primary instinct, before the instinct of survival. The instinct to survive is based on fear, not faith, and this has developed through disconnection from spiritual knowledge as human beings have disconnected their consciousness from All That Is. Fear for survival narrows the range possible through which to experience the parenting instinct.

The lesson to be learned is that in the shift in parenting from its divine essence to its present basis, the sense of the survival instinct as a necessity has developed because of the nature of the physical plane. The nurturing parental instinct—with free rein to develop out of the plane—has become a challenge to manifest clearly in the plane because it is blocked by the fear-based survival instinct.

See then the preciousness of the possibility to express the parental instinct completely by creating parts of the self through offspring as whole beings without the fear for survival mentality infiltrating the system. Rather, creativity can imbue the system, with the faith that the line continues whether or not it is physically manifest. That will be the key for optimum development of the parental instinct in the coming century—to nurture the parts of self expressed in one's offspring, nurture the whole spirit based on faith. This is the clearest expression of the divine plan.

In the beginning, this innate part of the human race's makeup was a seed to manifest in each soul. And there never was any fear because there was complete faith in the eternal nature of All That Is.

We will say in closing that the instinct for nurturing—in its most universal range—can be expressed with any personality one meets, as long as there is the recognition that the source for the nurturing energy is eternal, endlessly flowing, constantly growing. One recognizes those connections in channeling this nurturing to others.

The only question is how large one's channel can become

to express this instinct in its divine nature. It is physically expressed in its most finite sense through the womb. Beyond this, it is part of the universal blueprint. We may open it up now.

"Is there anything specific for the channel?"

One moment. For the coming week, focus the nurturing instincts on the self, confirming faith in the path, not on survival or fear of the unknown. For these are as the falling stone, falling away, felt now as pressures in the being physically. The fears and doubts as to the rightness of the path now taken are falling away.

Focus the nurturing on the self, surround the being with nurturing from others, and this period of confirming the path will be flowing smoothly within a week. Just be gentle through this period. It is a righting of the course of the ship, so to speak, lightening the load so that the ship can sail more easily in the water.

Let us say in closing that there is a full moon howling and the energies are swirling. We send blessings and protection through the night and the days ahead, to maintain balance through the structure.

▲ ▲ ▲

Commentary

This reading had a nice energy flowing in to aid in stabilizing my psychic structure, since I was going through some changes at the time that manifested as physical pressure in the head. There was a full moon at the time, with a crazy energy in the air. But afterward, all within was calm.

7

EXCERPTS FROM PERSONAL READINGS

TRIBAL CONNECTIONS

October 1, 1982
Sunnie, age 28

Suzanne: "I'm going to count from 1 to 10, where you will please focus and do a reading for the personality Sunnie, presently in Canton, Ohio, on the probabilities and potentials for optimum emotional development in this lifetime."

▼

Yes. We are now perceiving the personality's direct reincarnational links along the chain leading to the present life. As we view the factors, we see several that have led to the strengths and challenges inherent in the present personality.

First, we see a very strong development among the tribal peoples of Africa. The personality inherently knows this. The strong tribal bond carried into the present as the need for strong ties with family and friends. We see a direct link to the present in a mature sense of responsibility and duty to the tribe. Also strongly developed here were roles as warrior, kinsman, and mother.

The mainline development now is the natural impulse for the maternal instincts to be developed again. But there is latent

114

within the being a need to develop not the maternal side of the nature so much as the feminine, receptive side. The societies which the personality links to the present were primarily matriarchal, and the feminine was expressed maternally, but not in a passive, receptive, intuitive way. That is the challenge to development in the present life.

We see a natural ability to deal with children and animals—but the ability to open up and interact with other humans only at arm's length. This is due to the fact that the personality at present has not removed the blinkers to perceive that the tribal connections she once felt also exist in the present lifetime, in the expanded sense of those she likes and feels she can trust and depend on, who have a strong sense of responsibility to the tribe. As we move into the Aquarian Age, this tribe of humanity will truly, in the broadest sense, become her tribe. Gradually, as the personality opens to encompass all humanity with each individual she comes in contact with, she can recognize that they are also part of her tribe. Opening this awareness will complete the perception she already has of the connectedness of all energy—in children, animals, and nature.

It is now time for her to recognize—without cynicism, mistrust, or fear—that the next step in the evolution of self is to perceive other human beings as her tribe. (Some more than others, however.) This will be the next step in opening the self.

Allow the self to grow in the next two to three years, expanding outward in friendships, at work, and in the professional sphere. We see during this time, if the proper actions are taken, that there will be opportunities and offers made for the personality to break the bonds of emotional dependency with the nuclear family and move to another area, not necessarily staying in this hemisphere. Take the leap and move where the intuition pulls. Take action, for here is the ability to make the connection with humanity as the nuclear tribe.

Then will the personality, with a developing inner fullness, make the connection to someone who will meet the requirements inherent in both soul vibrations. This is an old friend in the same nuclear soul family manifest this time around who will see the personality clearly in all her potential—in all her strong, maternal, deep intuitive connections to the earth—and feel drawn and connected to these qualities.

We see, five to six years from the present, the probability for a marriage. Following, there will be a time of development in career, in terms of animal intuition studies. At the same time, the personality will carry the first child; there will be two or three. This is along the main tract of probabilities set up by the entity for optimum personal and emotional development before entering the plane. Understand that these linkups involve, at each step of the way, taking the right intuitive turns with openness and willingness to acknowledge and connect to others as part of the same tribe.

The suggestions for the optimum enjoyment of daily life, leading along the path of emotional fulfillment, are to, first, take studies or courses that will give the personality more potential to travel to other places for career purposes. Also, if opportunities are offered over the next year's holidays, spend them with friends or families other than the present nuclear one. Explore this and see the connections in the human tribe, not just the present nuclear family. These will enlarge the vision and allow the blinkers to be more translucent, shall we say, regarding those with whom the personality interacts. One moment.

Before we close, it is important to mention that the relationship of the present personality with the mother in this life has a double bind. On one hand, to fulfill the karmic obligation, there will always be a sense of duty and loyalty involved. This is as it should be. But recognize that to fulfill the personal potential for growth in this life, it is essential (while expressing love and respect to the mother at all times) to fulfill the self in this life. The double bind is that it is important to both express love and detach, for you will not be able to fulfill yourself emotionally under the wings of this bird.

We send blessings to the personality and we see that there is clear sailing, clear vision, and much good energy being sent to you by your guides along the earth's vibrations and in the dream state. That is all.

▲ ▲ ▲

Commentary

At the end of 1993, it still remained to be seen whether the optimum probabilities of marriage and children and a more universal tribal sense would occur for Sunnie. She still had not broken away from her emotional dependence on her mother and her nuclear family, and she was stuck in a side trip, so to speak, of worrisome genetic health problems.

But I have faith that these probabilities are open for her. She still has time to follow the reading's suggestions and break her patterns, even though it will have taken years longer than if she had been willing to act sooner.

With these readings, my experience has been that many people have a great deal of resistance to the challenges, work, and discipline necessary for their optimum soul growth— which entails the falling away of parts of the ego as they know it. Therefore, it usually takes years longer than the readings indicate for optimum probabilities to align, though it doesn't have to.

SERVICE VERSUS SLUGGISHNESS

December 12, 1983
Mary, age 57

▼

It is time now to more actively express your compassionate nature, as this will alleviate all feelings of inadequacy, low self-worth, and the sense that the personality's potential has not been fulfilled. It is time now for you to, first, take action to meditate and pray—receive guidance as to potential directions where you can go to get out of yourself.

We see this as coming in a convenient geographic area that will be very energizing for you in service to those who are in greater pain and need than yourself.

It is time now for you to begin fulfilling the potential developed through the reincarnational cycle to serve others in a more active way. We will not specify now, but the suggestion is that you tune in to your guides, your higher power, and be receptive to direction. This will expand and fulfill your purposes here, your personal spiritual development. But it also will activate the positive vibrational energy within your being along physical, mental, and emotional lines.

In serving others, you will heighten and strengthen all lines of personal development. It is the optimum direction for you now on the soul level personally, but it is also to plant seeds and, through the ripple effect, influence the race positively. Within four to six months, it will allow great peace and serenity into daily experience. The range of areas for this service, based on the personal vibration, is quite varied. We leave it to you to choose the area of primary interest. But it is now time. Another question?

Mary: "Is there anything regarding my health that you wish to advise me about?"

The general health is adequate. However, in the vibrational tone of the entity as expressed through the personality, the energy level is sluggish. The need here is to affect the mental and emotional health through meditation and daily affirmations of faith and purpose. These will allow the energy level to rise, recognizing it is an affirmative action to meditate and pray for guidance that will raise the vibrational tone to a more balanced level with the entity.

Tune in to the entity of which you are a part for guidance and tune the physical tone along this line. The physical being will benefit down to the cellular level and, as time goes on and more action and initiative are taken in the world, the health and energy will become better.

▲ ▲ ▲

STYLE, INTELLECT, AND IMAGE

February 16, 1983
Leo present

"I'm going to count from 1 to 10, where you will please focus and do a reading for the personality present, Leo, on the present nature of his physical and emotional states, primary reincarnational input to present development, and suggestions for optimum directions for the immediate future."

▼

As we view the present personality's development, the first thing we perceive is that as he manages his own creative and emotional energy, there is an overemphasis on, shall we say, style. As we perceive the personality's movements through life, as he channels and tunes the energy that flows through him with his vibrational nature and sends it out into the world, we see that in this emphasis on style, the content of the interchange has become the packaging. It is true to the mental view or image of the self, but not as true to the soul vibration from the compassionate level in terms of the view of others. Of course, this is always the mirror reflection of one's level of compassion toward oneself.

It is as if the style of communicating and giving to others has become so entrenched that it closes down many areas of personal fulfillment available in this lifetime. New ways of dealing with the personal energy, particularly on the emotional level, do not fit the stylistic mold of giving developed in the self-image—an exterior manifestation that sometimes mirrors the vibration of the entity from whence the personality springs.

In this case, however, we see that the image, the style, and the development of this personality's interactions are reincarnationally connected through several other personalities in different time-spaces within the plane, with whom the present personality works and interchanges. But all these personalities are not a true reflection of the inner soul vibration—and herein lies the crux of the pattern now unfolding.

It is time to break open the package through which the personality views the self and which colors his view of the world and of those around him. Crack open this perception of the way things are and recognize that, while there will be a very vulnerable feeling for a time, it is breaking a karmic pattern. Until the inner source energies are allowed to flow without following the old stylized conduit, to flow out based on feelings of the inner source self, this will be a vulnerable time. But one can experience this as a rebirth on the spiritual level. On the level of the reincarnational cycle, it can be perceived as the start of a new cycle *within the same lifetime.*

There is in this pattern the security in the inner knowledge that intellectual development has always stood in very good stead. The oversoul of this reincarnational line has viewed many personalities striving for domination through the ego—the power chakra, the creative/sexual chakra. But this entity has clearly seen that the development of the intellect contains a serene personal control over the immediate environment that is fulfilling. For it is not a base physical vibration that in some incarnations (not primarily linked to the present) the personality has experienced in his repertoire. He has chosen as his style this time not to express those as his primary image. They are, however, latent within his being.

If the personality chooses to maintain the status quo in dealing with others—always his free choice—there is the probability that the creative energies will stagnate and cause, shall we say, challenges to arise, crises to arise within the physical area to point out that it is time to break the vibrational shell.

It is not necessary to develop a physical crisis if steps are taken to allow the creative and emotional energies to flow through the being and outward to others in the work with more compassion and more heart. It is not that the personality does not understand deep feelings of compassion and love through the heart chakra. Rather, he chooses not to express these in his work and in his life, as it is not [said vehemently] part of the image he has chosen to protect.

▲ ▲ ▲

THE FLOWERING OF THE INNER FIRE
May 31, 1983
Sophia present
"I'm going to count from 1 to 10, where you will please focus and do a reading for the personality present, Sophia, on the present nature of her personal development and her options for optimum growth in this lifetime."

▼

In this case, we see that the self from which this tree springs has within the conscious knowledge and the growth of the full-flowering tree from whence it formed its pattern. Here it is not so much a question of growth, since growth and knowledge are inherent in the seed of this personality. Clearing away the debris—the emotional blocks formed through the reincarnational cycle—will allow the seed to fully flower. Growth in this lifetime does not need to be learned or developed; it is inherent. Rather, it is clearing away the blocks for the flowering to occur. One moment.

There is something here in how the personality utilizes her personal energy. In terms of her inner knowledge and communication with her Higher Power, it is as if she is dealing with a more true form of her personal power. It is *not* the usual form of energy that most personalities have available to deal with their fellow human beings. Therefore, in her growth, the personality has allowed this highly combustible energy to be channeled through inner knowledge, meditation, and communication through the inner realm. In daily dealings, she has chosen to dampen this fire so that she will be able to play with her fellows. Coming now is a time when the dichotomy will become more uncomfortable.

Because of positions of power along the reincarnational cycle, this soul has chosen in this life to channel personal power in ways that will develop humility. A point is coming in the next five to six months when the lessons chosen for this life's first part can be swallowed whole, incorporated down to the being's very cells, so that the personality may choose to move on. Once the lessons of the cycle have been absorbed, the inner fire can be utilized in the external world in a positive way.

Therefore, we see in the next six months the flowering of the inner fire outward, a time to record all perceptions of self from the earliest ages, accepting self at each age and letting go of parts of self, valid reality perceptions that are no longer operative. The next step is to allow the growth that is inherent to flower. There is no need to learn. There is no need to acquire knowledge. The growth is inherent. It needs room to flower. It is blocked by old perceptions of self that were chosen by the personality to develop on many levels—compassion and humility for the human form.

A choice is now coming for this personality to continue along the same line or switch tracks, becoming able to enjoy dealings with the external world, as she has experienced in small measure with the till-now small professional dealings in the last five years. A time is now coming to expand the inner fire outward into the world for a period of two to three years, so that the changing perceptions of the personality's power will have a chance to travel new avenues. There will be a reconsolidation, a new level of confidence in the inner fire that can then be channeled more toward humanitarian pursuits. This will allow for a time not only of the voice and the face, but also in changing the perception of self. For we see that the mainline probability for the remainder of this life is to express the core of the personality—if the lessons to date are fully absorbed down to the cellular level. We see the remainder channeled toward intense enjoyment of daily life combined with intense humanitarian communication. We will open for questions now.

Sophia: "I would like to know more specifically the professional area that was referred to, and my options."

Yes. We see it involving voice and face, using the ability to positively communicate and/or sell, as in public service, movies, or messages, announcing on radio or TV. Even in the commercial realm, we see possible short works on film that will be put to educational use for children, teaching through the positive inner fire. You will be able to utilize the inner fire, communicating learning processes to children and others. These connections will open up in the next six months, if you take the necessary actions and place the results with connections that are beginning to line up.

Though this process will take a year to unfold, it will be enjoyable as long as there is no worry about exposing the self. The self will be developing anew. The parts of the self released will not be operative in this new venture, except in the beginning, in shadow form. And actually, in taking external actions, this will be the core in forging the personality's new vibration. It will not have to do with self-worth or no self-worth, with self-judgment or no self-judgment. It will have to do with being in the moment based on the inner core vibration—which at this point is a very hot white fire. Next question.

Sophia: "Will I . . . will it be obvious when these . . . what are they called . . . blocks . . . knots . . . when they come up to be dealt with, will they be obvious?"

As we have suggested, start with the writing—from the earliest perceptions of self—and start seeing their validity at the time. Acknowledge and accept the validity, and then let it go. It is primarily an inner process that will be able to be communicated over a period of several months . . . one block or knot a week . . . communicated to those close, working it out and talking it out. And in letting it go through prayer and meditation, being willing to let go the perception of parts of self that are no longer valid.

It will be a lightening of the load within the being that is blocking the inherent wisdom of the core energy. The lessons of this lifetime to date are ready to be absorbed into the being, making it possible to move on from a new base, the core vibration, rather than the vibration the personality formed through this lifetime to date. It will be a vulnerable period, but it is the next step in this personality's optimum growth process. Next question.

Sophia: "I would like to ask about my physical well-being and the difficulty I seem to be having with weight and appearance—an inaction up to now."

Yes. As we have said, in the next six months, parts of the self no longer operative will be able to be released. And this also—as you will see in recording the perceptions of self up to this point—involves perceptions on the visual and external levels through each block. In letting go of these perceptions of self, the view of the potential for visual change will also fall into place, as the perceptions of the past Sophia are released.

In seeing each block as it formed, each step along the way, the inertia in taking action will be lifted as you let go of prior perceptions of the personality. It is a combined process, integrated at each level—each knot unwound, each block cleared, each part of self let go—that will lighten the load that blocks the ability to act to change the external image. It will be based on a new internal image projected outward. It will be gradual over the next six months.

Let us say that the complete lifting, turnaround, and letting go process that the next six months can entail is your choice. If you can lighten your concept of yourself to just the inner core vibration and begin to develop the personality from this, all others will move with your new flow. You are, shall we say, the only impediment to this lightening process. Everything you need to fulfill your optimum growth in this life is contained, intact, within you right now. It is only necessary for you to clear away the debris that is no longer operative. And this debris is parts of your personality, so it will be a period of some vulnerability. But we send you strength and blessings for the next step in your personal dance.

▲ ▲ ▲

COMPASSION VERSUS VIOLENCE

September 7, 1983
Gordon, age 33

▼

Gordon: "Sometimes I think of myself as a very spiritual being. At other times, I feel capable of enormous violence. Those two seem contradictory, yet they both exist in me. Can you help me see through this dilemma?"

Much of the violence expressed is a projection into the world of the violence and anger the personality feels for himself. The lack of compassion for the self is, in this case, turned inward. There is a need to acknowledge the spiritual path on a daily basis and to integrate this vibration into the belief structure.

The key that will help dissolve the violent feelings and episodes triggered by alcohol, in loosening inhibitions, is a more compassionate view of the self, acknowledgment of the potential within, and the self's uniqueness. With this more open, compassionate view integrated into daily life, others in the world will be mirrored with a more compassionate view, and this violent part will dissolve. But recognize that it is a flailing of the self projected outward.

As one chooses to love the self more and accept the self exactly as is, with all the assets and shortcomings that need to be worked on and changed, to accept all parts—as is, right now—with compassion, then the violence will dissolve. It will no longer exist. It cannot exist in the same space with feelings of compassion and love for one's self.

▲ ▲ ▲

THE KOREAN AIRLINE DISASTER

▼

Gordon: "Do you have access to information about the Korean airliner that was shot down recently by the Russians?"

We do not have the perspective at this focus to view the probable ramifications of the destructive act. Our level is more personal: we can tune in to the vibrations on the airliner itself. There are a lot of, shall we say, cancer-causing vibrations, negativity, and fear, and every personality made a subconscious decision to be on that airliner. Each was drawn into the interaction, the situation, equally.

All the passengers, on the deepest levels, agreed to express their negativity and their fear of the world as it is by this symbolic act on their part—as a sacrifice and a symbol of the direction in which this probability is leading the world.

▲ ▲ ▲

COMMITMENT TO THE LIFE FORCE

September 4, 1983
Sophia present

▼

Sophia: "What is the present state of Luna's health, and how can the channel best deal with this situation and its ramifications?"*

What we see, in viewing the physical being of the dog Luna, is that there is a toxic state caused by the ingestion of metals that has irritated the intestinal tract and has been absorbed into the cells of the bloodstream. There is a need to flush the system, as the toxicity has infiltrated the cells and is affecting the behavior of the animal on all levels. It is necessary to confirm this with a blood test first, before more medication is given.

Medication for anything other than clearing the toxicity and stabilizing the intestinal system is not necessary. It is suggested that the channel clear up the investigation and work on the cure by taking all actions necessary to flush the system and stabilize it, for it is now affecting the brain.

The damage done to the physical being of the animal is reparable, but there are other probabilities aligning here. It is suggested that the channel follow through thoroughly and with great intent to clear the toxicity, with the faith that if she takes all necessary actions possible, carefully examines her own attitudes as to commitment to the life force in herself, and shares and showers this vibration on the beast, the probability is that the animal will recover.

At this point, we see that there will be lessons learned from either outcome. In recognizing this, explore the attitudes about

---

*At the time of this reading, my dog, Luna, a female beagle, was extremely ill and not responding to conventional treatments.

commitment to the life force very carefully in the self and with others, through the relationship with the animal.

The key words here are commitment to the life force, and faith.

▲ ▲ ▲

Commentary

Upon returning from trance, I said the probabilities for Luna's recovery were very close to 50-50. Luna recovered fully, after a month of gentle hands-on energy healing, and at the beginning of October 1983, I noted in my journal that I experienced a greater enjoyment of Luna, the life force, and the moment.

PAIN VERSUS PLEASURE

November 17, 1983
Sophia present

▼

Sophia: "What's happening with Joan?"

The personality Joan is doing everything possible now to hit herself over the head.

[Laughter from Sophia.]

It is part of the process of clear seeing. The personality enjoys certain parts of the creative and psychic processes more than others. To be specific, she enjoys creative bursts in painting and the actual psychic readings. The other elements of these processes are not as enjoyable.

The personality is coming to terms with the recognition

that all parts of the process are necessary to manifest them in the plane so they can serve their proper function and find their proper places—on their own. All parts of the process are necessary. Recognize this, accept it fully, and balance this with other parts of life that the personality does enjoy, especially interpersonal relations and contact with nature.

Also, recognize on the highest levels that the purpose is being fulfilled through unwinding the processes involved with the creative and the psychic work. Rather than viewing some parts of life as pain and some as pleasure—as the personality is acting out so well*—recognize how full life is with aspects the personality does enjoy. Without analyzing or questioning, she can balance and counter these and, as she does so well in the dream state, make each waking day a counterpoint of fulfilling purpose with enjoyment, at whatever point in the process, because all are parts of the process.

Also, enjoy those parts of life that give the personality pleasure in the physical and particularly in the emotional area, and accept these with grace. Enjoyment is part of the balancing process that makes work in the creative and psychic areas possible, the balance between enjoyment in areas not for the soul's fulfillment per se, but for the personality's flowering. And not to beat up the self for the relaxation periods necessary for the work to be of the highest quality. It necessitates the maintenance of the physical structure on many levels that cannot be analyzed by the personality but can only be experienced and integrated.

▲ ▲ ▲

---

*I had been suffering from migraine headaches.

Commentary

As has been the case on numerous occasions, the reading released much of the psychic energy that was causing pressure in my head. I felt much better immediately.

ENJOYING GIVING

May 12, 1984
Edward present

Edward is a professional caterer who, over the last five years, has become very involved in volunteer work with the Gay Men's Health Crisis, helping AIDS patients. Through this, he has found a sense of purpose and fulfillment.

"I'm going to count from 1 to 10, where you will please focus on the highest available channel of clear seeing and do a reading for the personality present, Edward, on the present nature of his physical, emotional, and vocational development and the optimum probabilities aligning in these areas."

▼

Yes. We are now viewing the way the personality present deals with his personal energy and his gifts. We see that the personality perceives his various talents and gifts as burdens to carry that, at times, feel heavy to him. Periodically, he is able to gather them all together, so to speak, and move as an Olympic discus thrower spins before he throws. Then, during the spin, the effort of mobilizing the gifts becomes too great and he must rest. When the desire to activate them again becomes powerful within him, he spins them around, all together, and then rests. One moment.

First, we would like to discuss the core vibration for the personality's potentials in time. Recognize here that the abilities of this personality—the creative, the aesthetic, and the discrimination in aesthetic areas—are not something finite. Rather, the abilities are flowing infinitely through the personality to use his talents, enjoy them, and let them go.

Many of his talents are not being used optimally yet, because he is holding on rather than letting them go, giving them freely for enjoyment, to feed and nurture those to whom he can give with his skills. It is not a question here of being depleted by giving and utilizing his energies and his talents.

Rather, recognize that in activating abilities in the creative and aesthetic areas—catering, home furnishing—we see that if the personality can make the decision now, if he is willing to give his skills, talents, energy, and time freely, he will be replenished from inner sources. He will feel more purposeful, more activated, and the balance will be equitable, in enjoyment of the giving.

We see that the key with this personality in all areas—physically, emotionally, vocationally—is in developing the now latent potential to enjoy giving of the self—not just on a superficial level, but in every act, with the whole being. It is in enjoying this and letting go of the result, simply experiencing giving of self through the personal energy manifested in daily work, in freelance activities, and in time for recreation. One moment.

The experience of this personality in this lifetime is to enjoy interpersonal energy and giving of personal energy as much as the energy interchange on the aesthetic and mental levels. Develop an openness, a playfulness in energy interchanges, enjoy the varieties of vibrations the personality will encounter in the coming year.

The personality can choose now to start taking actions for the self—giving freely of the personal energy and having faith that there will be no depletion in any area, external or internal, as long as there is faith that these will be replenished from higher sources.

▲ ▲ ▲

THE AESTHETIC SELF-IMAGE

December 29, 1983
Sophia present

Sophia's heaviness had been an issue for her for many years. Though she was interested in losing weight, she was also exploring how it helped her maintain a kind of power and control and protect herself from feeling vulnerable with men.

▼

Sophia: "Can you suggest an optimum overall plan for physical well-being, combined with the personal aesthetic self-image, for the personality present, Sophia? And can you please be specific about its implementation?"

First, viewing the physical being as it is now, let us say that the physical health is excellent. Recognize that any changes desired are motivated not by ill health but by a desire for a more healthy self-image. The health, regardless of whether a change is made or not, can be maintained strongly within the current pattern. It is not necessary to change any of the daily routine, through exercise or diet—for the health. The health and the physical body have adjusted through the years to a maintenance of well-being with the current patterns intact.

So what we are dealing with now is the consciousness of the cells of being and the health of the being's vibration, rather than the physical health per se. First, recognize the strengths in the area of self-image and those areas in which inadequacies are felt by the personality. These feelings of inadequacy have infiltrated down to the consciousness of the very cells of the physical being. And this is, of necessity, the primary focus in any overall plan.

So the key is to first examine the motivations for the desired changes. Once the motivations are grasped, the key will be the intensity of the desire for this change in self-image. No other means or method—no advice or medication or nutrients or supplements or exercise programs or diets—can be utilized until the intensity of the desire for change is accepted, swallowed whole, down to the cells of being. The cells of the being and their consciousness need to be motivated by the being's core and the personality's consciousness, to change their vibratory state to a lighter, more refined tone.

If the desire, in its intensity, is incorporated into ongoing daily priorities, then the next step will be a rather radical change in dietary pattern. Supplements are not of primary importance here, but they are helpful for ten percent of the feeding process for change. The primary suggestion is to lighten the diet: no refined carbohydrates, no fried foods or fats that are too concentrated, and more reliance on fresh vegetables salads, lemon and lime water, seafood, kelp supplements, and even some algae or seaweed for the stimulation of the glandular system.

The key here is that the change in dietary pattern be based on desire and the recognition that this change is not for six months to a year but is part of a full plan for the remainder of the lifetime. It involves commitment to the desire to change the aesthetic view of self. It will, without doubt, be possible to do this, if implemented with a commitment to change. The lightening of the vibratory nature of the foods ingested, combined with the desire within the cells of consciousness—this combination and the faith in it will be all that is necessary.

The key is, first, faith in the commitment to the priority of the change within self. It does mean change of the dietary pattern for the remainder of life. It is the personality's choice.

▲ ▲ ▲

THE PHYSICAL BEING AS A HELPMATE

February 7, 1984
Sophia present

▼

Sophia: "What's happening with Sophia right now?"

One moment. The physical being is now undergoing a split based on expanding the self-image, and a dichotomy of feeling about it.

On one hand, the personality views the physical being as a horse that one rides through life—that must be taken care of, fed and nurtured, to allow mobility. On the other hand is a view that the physical being is a part of the journey, itself the path up the mountain, a burden that must be carried as part of the experience of life.

These images can be combined, as they are based on the vibrational patterns of the reincarnational cycles. View the mountain as your life and the being and the horse as the entity living in physical reality—with the horse, with nature, together climbing the path of physical existence. Rather than viewing the physical being as one of the challenges to be met, a priority in fulfilling this personality's potential, view the physical being as the helpmate, the friend, the loving companion of this entity. Love, nurturing, proper feeding, and communication with the physical being will meet the challenges along the journey with a unity of body and spirit.

So, rather than viewing the physical being as one of the challenges, view it as the helpmate for the challenges ahead.

We can stabilize the physical being of the channel at this level now to do a short energizing of the physical being of the personality present.

▲ ▲ ▲

The reading ended with Joan doing some hands-on energetic body work for Sophia.

THE VIBRATIONS OF FOOD

May 4, 1984
Sophia present

"I'm going to count you up from 1 to 10, where you will please focus on the personality present, Sophia, and do a reading on the present physical condition, with suggestions for optimum physical maintenance at this time."

▼

[Two-minute pause.] As there are many levels at work here, we have three source energies combining from different vibratory viewpoints for a consensus in this reading. The physical being manifests the being's attitudes and beliefs about reality.

The core belief at work here is a revolutionary one for this personality in this lifetime, and it is necessary to integrate it into the personal view of reality to realize optimum benefits.

Some blockages are still unwinding from the personality's past choices in the second chakra—the creative/sexual area—in reacting to reality as it appears rather than creating it. The beliefs about reality are from the past personality structure, a belief structure that is no longer operative for the present personality's personal and physical development.

View the daily diet, the daily routine, exercises, and actions as clearly and comfortably as one chooses with whom to interact and exchange energy. Realize that each food ingested is imbued with its own vibration, as the personality's vibration in turn colors the food. Align these into a positive view of the ingested energy's potential, as the personality does so clearly with personalities she works with.

So allow this skill and discernment to work in the area of physical well-being. Choose each activity for the physical being, combining some physical exercise with a conscious belief in diet for its health-giving properties. If the personality does not feel that certain foods are health-giving in terms of energy vibration, then choose to eat what the personality perceives as the most healthful and energy-giving.

Use the discriminating sense, and change the belief structure so that you, the personality present, Sophia, are the activator and motivating force in the physical reality of your body and [said very strongly] *are not acted upon.* Each movement in the daily dance and each food is imbued with an awareness of its energy and health-giving qualities. We will go into specifics now. One moment.

We see the use of lemon as beneficial—before, during, and after all meals—for stimulation of the digestion. We see beneficial results in combining light protein, as in fish, with greens; the darker the greens, the better. We see the stimulation of the glandular system with kelp or seaweed. Also, a cleansing vegetable-juice fast one day a week, mixed with spring water and lemon on this day—not carbonated, but spring water—moderate amounts of carrot and spinach juice, a touch of parsley juice—one day a week. Combine this with periods of meditation, some time in the sun, in the air, and complete relaxation and attunement with the Universal Forces as they move through and motivate the physical being.

Of course the key here, the necessary attitude to activate now, is a change from past belief structures. The personality needs to make a daily affirmation, and feel it within, that she herself is the activating and motivating force [said strongly] behind her own physical reality. Each substance ingested, if viewed with healthful, energy-giving qualities, and each activity engaged in, if viewed with the energy and life-sustaining qualities attached to it in the doing, will be the catalyst to stimulate the being into a lighter form.

As the personality becomes responsible for activating and motivating the personal reality in the physical form, and truly *believes* this is the reality, the bottom-line truth, to that degree will the physical being change, energize, concentrate, and lighten its form. Any questions?

Sophia: "What is the rash that has been on my legs for a few weeks?"

It is a manifestation of toxic elements from ingesting artificial supplements, specifically B_2 and B_6. Some of the digestive aids are counterproductive. In the physical manifestation of the next step now in process, the responsibility for choices made does not depend on the personality's faith in a nutritional advisor and maintenance of the diet and supplements suggested. Rather, a sign of the next step is to transfer this faith to the self, to one's own intuition. Just as the personality chooses to be with certain entities, so then faith needs to reside in the self.

▲ ▲ ▲

Commentary

Sophia's rash disappeared a few weeks after the supplements were adjusted.

ROLFING

September 4, 1983
Sophia present

▼

Sophia: "What part does rolfing play in my life?"

That is a very interesting question. How fast do you choose to move? It is your choice: It can play a small part or an expansive part. It is a tool, a mechanism for physical release. If the desire to open up is consciously acknowledged and the choice is to expand and grow, then these physical manipulations can be effective down to the consciousness of the cells of the physical being, releasing emotional and psychic knots and negative impulses and images.

Optimally, it is a process that lightens the load—the negativity absorbed by the cells of being by past experiences. In the choice to release these memories and images on the cellular level, there will be a clarity and, for a period of six months, a feeling of emptiness—if the desire is to grow. But the releasing process must begin with the acknowledgment that the new energies the personality would choose must align themselves with a new core vibration with clear expression, with no influence from past knots.

So it is the personality's choice. It can have a minor or major influence, based on the desire for momentum.

▲ ▲ ▲

PHYSICAL TIGHTNESS

September 7, 1983
Gordon present

▼

Gordon: "I would like to ask about my health."

In this case, we see that the structure along the spine and chakra system is very tightly wound. To help with the opening process, we see some therapeutic physical manipulation, such as chiropractic or rolfing. Some way of loosening up the tightness will help loosen the rigidity of the belief structure also and will allow more lightness into the heart area, which will be beneficial on all levels. Besides this, the health is very sound.

Although the physical health is sound, we see that some limiting negative beliefs, affecting the cellular nature, at times cause the personality to feel more sluggish than is optimum. This is the effect of the thinking.

▲ ▲ ▲

SMOKING

October 14, 1983
Sophia present

▼

Sophia: "Has smoking run its course in my life?"

We see that the personality enjoys the effects of smoking and the drug involved, and so can choose to continue this habit indefinitely. The choice is based purely on the recognition that the smoking habit does dissipate and diffuse large amounts of personal power and energy and indulges the craving for oral gratification.

So it is the personality's choice here to take the energy that becomes available from letting this habit go and channeling it in new directions. If she chooses to quit now, the increased energy will be uncomfortable for the personality to deal with, unless she consciously chooses in advance her desires and the directions in which to channel this personal energy.

If the choice is made in the next two years, we suggest that one-third of the newly available energy be channeled through the physical being's activities; one-third be channeled through internal processes, such as breathing and meditation; and one-third be channeled into developing the available potential to create and communicate in social interaction through career.

In this way, the smoking habit will no longer be necessary. In fact, if the energy is thus constructively channeled, in its proper time the habit can be let go and not even missed, except for occasional relapses when the internal energy builds up. Recognize that the spiritual program can be utilized when this occasionally recurs. But, again, the personality can choose to recognize what the habit does and, if it is released, where it can be channeled.

▲ ▲ ▲

REMINDERS

August 6, 1983
Sophia present

▼

Sophia: "What is the story on Sophia's right hand wart?"

From its location, that is the reminder that the hand held the staff of power and sometimes misused it, that the hand held the spear and at times misused it. In this reminder, recognize that power and aggression can be channeled creatively through service.

The reminder is only a small blemish, for the entity has unwound this misuse through the karmic dance. It is only to remind the personality that misuse of the source energy sometimes reaps unsightly rewards. In this case, the reminder is merely small and unsightly, rather than in times past, when the reminders were more maiming. We will leave it at that.

▲ ▲ ▲

RENEWING INNER AND OUTER THROUGH COSMETIC SURGERY

May 22, 1983
Sharon present

▼

Sharon: "I want to ask about a special date I had in mind to do a face-lift: July 6. Is it a good time in my life to do something like that, and would it be a good thing for me to do?"

We see that if the personality feels ready to spend the time recuperating from this to reconnect inward, by reading and meditation, if the process of inward renewal is connected to external renewal, this would be a fruitful time to do it, yes.

Sharon: "When you talk about connecting the inner as well as the outer, tell me more about what that means."

It is possible that during recovery from surgery on the face, just as the face will look not just younger but in some ways different and new, it will reflect connections from readings— inner work that the channel will suggest. It will flow from these that as the face is being made over, it will reflect inner work. By October, as you look in the mirror, you will find yourself feeling new both inside and outside. Then the connections will be felt and you will laugh, for you will see that if only the external is worked on, without connecting the emotions and the inner to All That Is, then the surgery and recovery process would have a certain disconnection or sadness. Add new levels of depth to your existence. You have explored only the external long enough. It is time to balance it out with inner connections.

▲ ▲ ▲

PHYSICAL BLOCKAGES FROM EMOTIONAL INACTION

June 16, 1984
Anna present

▼

Anna: "What information can be given to Anna concerning her preoccupation with the area of her breast and heart, and greater personal expression?"

One moment. Life is to be lived now to the fullest. Each small blockage in the breast area is a physical expression of time spent saying "I won't" and "I can't." Such expressions form these areas or masses. It is not so much about an implosion of negative energy—fear of disease—but expresses actions not taken to fully experience potentials in past situations.

The challenge now is to accelerate potential, to experience and take action, stretching the boundaries of the self's vibratory tone. It is the act of drawing a line in the ledger of this life, deciding what you want now and enacting it fully. The being, in its emotional flow through the years, has been through some internal rough waters. What is left now on the shore are some pebbles thrown up by the ocean. Let the emotions flow; let the pebbles dissolve back into the being.

Have compassion for the self now and faith that the cysts in the breast are only a symbolic reminder, a manifestation of past emotional storms not fully expressed. Resolve and commit to fully express the feelings and the tone, and these will dissolve. Recognize that these emotional energies can flow in actions taken that benefit not necessarily others, but the self, taking action with self-love.

▲ ▲ ▲

OVERACTIVE THYROID

February 5, 1983
Adelaide present

▼

Adelaide: "Is there an area of my health that I should be careful about?"

We see a certain imbalance or overactivity in the thyroid affecting the sexual area, which is also the creative area. It is suggested that the diet be focused on naturally stimulating foods, not spicy or artificial, but natural foods—whole grains, greens, and citrus. Also, to flush the system of certain poisons, drink the broth from greens such as turnip, spinach, or collard. As a calming influence, we would suggest also some fresh yogurt mixed with fruit, preferably taken on arising or going to sleep, three times a week. Because of the overactive thyroid, the glands related to skin and hair are also overactive. For this we would suggest squeezing in lemon when one drinks spring water or tea. Also use cider vinegar on salads and perhaps even rinse the skin and hair with this—diluted, of course. Also ingest it, to balance the acids overproduced by the thyroid.

The glandular overactivity will calm as the balls you are juggling become centered into one main ball that you will be able to toss, serenely, back and forth.

▲ ▲ ▲

TUNING THE SINUS SYSTEM
October 24, 1983
Leo present

▼

Leo: "Is there anything I should know about my health?"

For the coming season, to tune the physical being optimally, we see the addition of some fresh parsley and alfalfa and the occasional use of goldenseal root to clear the sinus system, to best channel the physical energy. Just for tuning now; nothing serious here. This is the primary system to which the tuning will align—the third eye. This will also help tune the thyroid.

▲ ▲ ▲

INTUITION AND DIET

August 13, 1984
Cynthia present

▼

Cynthia: "Is there any method of body maintenance that will help?"

Only if you believe it does. The optimum physical maintenance is, each day, to attune intuitively to one's needs, based on internal and external manifestations. Utilize the health-giving forces of nature—exercise and food based on that day's needs. And follow the intuition. Learn to trust the self to determine optimum nurturing.

▲ ▲ ▲

USING WHAT YOU KNOW

August 13, 1983
Joan present

▼

Let us say that the channel's dietary habits are not conducive to the proper maintenance of this channel system. It is suggested that the channel view this as a reaction mechanism, a resistance by the personality Joan to the responsibility necessary for the work ahead.

We are not suggesting a new diet, for the personality is intuitively aware of what is required each day for the optimum maintenance of the physical being. Rather, examine the behavior pattern, clearly seeing the path ahead.

▲ ▲ ▲

Commentary

Regarding this reading, one of many I have received over the years about my diet, I can only say that this area has been particularly difficult and emotionally charged, as it is for many people.

Before I was willing to take responsibility to maintain my body as a spiritual vessel, I had to bottom out by making myself ill with numerous physical disorders. I knew for years what I should have been eating, but I just refused to do it.

Gradually, as I strive to take responsibility in all areas of my life, including diet, the results (surprise!) not only are great physically but promote daily improvement on all levels, with a feeling of increasing clarity and lightness.

Each day, I try to tune in to what my body needs and to nourish it, with love. When I do lapse into old eating habits, usually for emotional comfort, I now know too much to completely overdo it. I have also learned to accept my own humanness with a bit more compassion for myself and others.

Part IV

EXPLORING THE
PSYCHIC SENSES

1

JOURNEYING ALONG
THE SPIRITUAL PATH

"People who are starting to explore the psychic side of their natures . . . feel the instinctual urge to continue their travels because, from the moment they open the inner doors, they are blessed in all their journeys."

July 24, 1982
Suzanne present
"I'm going to count from 1 to 10, where you will please focus and do a reading of the channel's choice from the highest available channel of clear-seeing."

▼

I am not the highest available channel to date. But I am—today, for you—the highest available channel of clear-seeing in realms within the vibrational boundaries in which you are dealing. The source you cleared through previously has graciously allowed me to utilize this channel, as my perceptions of the physical plane are of longer standing. In fact, dealing with time's arbitrary nature in its long-range perspective, you could say that I am a historian of the movement of energy, the currents and cross-currents of universal flows—how they tune in, move through, and affect the systems involving the realms on this side of the earth's vibrations.

We are always pleased to see elements of the human spirit expressed in the desire to explore greater parts of beingness. While it may appear to people starting to explore the psychic side of their natures that there is no material point to doing so, once the door is opened, they feel the instinctual urge to continue their travels because, from the moment they open the inner doors, they are blessed in all their journeys.

This vibration is automatically sent to anyone in the dream state or in psychic work so that they, perhaps without rational reasoning, feel compelled to continue because new energies begin to feed them, making their lives fuller within, rather than fuller in the material sense, which is perhaps satisfying to the ego, but external and in some cases a burden.

There is a responsibility involved here as the development grows. It is as if one were a train laying down tracks along a new path. As one travels, recognize that once one leaves the way station and begins a new path, building as he goes, that if he pulls up and stops the tracks, he has not finished the journey. Once the path is started, there is a responsibility not to let it go in limbo. Once one has tasted that there is more, then the internal feelings of failure are much deeper than they would be on the materially bankrupt level. For those who start the spiritual path and fall back or stop, the feeling of spiritual bankruptcy comes when they reach a point where they see that in the path is a responsibility, because once the path is open other trains will follow.

Following is some personal information for the channel. At this point, the track, in its probable state, is completed and you are moving along steadily. The most important thing now is to build momentum—in readings, in interaction, and in paintings. The building of momentum will multiply the energies available. The tracks will be laid automatically, as the path is already created and the train can roll through.

All signals are go now. Optimum health is being fed into the instinctual system through diet and exercise, following the intuition for daily enjoyment. Every day, some psychic and creative work should be done. This will bring peace, and as momentum increases, the regulated inward flow of high energy will seem natural.

The system is being very delicately altered now to contain more massive amounts of energy, available to flow into the plane for the expansion of consciousness. At all times, the vibration should be to enjoy the creativity within and share it with others. With the quiet knowledge within the being that the path is open, it goes all the way through, and the momentum has started.

We are sending you many things which you feel, which will stay with you, as we will now.

We send blessings to this open channel system, as we are recording the probabilities from this point as signposts to aid you along your way. That is all.

▲ ▲ ▲

Commentary

After the reading I had strong feelings of completion, blessing, and oneness.

"The source you cleared through previously" mentioned at the start of this reading is a reference to a really far-out channel I had picked up (or that picked me up) five days before. I've never heard from this channel again, but I know it's out there and I can still sometimes feel it.

That reading, titled "From the Other Side of the Universe," is in Part VI, Chapter 6.

2

DREAMS AND CREATIVITY

"The desire to help others or help oneself, without knowing how to begin, can always start to be fulfilled in the dream state."

Commentary

I have been working with my dreams for over fifteen years now, with sometimes amazing results. At times, I feel more at home in dreams than I do in physical reality. Dream work also helps me connect with a client or colleague on deeper levels.

For several years I kept a detailed dream diary that helped reveal the patterns of my personal symbolism. These symbols have become an evolving frame of reference on different levels of reality for my current focus, whatever it may be.

Before going to sleep, I feel grateful for what the day has brought me and give myself suggestions and affirmations. Feeling at peace with myself and the knowledge of my eternal nature, I am then ready for my nighttime adventures. They can be exhilarating or scary, rejuvenating or restful. Sometimes I awake from a dream that has given me what I need to change my life.

On some nights, I work hard in the dream state with clients and potential clients, sometimes waking up feeling drained and spacy. Over the years, many I work with in dreams have mentioned that they sensed our connection and felt my presence with them, as I sent them energy or thoughts. This has often happened with those about whom I have no conscious memory of dreaming.

November 17, 1983
Sophia present
"I'm going to count from 1 to 10, where you will please focus on the highest available creative source energy and do a reading on the nature of creativity and dreams."

▼

Dreams are the laboratory where all aspects of physical reality are played out—probabilities, variations, future and past, and mutant strains. The dream state is the reality in which the emotions are given free rein as the motivating factor for creating reality—not necessarily, in the dream state, based on belief structures but colored by emotions, as is the case in physical reality.

In dreams, the stabilizing and operating qualities of the personal and en masse belief structures are explored. Usually, if a personality is moving toward a point in the personal growth process, emotionally or spiritually, in which the belief structure in one area has become too shaky to maintain operational standards and correlate with the personality's perceived reality, these beliefs will be played out, examined, and dissected fully in the dream state before the new belief pattern will be interwoven into daily life.

All negative emotions are first played out in the dream state. Fear, especially, is one of the hallmarks of dreams for those personalities who live with much fear. It is the only way to release enough of this emotion so that in daily life they do not draw to them, very quickly, from their fear further reason to fear. In these cases, dreams are the maintenance or the medicine, the laboratory that allows the personality to experience physical reality until the belief structure can be stabilized in a more positive emotional framework.

In its most positive light, one can utilize dream reality as a laboratory for many experiments never before conceived of in physical existence. It is a place where seeds can be planted and watched as they grow, to see whether they in their season become mutants or come to full flower with straight stems. It is a way to explore the inherent potential that a personality feels coming to the surface, to see if the time is ripe for their flowering in physical existence. Allowing them to flower in a dream and nurturing their growth from there forms the basis, on entry into the physical plane, for a firm belief structure of faith.

The use of symbols is utilized more as a language in dreams than in physical reality; only in dreams, symbolism is seen more clearly. There are just as many symbols in daily life. In dreams, however, personalities free from the bonds of physical structure and their belief patterns can play with the symbols and realities surrounding them (created by their emotional desires), utilizing these energies to create probabilities that do not seem possible in physical existence.

Shall we say then that, for human beings in the plane, the dream state is the area in which the field work is done. It is the stepping-stone between the creativity of All That Is and its flowering. It is the place where personalities can develop their own potential as co-creators of physical reality by experimenting and closely monitoring the results. It is the reality in which the seed of all creativity is born, as it is expressed in the plane through the arts. It is the reality in which all human beings who are fearful can learn to deal with this fear and move on. It is the reality where human beings go every night to remind themselves of why they are here. This gives them the source energy—emotional, mental, creative, and spiritual—to move on through the next day. Whether they are consciously aware of this transfusion or not, it does occur.

It is reality on a mass level that has formed all the clichés of "brotherhood" and "love of mankind." It is what keeps us all from killing each other on a daily basis. If all mankind could meet consciously in the dream state and work out the potentials for peaceful and creative co-existence with each other and with

All That Is—and then not awake so much as merge these two realities—we would then have one of the probabilities available for the race. And this too is being worked on in dreams by those guides whose function it is to work in the dream state with personalities.

This is also the realm of communication in which the source self of each personality can get information through to the personality when it has blocked the inner voice.

Let us say in closing that the desire to help others or help oneself, without knowing how to begin, can always start to be fulfilled in the dream state. If one truly has the desire to help one's self or one's fellows, and for whatever reason—fear or inertia or blockage or disease—cannot consciously or actively do this in the plane, the dream reality will allow this desire to be fulfilled. It is the channel through which the personality can come to fullness with the desire and then channel it back into waking reality.

▲ ▲ ▲

3

THE KEY TO THE AKASHIC RECORDS

"The essential qualities (to read the Records) are: clear channels, confidence in one's instinctual urges, and a desire to travel to far places."

Commentary

This reading was done when I first began to channel. Quantos, a record keeper, was one of my earliest channels. His cousin is vibrationally similar, but this is the only time I have heard from him.

    In 1982, as my open communication between planes evolved, I developed a direct contact in the Hall of Records with what I call the Sympathetic Bridge Recorder. I use this channel for soul readings, reincarnational and karmic, as her vibration is more emotionally attuned than that of Quantos, which is more detached.

January 17, 1977
Jim present

The following is an excerpt from Automatic Writing Session No. 5. The Akashic Records, which are referred to in the reading, are the eternal history of all souls written within the ethers of time-space.

NEW DIRECTIONS

▼

The theory that the Akashic Records are read through time—as if time were space and space were the soul—is concurrent with the belief that one can connect if one allows the soul consciousness to become the only space.

The attitude of divine intervention is necessary only for those with a need for a hierarchy of back pats. The essential qualities (to read the Records) are: clear channels, confidence in one's instinctual urges, and a desire to travel to far places. The amount of energy expenditure must not allow you to forget how much more important self-confidence is.

Internal demands for this journey start with the packing of the knowledge one will need for the trip. Ask yourself what you will need. You will see that if you need to carry anything along, you are not ready.

This journey necessitates disconnection of all psychic baggage, or at least the ability to travel light during periods of expansion. Intercommunication between soul and body must be on silver threads—very, very light. All excess weight will equate in inverse proportion to the amount of information available. [Any psychic blockage or baggage will interfere with the clear channeling of information.]

The inner guards for the Records are your own inner locks. There is no key, except to realize that there is no lock at all. The key is there within, turning round and round, and you are all there is to unlock. The Records, the information, are there. The interpretation is infinitely individual, and there hasn't been a good definitive review done. The alterations are constant and often simultaneous, enhancing awareness of the humor of time and the way to carry on a meaningful relationship.

Transgressions of faith are only an issue when one lacks confidence in one's own power. Instinct must be allowed to rule, regardless of energy level. The results are comparable to those that come when one's own psychic powers are felt as fully and clearly as one feels one's teeth or eyes or hands.

More personally, the initial thrust into the realm of communication between planes is opened again, and defections of energy into other areas will not hamper production. Costs result only if frequent energy expenditures are made in running from oneself. Allow no time for self-doubt, only for reflection.

Actions are being called upon, events are shaping up, arenas of new landscapes are unfolding, and, unquestionably, the amount of progress of our work together will be dependent not only on you = us and all that is happening, as energy is constantly shifting and the quintessence is not lost, but only the fire smoldering.

Till the next,
Quantos's cousin

▲ ▲ ▲

4

PATHS OF ENLIGHTENMENT

"True enlightenment is not reaching the top of the mountain. It is in experiencing clearly, on each step of the journey, that there is no difference between the mountaintop and the point one is at in the greater scheme of All That Is."

July 19, 1984
Sophia present

"I'm going to count from 1 to 10, where you will please focus through the eyes of the Sympathetic Bridge Recorder and do a reading on paths of enlightenment—now."

▼

There is no time like the present for enlightenment, and all paths lead to the top of the mountain. Experiencing enlightenment does not mean that your reincarnational cycle is over. It only means that you see very clearly, without a doubt, why you are here, where you came from, where you are going, and that it is all right.

Established spiritual disciplines in the various religions of mankind—ancient esoteric practices and schools—all have paths that lead to the top of the mountain. These paths are well-worn, with clear markings, way stations, road maps, traveling companions, and supplies for the trip.

But even if one is traveling a path toward the top of the mountain that many have traveled before—whether it be an avatar, such as Buddha or Christ, or the renunciates so common in the Far East, whether it be those saints who have dedicated

159

their lives to the service of mankind or within structured current religions—each step will be uniquely individual, even if the stepping-stone has been trod on before with spiritual success. The impressions of each step, of each upward movement, are unique. And enlightenment, when it does descend, is a uniquely individual experience of Divine Energy.

We have been asked to focus on various disciplines and schools along the road to enlightenment. There are many. Astrology is a soul science and, as such, is primarily of the mind. It is a science in that it has direct and finite correlations to universal vibratory patterns, and through its study one can come to understand, on the personal level, their vibratory nature and purposes in the esoteric focus on the moon's nodes and along the Sabian Symbols vibrationally.*

This is primarily, though, a mental tool. It can be used as a mechanism of the higher mind for purposes of interpretation. But alone it does not transcend to levels beyond the mind, and as such becomes baggage for the trip. Once it is digested and understood, it can be outgrown and discarded. It is not a necessary tool but, for those overly focused on the mental, a useful one in the early stages of spiritual expansion. In many cases, it trains the mind to certain disciplines and allows the spirit to desire more direct knowledge.

We then move on to one of the primary tools of the present age for the expansion of consciousness along the spiritual path. That is the exploration and development of the psychic senses and, through this, a direct knowledge of purposes and probabilities—past, present, and future—and direct experience with All That Is. It is a stepping-stone to becoming a co-creator with the Creative Forces.

To put it simply, what this development means, again

---

*The moon's nodes are the vibrational focus of the karmic direction—where one is coming from and where one is going. The Sabian Symbols are an updated psychic tool of symbolic messages, uniquely keyed to each of the 360 degrees of the zodiac. See *An Astrological Mandala* by Dane Rudhyar (New York: Vintage Books, 1973).

using the analogy of the mountain, is that, as one follows one's personal, solitary path or one's structured, guided path up the mountain of life, it is the ability to transcend the mind/ego and listen to the inner voice to know which step is next, to know when it is time to rest, when it is time to travel with a group, when it is time to change direction, cross the waterfall, go under it, or swim through it.

It is mankind's heritage to have the psychic senses as closely at hand as the five physical senses, to have, in every step, communion with nature, with one's fellows, and with the higher forces. It is a natural function of the race, now latent within each being. The key is in the "now." For true enlightenment, in this new definition, is not reaching the top of the mountain. It is in experiencing clearly, on each step of the journey, that there is no difference between the mountaintop and the point one is at in the greater scheme of All That Is.

If the psychic senses are trusted and heeded as intuition develops along the journey, they tell one how to clear the view to become lighter for the journey, when to be of service and when to stay clear, when to unwind karmic bonds and when to work them through. It is the sense of knowing one's vibratory nature and understanding that the four elements—fire, earth, air, and water—are connected to the journey and each individual's vibratory makeup.

So, then, there will be times in different lives when a personality will feel more comfortable journeying along rock and earth. Some will choose to swim upriver. Some will choose the path of fire, and some will choose to fly. And if one can tune through the inner senses into one's true vibratory nature and one's point of development, one knows clearly what element is most comfortable at a given time, and what step is the clearest move to make.

Once human beings are on a spiritual journey, focused on clearing, lightening, and moving back to the source at the top of the mountain, they have had moments of enlightenment—unlabeled as such because they have not passed the standards of any structured school or esoteric discipline. But within the moment of realizing the purpose and interconnectedness to All That Is, enlightenment is there.

To experience enlightenment, the optimum development is to enlarge perception in the moment, utilizing the inner psychic senses, to experience each step—no matter how mundane—with as much clarity and light as flashes of inspiration and understanding, so that each step on the daily path is an experience of enlightenment in beingness.

All mankind, each member of the race, is on a path up the mountain, no matter how circuitous it may seem in any given incarnation. Some are tunneling deep within the mountain; some are going down before they can go up. But for each individual, no matter at what point in the reincarnational cycle, it is possible to experience the illumination in each step of his own journey. In closing, we will just say that no person experiences true enlightenment on all levels just because they have followed the directions of some structured path. Enlightenment occurs through the desire and faith of the being and the readiness for this opening. If there were more trust and faith in the inner voice, the inner senses, the intuition, and the connectedness to All That Is through prayer and meditation, then even on the darkest nights on the mountain, the path would be illumined by clear-seeing beings, generating inner light as they move back to the source of their illumination.

5

IMAGINATION, PLAY, AND THE PSYCHIC SENSES

"Contained within each individual—the conduit from the lower octave of the physical senses to the higher octave of the psychic senses—is the imagination."

October 22, 1984
Sophia present

"I'm going to count from 1 to 10, where you will please focus on the gestalt of source energies now aligning and do a reading on imagination, play, and the psychic senses."

▼

Just as there are five physical senses, there are seven psychic senses.

The first is the sense of connection between the self and All That Is through the crown of the head. When activated, this sense allows the being at all times, on the energy levels, to be fully connected to the Godhead in himself.

The second psychic sense is located in the higher mind of each being. It is the part of the mind connected to the Universal Mind, whose structure is divine law and whose medium is the intuition, or the inner voice. When this psychic sense is fully activated, the being knows intuitively, without doubt, the whys and wherefores of every step in the physical dance—based not on rational thought but on the understandings of divine law communicated through the intuition from the source of the higher mind.

We then move to the third psychic sense, which begins the alignment with the higher octave of each of the five physical senses. The first is aligned with vision, the sight, the physical eyes, and focused as the third eye connected to the physical being, also connected not through any optic nerve to the brain but as a direct vision center to each personality's soul entity. When this psychic sense is fully activated through the third eye, it raises the physical vision to the higher octave, in terms of the ability to perceive on more than just the physical level. To the degree that this sense of sight is activated on the psychic levels, the being has the capacity to view physical existence on multi-faceted levels of vibration and purpose within the dance, absorbing into the being the fuller range of each energy interaction and event in the depth of physical existence.

Moving on to the fourth psychic sense connected to hearing: This sense, when activated, allows the being to hear on a higher octave, through nature and through man, the sounds of the universe. So, combined with the other psychic senses mentioned, the being has the capacity to hear more than is being said on the physical level, and knows and feels on the vibrational energy level what the true meaning of every communication is.

The next psychic sense is connected to the nose and also to the lower chakra system on the survival levels. It is connected to the ability to discern different odors and scents. On the higher octave, these smells can be picked up vibrationally in terms of negative energy, aggression, power, danger, etc. This is the beginning of the higher octave of the physical to the psychic sense. Moving even higher on this octave, we have the capacity to utilize the nose for breathing, as it is developed in the psychic capacity—breathing air, prana, energy within the air that contains different vibrations within the ethers. As the breathing psychic sense is fully activated, the being can utilize the breath to raise the level of consciousness to a more rarefied, clear form of beingness.

The next psychic sense is connected to the mouth—the physical sense of speech. On the higher octave, we have the capacity through the psychic sense to communicate to others through the language of choice more in the vibrational tones and words, psychically connected to the other senses, than is possible solely in communication through the rational mind. So this psychic sense, as it is developed in the higher octave, is a communication channel for the Creative Forces, in every breath, every thought, every tone heard and every word spoken.

The last major psychic sense we will mention is the higher octave of the sense of touch—connected here too through the heart chakra to All That Is. As it is developed, it is the ability to feel, through the skin, vibrationally connected to All That Is, to mankind, and to nature at its fullest capacity, with compassion, as the Compassionate Hot Wire is the feeling tone for this psychic sense clearly manifested in the earth plane.

Contained within each individual—the conduit from the lower octave of the physical senses to the higher octave of the psychic senses—is the imagination. The imagination is the tool, the method, the means, the bridge contained within each being to raise the senses to the higher octave. It says, "What if?" and, "Perhaps there's more here than meets the eye. Perhaps there's more going on than I feel, hear, or sense." It allows this curiosity, this questioning, to flow from the lower mind to the higher mind.

It is the capacity found in children to experiment and play-act with curiosity, pretending they are someone else or somewhere else, and it is in allowing this skip in physical focus, this stretch activating the imagination, that the psychic senses are allowed to activate and flow in.

So the keys to activating the psychic senses that are now latent within each being are to let go of the rigidly structured physical focus—based on rational fact and reality limited by what the five senses can reveal in terms of society's finite acceptance of evidence from the five senses. (In fact, it is suggested that one of the necessities of the evolution of the race is to raise its consciousness by activating these senses for a more comfortable alignment in the coming century.) And to allow each being's imagination and childlike nature to come forth again, and imagine in the play of daily life what else might really be going on. To play-act, to imagine, to allow the inner voice to whisper to deeper levels of beingness to come into awareness.

We will, in closing, give some suggestions for how to utilize the bridge of the imagination to activate the psychic senses more fully. When in a comfortable situation, whether alone or with others, one adventure or experiment to pursue is to allow the imagination to form the being in another place or another point in the history of the race, communicating or feeling the same on the personality level and shifting the time and space sequence.

Another key is the being's openness, the willingness to experience these senses through the crown and the pores of the skin as polarities to be open to all feelings of universal sensation and creation, and to allow these feelings of connection to be expressed as joy in being. This too will activate the psychic senses more and more, as interconnectedness to Universal Forces—to man and nature—is expressed and felt. Through openness, the joy in beingness will activate the comfort with using these senses in daily life, as the beneficial next step in the evolution of consciousness that is wrapped within each being as a gift, waiting to be opened.

▲ ▲ ▲

Commentary

This reading was so ready to come through that it started even before Sophia could finish counting. Afterward, she said that it was the clearest channel she had ever heard.

I am continually amazed at the simplicity of the concepts in this reading—at once old and new. Before it, I never realized in such clear terms how the psychic senses really are integral to each of us.

6

EXCERPTS FROM PERSONAL READINGS

SOUL FAMILIES

October 24, 1983
Jack present

Jack is a very successful writer of fiction who also teaches writing workshops. He had been married a few weeks before.

"I'm going to count from 1 to 10, where you will please focus and do a reading for the personality present, Jack, on the nature of his present development—creative, vocational, and spiritual—with suggestions for aligning with the optimum direction for growth in these areas."

▼

Have faith in the powers greater than thee, for as your openness to them grows, they are aligning themselves to guide you more fully.

What we see in the present development is very heartening, on many levels. We are speaking directly to the personality present, Jack, as guides of the powers that be as part of his soul network, aligned with his connection to All That Is.

In the last year, the personality has chosen to fulfill the self and allow the self to stabilize, emotionally and externally. The serenity that then comes is allowing inner workings to enlarge and become more receptive to the inner flow of this personality's energies.

So the personality gazes around his world, with a new contentment at what he sees. And this has always allowed the focus to turn inward again, to rebalance with the outward on a higher vibrational level, and in the turning inward, to examine what will best fulfill the potentials of this personality for the purposes chosen for this lifetime.

It is now time to remind the personality of the purposes and core vibration of the soul family of which he is a member. This is a large, illustrious family in which the purposes have always been in the realm of creative communication—to fulfill the self and ignite attention and receptivity in others. It is also to infuse those around the communicator with the knowledge, whether conscious or below the conscious level, that there is more to physical existence than meets the eye.

This personality's gift in communication involves conveying this message of the enlarged scope and purpose of physical existence. These gifts of mental development, language arts, and humor are fully deserved and developed through the reincarnational cycle. Humor and wit can be utilized not only through the planned seminars to ignite in people creative purpose and enjoyment, but also beyond personal fulfillment, the purpose for which the entity chose this vehicle in this lifetime.

Writing can now take on a new direction. We see a gestation period of four to five years until this next creative step is completely comfortable. Communication with others, through the personal, service, and teaching spheres, will align the personality to pursue this new direction. This will entail the writing of, shall we call it, metaphysical fiction, which explores in its full depth, with dramatic devices and humor, the nature of why we are all here, with the nuances of daily communication and fantasy involving visions and dreams in the characters' daily lives. In doing so, the personality will send messages into the plane that, while enjoyable and entertaining, will ignite in those who are receptive a broader range of perception. This is not to be slighted in any way. It is essential for our age to ignite this broader seeing with whatever gifts one has.

In the meantime, recognize that the personality's spiritual nature is aligned with its optimum future direction. Express the commitment to a vibrational direction daily, express what one knows on the deepest levels in all aspects of life, with the family and in the guidance role now aligning. This will enlarge the core vibration, and the feeling within the being will pulse stronger and brighter than before, as serenity, in the sure knowledge of the personality's eternal nature and the fulfillment of this life's purposes.

Jack: "Is there anything from past lives that I should know and be able to deal with in this life?"

At this point within this personality, there has been much integration of various roles developed on a mature level in the previous line or cycle. Be aware and appreciate and enjoy all the various facets of being to recognize that, while they are a gift to be used wisely, they are also well-earned through the reincarnational cycle.

▲ ▲ ▲

July 31, 1984
Sophia present

▼

Sophia: "What soul family or families do I come from?"

We see here a triple alliance. The primary focus is from earlier incarnations of hierarchical authority, administration, and power structures, to maintain order as civilization developed based on higher patterns of structure within the universe. Administrative abilities are still intact through this family connection.

The second connection in this alliance is to serve others, the caring family of those committed to recognizing the connectedness of all human beings; helping and guiding is the optimum fulfillment.

The third vibrational focus of this alliance of ancestral families and soul vibration is along the creative earth vibration, to utilize the physical gifts through the five senses, to communicate joy in beingness.

So we have a combined alliance—administrative, service-oriented, and creative—all inherent within the present personality, all developed through the reincarnational cycle, and balanced in the present incarnation, with the service vibration at the center.

▲ ▲ ▲

August 13, 1984
Cynthia present

▼

Cynthia: "Do I belong to a soul family?"

We are getting a dominant family here—the guides, healers, and teachers, within and beyond the plane. This also means that the personality in the soul form between lives is a guide, healer, and teacher on other planes. The second family connection is the one of creative communication, through music and other creative arts, utilizing the five senses to communicate joy in the plane. These are the primary soul family connections that we pick up.

▲ ▲ ▲

THE POWER OF COMPASSION

September 9, 1982
Winston present

▼

More and more, you are in a position to deal with those around you on a new level of compassion, taking into consideration the vibrations of the entities in your immediate environment.

The key here is to clear the vision and see not what these people have to offer you, see them not even in terms of personal power as your equal, but rather on the intuitive level; if there is a pleasing vibration to the personalities in your life, then interchange and give freely of your own personal energy and vibration.

There will be an opening up of the heart chakra, with nothing to be gained but the interchange among compatible personalities, with a naturally flowing generosity of spirit—with nothing to be gained. This is the smoothest path for opening the heart chakra and allowing the mental debris to be swept away.

You are working from a pattern in which the vision has been limited. This pattern does not allow the personality to see clearly that in giving one's personal energy to others, one's self is not diminished. If giving and flowing continue, the self will not disappear. Rather, it is in compassionate giving to others that one is filling self in a cycle.

The vision has not seen this clearly up till now. But in recognizing and slowly lifting off the blinkers in daily life, in giving to those one likes, there will be enjoyment. The self will feel fuller rather than diffused, the vision will clear, and the belief structure will change. So giving of one's self does not diminish the self but rather multiplies the energies flowing in from the Creative Forces.

As one becomes a channel for compassion, recognize that all the energy, power, and vitality that you possess is not yours. It is contained in you, yes, but you are a channel, a vessel. In only giving to others to aid your self, the channels to you from the Creative Forces are limited. Only in giving to others freely and not for the self can the self be transcended. As we now view it, this is the next step.

We are suggesting the path of least resistance: to remove the blinkers on the vision and see the connections to all human-kind. We will repeat: In daily dealings, in personal life, in group associations, and in business, give freely to others because of the vibrational energy interchanged based on compatibility and connections on the intuitive level, rather than on the level of power given and power returned. Helping others with enjoy-ment is, shall we say, the least painful way for the personality to move.

Those who you view as guides or teachers in the plane are those who see clearly, without the blinkers you have, the poten-tial power of compassion that you have within you. As the transformation of your soul occurs, there are many souls with different functions in the plane who can guide you. In doing so, they are following their own path—growing and building—for they see clearly that in guiding and giving of themselves, the energy is never lost or dispersed. Recognize that it is not neces-sary to give back in the same direction given to you, but to pass it on as you move along your path.

What others have given to you, give to others. The cycle remains unbroken. It needn't be reciprocal between entities. Just pass it on.

▲ ▲ ▲

CREATIVE CATALYSTS

February 16, 1983
Jack present

▼

Jack: "In order to take a new direction in my work, as the reading suggests, what sort of books should I write next?"

The most exciting creative endeavor to explore, if not for the next work then for one developing as the personality develops, is an exploration that the personality is himself moving toward—with, of course, the necessary plot entanglements to maintain a level of interest.

This explores the elements within each human being of the full repertoire of roles, both sexes, with the nature of sexuality explored in the personalities in the book, their full range between feminine and masculine and as they develop within the personality present. There is an emphasis here on men's ability to start taking action based on intuition and women's ability to start moving out into the physical plane as a new kind of warrior, based on the feminine qualities of compassion and intuition.

This will be not only entertainment, which is of course the hook, but also an exploration of the personal path, the path many personalities are now looking toward. It is necessary through the creative repertoire of the race that there be catalysts, which your work could be in this realm.

▲ ▲ ▲

THE SOUL'S MUSIC

September 7, 1983
Gordon present

Gordon is a very gifted musician and composer.

▼

Gordon: "Would it help me to know who my spiritual guides are? If it would, may I know who they are?"

We get the name Rachmaninoff here. There is the Russian influence and the piano and violin influence. This vibration was a teacher of this personality, now either your guide or a counterpart personality, another probability that your soul lived. In the nineteenth century, the teacher was involved with meter and structure and practice, practice, practice.

Also, going back further, we see that the line to music in the present has developed from a yearning to express the music of the soul through various personalities who were wanderers and warriors along the seas and the land. In this lifetime, the integration of the longing for soul expression with the structure of this Russian guide is integrating in this present personality *for the first time.*

It is not something to sit down and analyze. Rather, tune in to the inner music of the soul and utilize the need, from the Russian influence, to work at it. It is in being more inwardly open, listening to the soul's music, that the greatest joy from this creative potential will come—the openness to the soul's music based on the wanderings of various parts of self. The fulfillment in music will come as the being opens emotionally to others more. Another question?

Gordon: "I am confused as to the path I should take—popular music, jazz, or classical forms. I feel that I can express myself in all three, yet I'm confused. Can you help?"

The key is to listen and be open to the inner music, to the inner desire to express the soul's vibration through self and through the music. Whatever medium works to express inner ideas, inner emotions, inner longings, is the music to work on.

The style is a personal choice. The joy of expression will come from finally tuning in and being open to the inner music. And the chosen expressive style will find a place externally as the being opens up more. But in terms of creative expression and the fulfillment of this potential, the style is only whatever choice best expresses the inner creative workings. Does this help?

Gordon: "Yes."

Another question?

Gordon: "Sometimes lyrics come easy and sometimes they come hard. Is this also a reflection of how attuned I am to myself?"

Words are not easily expressed by this personality, but the feelings and ideas are there within the music. In time, as the personality opens more, inner and outer, the words will come more easily. But recognize that the development has been toward expression through the music rather than the words, the expression of ideas and themes through melodies. As the personality is able to more openly communicate with those he trusts, the feelings behind the melodies will become more articulate.

The ability to express the inner music through melody is a talent that is not yet fully developed in this life. He will find those who will catalyze him to develop his own abilities, to utilize the themes that are being expressed more verbally. He will need to trust others to help him become more verbal.

▲ ▲ ▲

ENLARGING THE VISION

May 4, 1983
Jacob present

▼

Jacob: "What must I do to clear the vision?"

As always, the beginning of any flowering such as this is an inner process, as the being well knows. It is suggested that in meditation, in viewing the self, and for work to be done in the dream state, suggest before sleep that the personality will dream of clearing the vision of self toward self and self toward others. Start in the dream state and then, in daily meditation, start viewing the self as a bud that will flower if the personality will allow the sunlight of compassion to flow through the being—compassion and love for the self first.

Recognize that there needs to be a flowering. The bud is now closed, but there is a flower within. Feel the compassionate light of the universal Creative Forces flowing into the being so that the flowering will allow this light to flow to others.

It is a mechanism of the heart chakra, and it is imperative to start with the compassionate, generous view of self to self. The dream state will help lift some of the darkness. Just be willing to enlarge the vision of self. In fulfilling the track of this lifetime, we see it is the only clear way available—not easy but, with willingness, possible. More questions?

Jacob: "Can you explore the throat area mentioned more deeply?"

Yes. We see some blockages here. We suggest that the vision view—figuratively and in reality—a compassionate white light flowing into the whole chakra system, especially to the area around the throat. It may be suggested that for a period of, shall we say, three months some therapy be considered, such as acupuncture or shiatsu, to open up the energy flow in this area, as there are some blockages on the energy meridian levels that have become rather dark.

Jacob: "In my throat?"

Yes. It is leading up from the heart chakra, but the way to the heart chakra will be leading in through the throat, not from the lower chakra system.

Jacob: "Why am I here?"

It is the primary purpose of this lifetime to unlock and enlarge the capacity for vision and to share this with others in being a channel for the compassionate view based on the personal vibration of your original source energy and where you are going—which, eventually, is back to this source.

Develop and enlarge the vision in the present moment. See the continuum you are on as you move through it, and share this with others. And recognize that the greater source that feeds you and from whence you came is, in essence, the same source that connects you to the race. In enlarging the vision to perceive this continuum, you will find fulfillment in this lifetime. The key word for you is vision. More questions?

Jacob: "I don't understand about the word 'vision.' "

It is the capacity to see with the inner eye of the soul— more than mere physical reality, but the full spectrum of realities available through time-space. In essence, enlarging the vision means enlarging the view of self, so that self can be a channel. It is the recognition that, except in physical reality, the eyes are not connected through the optic nerve to the brain. The eyes are connected to the soul, which is connected to the source from whence you come. This eternal vision is what can be unlocked in this lifetime. And you *do* know of what we speak— well.

▲ ▲ ▲

GUIDES, MASTERS, AND GUARDIAN ANGELS

August 13, 1983
Cynthia present

▼

Cynthia: "Do you know who my guardian angel or master is?"

Listen very carefully to this. Through this lifetime, you will meet several entities in positions to guide and reassure you. If you choose to perceive one of these entities as anything more than a guide, you will not be able to maintain balance at the core. The optimum master of your own being is *yourself.* You develop mastery through connecting with your own higher sources to your entity and soul.

If the purpose of this lifetime is to attain and maintain balance, that must come from internal sources only. External sources will bring pleasure, guidance, catalytic energy, and reassurance, but mastery for this lifetime, for this personality, must be developed from within the being. Otherwise you will spend too much energy and time spinning.

▲ ▲ ▲

MEDITATION

▼

Cynthia: "I am associated with a friend who might possibly be a teacher to help me balance my personality. Is this true?"

This personality can reassure and guide you on your personal path with meditative qualities to align with your inner sources.

Cynthia: "Is it possible that she will lead me to the woman who heads a light group, to be part of that also?"

Again, at this time we see that the light group will reassure and offer guidance. External sources will offer external points of reference, which will keep the personality spinning. For the truest, clearest alignment, it is necessary for all beings on this path—the path that is One—that it must be done within the being, alone.

Cynthia: "Would this be through spending enough time in meditation?

The key here will be the quality of the meditation. Beginning with a half hour twice a day will be sufficient. Balance this with metaphysical readings and the reassurance and guidance of others in the psychic and spiritual fields. But do not let external guidance spin the personality in too many directions.

There are many points of reference for the spiritual traveler. There are many paths up the mountain. For this personality—at this point in this lifetime—alignment with inner sources, acknowledging the inner truth of beingness, is necessary so that choosing another's path will not, as years go by, lead to imbalance.

Cynthia: "I feel it's imperative at this time to control negative personality traits. Will that help make meditation more fruitful?"

Control is not the issue here. *Letting go* is the issue: letting go of all external parts of the personality that are no longer operative.

Let us just say that your entity has been giving you shock treatments, eliciting your desire to open up the connection with him. This is aligning circuitry optimally, running not just from the entity outside the plane to you, but also so that you will be able to channel, from a balanced position, energy back to your source—an open system.

Part of the process is not just to feel balanced within your being, connected in balance to the physical plane, but also, as a being within the physical plane, to feel balanced beyond the plane. As balance in the physical plane develops, the next step will be the next step.

▲ ▲ ▲

THE FEELING TONE THAT IS YOU

▼

Cynthia: "At what vibration does my core generate?"

Let us put it this way: Each entity, each soul, has a unique vibration all its own that is the seed contained within each personality in the reincarnational cycle. We suggest that you get in touch with the seed that is always in you. It is the core vibration that is your eternal nature and your individuality in the universe.

It does not have a name or a label. It is a feeling tone that is you that transcends physical focus or personality.

Cynthia: "Provided that the personality is balanced, is it possible in this life to combine all the creative energies, as well as have a personal life and children?"

To the degree that the personality is able to maintain balance from the core vibration, to this degree will all the talents and potentials for fulfillment be possible.

Cynthia: "If I balance the personality, will it be possible for me to see other planes of existence?"

Not just see—experience.

▲ ▲ ▲

The following five excerpts from my own personal readings were done over the period of a year.

TIME OUT

August 28, 1983

▼

Just a reminder—since the channel tends to forget—that the time now for the next two to three weeks is an inner flowering, an inner growth process, time out to be in touch with the self on the deepest levels experienced in this lifetime. And recognize that this is not exactly "not doing anything." Recognize at all times—in quiet moments, in meditation—the validity of the connectedness of this process.

▲ ▲ ▲

INTUITIVE TRUST

December 29, 1983

Sophia: "What is the primary focus for the personality Joan for the coming year?"

▼

Life will hold many surprises in the coming year, whether the personality Joan is open to them or not.

The key here, the primary focus, will be to utilize both the external and internal energies available, to stabilize the personality on an integrated level of awareness and acceptance of the path ahead. That way, the events moving toward the line of probabilities will not blow the personality off the track she is now on—if the personality focuses on stabilizing and integrating the level of awareness, utilizing all energies available from all sources that she can intuitively trust. Surround the personality with those she trusts intuitively, both along the channel system and externally, in daily life.

Stabilize the physical being daily with diet and exercise. Service to others in the coming year will be an energy recharge, directly linked to the stabilizing process. Internal stability and intuitive trust are key here. The work to be done will be done. There is no questioning or juggling of the probabilities in the area of painting or psychic work.

So focus on stabilizing the channel system as it manifests through the physical being of the personality Joan. And the surprises will not be at all disturbing or have any connotation except newness and enlarging the awareness and range of vibrational depth, if the personality's primary focus is on the stable core of being.

▲ ▲ ▲

RAISING AND STABILIZING THE VIBRATION
March 3, 1984

"I'm going to count from 1 to 3, where you will please stabilize on the channel's core entity system and do a reading on the current level of development of the personality present, Joan, with a specific focus on energy interaction."

▼

It was suggested several years ago that under no circumstances should the personality Joan allow herself to lower her level of vibrational dealing to a primary focus below the fourth chakra of compassion.

It is now time to reiterate that in refining the tonal quality of energy interchanges in the higher chakras, it is necessary to become more discriminating. To fulfill the purposes and do the work ahead, it is time to let go of all vestiges of primary energy interaction from the lower chakra system and raise the level of the whole system by focusing through the heart chakra and the third eye, using these clear vibrations as the channel to revitalize the lower system.

In terms of development, it is time—with the nuclear family and with the core group or network with which the personality frequently interchanges energy—to deal straight across from the higher vibratory tones. Any resistance to the new level now aligning will cause massive splits in the being's connection to her source self.

▲ ▲ ▲

NOT ANALYZING
March 28, 1984

▼

The key for the coming month is lightness. Take nothing with too heavy a ramification in rational or analytical terms. Rather, blend and flow through both creative and psychic work and in daily interaction, with a light vibration that will allow the entity and the present personality to find a balance point of comfortable beingness.

This lightness, this blending and flowing, without the rational mind to give it all depth and meaning, will utilize the development of the beingness in a way that will be optimum for the feelings of freedom now developing and for the utilization and clearing of the channel system, not just for the work but also in daily dealings.

We send blessings to the personality present [Sophia] for the commitment to the present endeavor, and blessings to the channel for maintaining this opening.

▲ ▲ ▲

INTEGRATING ON A HIGHER LEVEL
July 19, 1984

▼

Sophia: "What's happening with Joan?"

The personality, the channel, is experiencing an immense amount of personal power in the psychic realm. She is utilizing the energies well, without much connectedness on the personality levels as to the effect of where these energies are going. This transitional phase is now evolving and, while it is important to experience this surge of personal and psychic power, it is also important to maintain a balance between time alone and time spent with people and structure. Balance between the inner and the outer and maintain the health and diet patterns through this period.

The energy is coming through now because the personality has asked and trained for it. Through this period of integrating a higher level of this energy, the key is to be very aware of the effect on people toward whom this energy is going, and not to generate this energy outward without acknowledging the humanness of the recipients.

▲ ▲ ▲

Commentary

I returned from this trance trumpeting a bugle call and said, "I feel electrical currents running off of my hands. I feel like Frankenstein's bride." Sophia laughed. This reading also contained information on paths of enlightenment, which appears in Part IV, Chapter 4.

Part V

THE PERSONAL DEVELOPMENT
OF THIS CHANNEL SYSTEM

1

EXCERPTS FROM THE EARLIEST READINGS: THE AUTOMATIC WRITINGS, 1976–1977

"Have faith in this—for you feel it within you—that the channel, from the start, was allowed CLEARANCE stamped on all your dual ventures."

In the fall of 1976, my roommate, best friend, and fellow traveler, Jim, and I bought a Ouija board with which to experiment. Nothing much was happening except a lot of slow, meandering gibberish. Impatient, I picked up a pen and started writing. This became reading no. 1.

READING NO. 1

▼

Each and every one of us has something to deliver. I am Joseph. Tonight we will start.

The question is not one of mental endurance, but of the nature of sensation, as in the sea. Forget everything for the moment. Certainly Jim is the coordinator, but you are the star, my dear.

Back to it. Quantos, who never loses it, will be our philosopher of the moment. He is all—ALL—in the sense that he never loses count. Somebody's got to. I am the guide. He is the rudder. And space will be our new sea.

Now a Christian regard is needed in this discussion.

Symptomatically, our civilization is suffering from a moral revolution. We are in it, but we are also here, NOW. Rapidly we will become accustomed to this new state of affairs as time—the workmate of space—becomes our new dimension to travel through. If we are to experience the true joy of the shift, we must smile as it takes place.

The spirit of Santos is the appropriate one to connect with—as He/She is the well-being of any such expansion. Closer now, we will start the field moving with an array of color.

▲ ▲ ▲

Commentary

At the end of this reading, I saw such a spectacular visual display of swirling colors that I knew there would be more to come. Periodically through the next year, I did twenty-three more readings, always with Jim present to stabilize the energies.

Quantos and Santos, two of my ongoing channels, were clearly present from the beginning. I have since come to experience them as part of my higher self's network outside the earth plane.

READING NO. 2: COMMAND PERFORMANCE

▼

Revelation exists at a stage of development akin to this— so do not worry where or who, but just what is. Question not what you can do for us but what we can do for each other. For thine is the kingdom, etc.

As out of the corners of your eyes you can see us, so out of the very centers of ours do you exist.

(Question not:
seize not = seizures
weep not = unweavings)

There is now evidence that existence can be a stepping-stone to grace, so we must work on our more constant communication. For this is the time, and NOW is the channel open. Resistance is not a kindness to your heart and feelings, but rather a last gulp and swallow of the physical that you so love.

As the eye and focus grow and contain the old, conditions for creative constant growth are being perfected. The eye turns ever inward to the soul. Reap this harvest of the pressures of pursuit. It will contain all in a single eye.

Symbology is a tool that is useful in this discussion. As the ball is caught, so to speak, picture hands open to receive spontaneously on either side of the head. That was an earlier model of the Sphinx design. If we are to delve into the time of Pharaohs and visionary dreams, we must first disrobe our purple robes and stand, arms upheld to the sun.

Results are a factor of recognizing consciousness and, as the results come in, you (we) will be surprised at the immediate application to daily life. Things will open up, and blue will serenely reign. Do not forget us now, for the foothold is prepared. Stitches in time keep the channels from closing!

So goodnight, my dear ones, from yours truly,

the HRO

▲ ▲ ▲

Commentary

I did not hear from "the HRO" again, as was the case with many of my earlier channels from the automatic writing period. But this reading definitely let us know that to keep these readings going, it was necessary to continue doing them and not resist.

READING NO. 3: REVELATIONS

▼

Questions of iniquity are an issue now. Before we start, understand that all are blessèd. It is their doubt that is as the falling stone. Art thou afraid at times? Do not be so, for you are on the threshold of the joy of the world, which the founding rock has birthed.

Return with us now to the time of Rebecca and Joseph and the coming into Egypt. The relationship of Joseph to the Pharaoh is the key one here. The trust that Pharaoh had in Joseph, Joseph must now have in the Pharaoh. The conditions of the time were such that because of the seriousness the trust served, the relationship became an open channel.

That will be your hookup as a working team.

▲ ▲ ▲

READING NO. 4: REVITALIZATION

▼

To be immersed in the physical plane is like the eagle at the sun's final setting. And for the cat, another eon's purr. For as the sun revolves around, so do you straddle both—one more above and one more below—in the inner seed connecting both in infinity.

Resolve now that all arbitrations are unnecessary. Consummate the inner vibrational instinct and there will be no doubt at the final moment before.

Situations reflecting your inner state, such as the apartment, exist because in the future you already have a larger one and have grown beyond it, causing conflict regarding on which stepping-stone you lie. One smaller one will be sufficient at this time for your needs—to expand creatively and orient yourselves with a new group of associate travelers. The question of space is one that, for you, is directly connected to mind space—space to create and develop—with pushing against barriers—there will be none, if you have faith in your ability to expand.

A congregation of fellow travelers is now being formed in its natal state. And there will be many well-remembered faces for both of you. Creative energy is in storage for you both, and it will very soon be time to let it explode—in all directions.

For the fully developed state of creative consciousness necessary, we will allow that the foundation is set for an early settlement of earthly financial needs and obligations. Have faith in this—for you feel it within you—that the channel, from the start, was allowed CLEARANCE stamped on all your dual ventures.

Canceled checks are necessary. Forged on the wings of time, they are our guideposts to the future, in that they tell you when the ebb tide is ready to flow, and when to flow with it.

Remembrances will flow through you these days as you check off signposts, like canceled checks, that tell you to move on. For if we are to experience the new with no fear, we must feel the past as secure, as part of us.

The past will shortly not exist in the terms you are accustomed to, and the future present will be our new order. And that, my friends, will make it very cozy.

Adieu,
the Circle

▲ ▲ ▲

Commentary

Among the important issues raised in this reading was my fear. Getting information this way was starting to shake me up.

It also dealt with my relationship with Jim, symbolized as Joseph and the Pharaoh. Jim and I had been unwinding romantically for about five years at this time; we had decided to stay together because of our great love for each other and our deep and enduring mutual bond. This reading said we had another reason to stay together: to work as psychic partners, with Jim stabilizing the energy as I channeled.

This reading was also the first mention of "fellow travelers," the psychic development group Jim and I started in our new, larger apartment in late 1977.

But the most prophetic part of the reading was about "an early settlement of earthly financial needs and obligations." I didn't have faith in this information when I received it, but seven years later I was given a small income from a family trust that I didn't know about until years after the reading. The foundation that this reading predicted allowed me to devote more of my time and energy to psychic work.

READING NO. 5

▼

Respect yourself. Qualities of leadership are good, are inherent, and are rightfully unobtrusive. Organizational thinking in the past has led to much confusion: a small band of true followers wins the war while a whole army plunges into the ditch.

Santos sends greetings.

Santos is the joy.

Quantos is the eternal moment's memory.

Now have faith in instinct, because the next few moves and choices and finds will be the right ones—NO DOUBT. Ascension to the throne will be, at the final steps, a breeze.

At the throne of the universal eye, all is seen, all is recorded, and anything can be utilized at one's discretion.

The atom is but a tinker toy, and all of us are children at heart. The modus operandi is exuberant curiosity.

Traditionally, the spirit of comradeship is of a warrior nature. It is still, but not at all in the sense of danger but of the discovery together of new lands. The idea of conquest is not appropriate here but rather of *rediscovery*.

The initiation of at least one to your circle of upward mobility is essential. It is the symbolic act of a loving care for all souls, wherever they may be. [Rest break.]

Recess is over.

The attitude is good.

Sensitivity to each other's emotional defenses is necessary and is being given a gentle nudge in the dream state, as in the waking state it is difficult to face head on. Your Kutztown experience is coming forward to meet you as a reminder of *purpose*—nothing more—as free will must be allowed to play its lilting melody. The contrast of natures is to understand that every question has two sides—both right—and that individuality is a stacked deck.

The foundation for our search for the nature of this time around is a sensitivity to the Santos spirit of our creation. For as you acquire the sensitivity to the hum, then all the little bees will continue to go about their lives and we can produce a quality of honey that will sweeten the shift. If the jump is going to occur, the moving must be pleasing and the way tempting.

The occult is a never-never land, but honey—ah, honey of the soul—is the sought-after reward of any earthly struggle. Keep in mind that messages from within such as this are colored, and that the coloring today is moving toward honey-colored—and there is a surprise on the inside!

Greetings from all—
the Class

▲ ▲ ▲

Commentary

This reading gave us the idea of inviting our psychic friend Jan to sit in on some of our sessions.

The mention of the Kutztown experience is important because, along with my 1994 trip to Egypt, it was one of the most pivotal events in my life (see the Editor's Introduction).

I have excerpted parts of the remaining readings to give a feeling of the various tones and channels developing through me in the early stages. Some of the material included is poetry, affirmations, and personal readings for Jim, Jan, and myself.

READING NO. 6: MAKING CHOICES
January 20, 1977

▼

Traditional ways of viewing reality are contradicted by the events of the inner mind. Reality as a means of escaping destiny only allows one to run from knowledge of one's own greater identity, and [they] are not responsible for their actions.

The attitude of nonchalance to face inner values is a means of madness or contempt. To deny one's greater self is to get involved in a merry-go-round of denials of the events you yourself set up as an obstacle course before entering [the physical plane].

For if the "markers" [i.e., choices] along the trail are disregarded, then one may lose track, start a new trail, or continue without seeing—but if you can consciously acknowledge the "markers" then you can make your own conscious choices and, in doing so, grow into a greater sense of yourself.

As you pocket in your mind each "marker" as you pass, the memory of all the "markers" blink like lights as outposts of the soul. "Forget not that I am always with you" wherever you may travel and the road is never lost—even if you choose an alternate route, as long as you acknowledge the "markers" you set up for your self along the way. [Rest break.]

The conditions for reinstallation of "before-earth plane consciousness" are to see the "markers," remember *why* you put them there in the first place, and go on to connect these memories with an extension of your life as "markers" blinking from more directions than thought possible.

The altitude of a blinking light is equal to the eye's distance from the inner light or soul.

The tone of blinking lights set out along the way corresponds directly to your own individual tone so that you will know instinctively which "markers" are yours. If the choice is difficult, move back into your self's consciousness before earth and you will know, without doubt, the purpose of the "markers"—and the reason the choice is difficult, for a difficult choice is in itself a very, very important "marker" that you yourself set up.

Restitution of "wrong" choices is to swallow the acknowledgment of choice *completely* with the mind—and, mind being the builder, the choice will be righted.

If the choice was made from weakness or fear, then the choice is not really wrong—*none* really are at this point—only a reflection that more time is needed at a certain stage to do the choice again, with surety that one didn't have before.

Memories of choices that were made from fear always are with you until you are ready to reverse them—for the positive contains the negative *always*—but sometimes the positive cannot come before the negative has been felt . . . and the uncomfortable inner doubt pushes you to see that you are ready. And you ARE. [Rest break.]

The vibration within your daily environment only is allowed to sway to and fro without reason when enough people let loose their hold on it—and many people would rather not have the responsibility—it breeds familiarity and some would rather not get too close to themselves.

Major revisions of self are painful to those who are afraid of pain—but inner shiftings, or rightings of the "ship," are always necessary as conditions shift. And better to be your own captain and control the seas too . . . than to drift. For the preeminent feeling of capsize causes fear—fear of many things—fear of pain, of death, of losing self. When, if one has the inner strength and judgment to *choose* to control oneself, one will find that the shiftings of inner wakes are not painful but only ripples within an ever-expanding you, and only a trifle rocky at times . . . to keep you on your toes.

Sincere regards,
Janos

▲ ▲ ▲

READING NO. 7: WINSOME LOSESOME
January 29, 1977

▼

Messages from on high notoriously favor melodrama as a tone of delivery. Castes of succeeding generations of living dead come through to chastise those following in their paths—a generation gap of misunderstanding.

For the attitude of atonement is a misnomer in time. It is a cult of living dead trying to relive their mistakes and right them through their bloodless relations. Sinister though this may sound to some, it is a direct result of a mutual understanding built up in the fever dreams of souls in fear of doing their own thing. Doing now, all of you, straight down the line, is more—much more—fearsome to some than a long journey down a stifling jungle river that winds round and round through marshes, never finding an outlet to the sea.

So, my friends, the moral is: lower echelons of living dead, in their own fear of new kinds of self-discovery, beckon the living into a fever game of mass discrimination. Listen—never to past undoing—but rather to the inner tick of time unfolding.

RAS-DO

Actions to better oneself in society must be looked upon as a misdirected guideline to inner growth.

Echoes of times past involve a lengthening of mutual awareness into a subsidiary of mutual fear. Conditions of cross-currents between continents involve a tightening of Christian ethics into a stranglehold of stifling rewards, not reflecting inner rewards, and ultimately negating the experience.

Together, inner growth brings rewards full circle—outer reachings for power in society bring ultimate frustration of goals established before input into the plane.

Strivings for outer realization of power can and do occur, without compatible inner development, but are the road not taken. For it brings the trip full circle. If one wishes to fulfill outwardly, one must attune to inner growth and transmit inner power out through the ethers of the plane. The strivings of material manipulations promote all the cancer programs. Don't you see?

▲ ▲ ▲

READING NO. 8: REFUGE FROM THE STORM

▼

In times of trouble I am here
so near the breath test
can flutter me like a leaf
playing a double take
on life
For if I am the breath's flutter
into life,
the leaf

will sing my praise
                          falling
Attest to me an oath
    of allegiance
and when the storm is felt
    the leaf will
        blow much sweeter
            going down
        into thy own sweet earth.
            ▲ ▲ ▲

READING NO. 9: TO A BLACK HOLE
▼

Sending it to you
    it all brings back memories
of meanings past remembrance
    in total recall
The essence of inner growth
    begins fresh
    like a pit of openness
giving way to a new birth
    in time
of knowing it
through sending it
back home

            ▲ ▲ ▲

READING NO. 10: ACTIONS NOT TAKEN
April 8, 1977

▼

Roads not entered
undivided Completions

So-called decision-making is as erratic for the race as gene pooling. Individual assessment of physical surroundings is a point within, waves of events fluttering without. And the choice is but a conscious move of the will to experience. Out of many insecurities these decisions are made at times.

Conquering doubt of the unknown, one can create new channels of influence that harken back to when you could choose and consciously experience several at once. Joan's experience into probable madness is a frustrative mechanism of a bird caged. The result is outer sluggishness and inner discontent.

The will must consciously choose to experience new energy to perform at a heightened daily physical awareness, and affirmations should be given daily for health, rest, replenishment, and well-being.

Jim is suffering from a stagnation of desire to become his own crusade, to be himself at his highest potential, and to allow his emotions to be more the motivations for his actions.

▲ ▲ ▲

READING NO. 11: RESIDUALS

▼

In conversation, you will often hear people say how they should have done something, and sooner or later some of them do it. Others who don't will eventually forget what they were supposed to do. The answer eludes those that shove opportunities so far into the corner that they are forgotten.

Remember that I am the power behind the throne of the living flesh and that action is a belief made manifest. Saying that all probabilities exist and happen at some level anyhow is as much of a cop-out as being ignorant to time sequence as mind transference in general.

Attitudinal shift from anemic to hypertrophic is evidenced by the coming together of beliefs into action in a swoop of regenerative energy. In this case, it is recommended that more time be given to conscious daily affirmation of goals, and that dream interpretation is utilized to its fullest extent by daily referral to symbols as working parts, to combat the insidious attempt of the ego to obscure your greater power.

For power is the message, means, medium, and the circle of time is closing in on a point very close to your central focus, and attention has been called—

SO USE THIS POWER NOW

and do not neglect the gift of the gods to refurbish you, continually and abundantly, as you search for the key to the light.

We are
the
Sons of Light

▲ ▲ ▲

Commentary

"Outer sluggishness and inner discontent" referred to what has been a personal theme, recurring periodically since this early 1977 reading. The suggestion that "the will must choose," with appropriate daily affirmations and dreamwork, remain guidelines for staying on my path.

READING NO. 12: AFFIRMATIONS

▼

If one knows, all know
If one knows, all know
If I have a problem, you have a problem
To every problem there exists a solution
If there is a solution, then I know it and can act on it
And so it is.

▲ ▲ ▲

READING NO. 13: CENSORIUM

▼

Attitudes of stress are unnecessary in this endeavor. But you must be willing to have faith in our input, for we can make adjustments for you through key links in the chain that can be motivated by a simple symbol, such as:

For Jim: Picture the pirate with the parrot, and the interaction between the high priest and the multitude. And find a midpoint without condescension—not without humor, but with respect for the All Knowing aspect within all life.

For Jan: Picture a fall from grace in society's eyes and too much respect in one's own righteousness.

For Joan: Picture the gilded cage with all comforts and fear of flying.

These are to dwell on, for I know you all well. You must realize that this summer has been ordained by you to be a stepping-stone, a starting point for your new makeup—a composition of souls which may travel at will to obtain knowledge long forgotten and utilize this knowledge to further the realignment of the race toward psychic awareness as the most important link to the earth, as a platform from which to expand. And you are the carriers of the chain.

I hope your spirits lift you higher, toward your remembered task at hand.

▲ ▲ ▲

Commentary

In the fall of 1977, Jim and I formed our weekly psychic groups (see the Editor's Introduction). The exercises I created in mine made for experiences that were both exhilarating and frightening.

The readings of this time were more sporadic and personal. Some enhanced our understanding of those we worked with. A few contained advice for me about painting.

By February 1978, I had decided to spend the summer studying art in Salzburg and then settle in southern Portugal with Donovan and paint until my money ran out. I was avoiding the responsibility of developing my psychic gift and hoping to channel all my energies into art.

Jim and I had been together for a seven-year cycle, during which we had evolved a deep friendship and working partnership. I felt it was time to try flying on my own.

Both the readings and Jim had impressed upon me that I needed him to stabilize my energy in that stage of my psychic development. Still afraid to channel without him, I decided to put all my psychic work on the shelf. It wasn't until almost four years later that the readings began again.

2

THE READINGS RESUME IN A NEW FORM, 1982

"In this journey it is imperative to remember at all times that the personality Joan is protected and inviolate and that the alterations of consciousness necessary for these readings to occur are at all times subject to the free will of the channel."

Since my return from Portugal, I had been living with Donovan, until September 1980, and waitressing to support my painting. The readings below clarified the reason for my periodic migraine headaches that began in Portugal and the frightening swelling in my leg that began in the later winter of 1982.

After two initial readings, I was off and channeling again, with Suzanne as stabilizer. The problem in my leg disappeared completely. As the second reading said, it seems that I needed a crisis to become open to doing readings again—to make this commitment to myself and have faith that I was on the right path.

Since January 1981, when I was twenty-seven, I had bottomed out, using too much grass and alcohol as coping mechanisms. But when I became sober and resumed these readings, I was clearer than ever.

Suzanne recorded all the readings in this chapter in longhand, but not verbatim. I had outgrown the automatic writing method, which required eye-hand coordination and kept me too physically focused. Free from the requirement of writing, I started to travel further out, and I channeled all these readings lying down, with eyes my closed. The words came through me faster than Suzanne could write them, causing a lot of back-up problems in my system. So, after a couple of slow, short, frustrating readings, the channel made a practical suggestion that hadn't occurred to either of us earth plane inhabitants: Use a tape recorder.

These are the only readings not recorded directly onto tape. Ever since, readings have referred to Suzanne as "the scribe," even though she functioned as such only in the beginning. But she graciously offered me the use of her laser printer for this manuscript, thus continuing her scribe function in a very contemporary way.

February 14, 1982
Personal reading

Suggestion for topic: potentials inherent in the probable realities for development of the highest soul productivity in the next few weeks.

▼

The base of operations is internal and now centralizing. The base of action is through meditation and then to take the action externally. The key to maintaining the highest energy impact is to remain open to communication between bases— i.e., operations and action.

There is no doubt that the impulses for action are correct at the highest levels. Because of the clear channel hookup now coming into effect, the personalized soul vibration will be magnetizing many old friends toward the channel.

For the first time, the key is to take internal action to release—letting go of all magnetic bonds, letting go with love and allowing the self to be, without pulling or anything external. Allowing the self to pulse outward with inner personalized soul power. Asking not, attracting not, pulling not, just being. This letting go of all but personal power will work in all relationships to attain the highest soul advancement at this time.

We send blessings, healing, and soul power for this endeavor, which is the next step in the path chosen by the channel as an enlightened traveler.

▲ ▲ ▲

March 1982
Personal reading

This reading was from a "plateau of clear-seeing as an enlightened traveler."

▼

Attention needs to be focused on the self and the realization of the path of the self. These days, through the carving of stone* and the connections with the outside world, are leaving imprints of soul growth.

Atar [my lover Paul] is dealing out his karma on the third level of power. He sees Joan's level of heart clearly enough to utilize it for personal aggrandizement. To allow no slip in development at this time, balance between stone carving and outside world through the center of the being.

Continue letting go and loving from the fourth level [of heart]. Let Atar see clearly that there is only one way to move and still see the connection. Do not lower yourself to the third level [of power].

The situation with the legs is stabilizing. You created this crisis so that you would pay attention to your physical being, and also because it is time to recognize that you have gotten all you need from waitressing. By the fall, the next connection to be made in external reality will be clear.

▲ ▲ ▲

---

*This referred to a large painting I was working on called *The Luminous Beings in the Temple Courtyard,* which had three-dimensional sculptural elements in it.

Commentary

I learned a lot from waitressing, coming as I did from an upper-middle-class Jewish background. Not only did it support me through art school and pay for my travels in Europe, but it also taught me how to be a worker among workers.

At the time of this reading, I had been working in restaurants for almost ten years. In the last year, "being of service" became my dharma, or natural karmic path, and I brought to it as much good humor and mindfulness as I could. When I recommitted myself to psychic work a few months after this reading, I felt I could retire from waitressing with honor.

April 15 and 16, 1982
*Personal reading**

"I'm going to count from 12 to 1, when you will alter the focus of your consciousness to the Hall of Records and do a reading through the eyes of the Sympathetic Bridge Recorder,† whose function is to maintain the records as a bridge between all realities."

▼

It is imperative for these proceedings to ensure faith in the channel that she is protected and safe, so that there is no fear of holding back in future readings.

The entity Atar [Paul] views himself, in his physical focus, as fallen. He mistrusts good intent because his power has come from manipulation of other sources. He is filled with fear of not being allowed into the reality of the Sons of Light that he has so long derided. The reason his guides view this as a change in plans is due to the free will of the channel entity, Loa-lai [Joan], in viewing the present bridge reality.

All those who are ready to move back into the cycle of

---

*Interrupted and completed on consecutive nights.
†The idea for this channel came to me in a light trance.

inner connectedness of the whole . . . [The reading was interrupted at this point by Paul.]

▲ ▲ ▲

The reading continued with the same countdown to the Recorder, with the suggestion that the channel be in a "space capsule of pure white light made up of personalized soul energy."

April 16

▼

In this journey it is imperative to remember at all times
that the personality Joan is protected and inviolate and that the
alterations of consciousness necessary for these readings to
occur are at all times subject to the free will of the channel.

All those ready to move back into the cycle of inner connectedness of the whole, see, or at least feel, the pulse of this
time in the plane as a potential evolutionary leap for the human
race in the expansion of consciousness as the beginning of this
earth cycle's final phase.

The experiment now in process between channel Joan and
Atar is at midpoint in its cycle. The keynote here is letting go.
There is much to be learned from each. For Paul: letting go of all
but self to find self.* For Joan: giving up self, letting go in the
giving, and feeling replenished from within.

Different stages of influence are, of course, at play here.
However, mutual reciprocity is really more on a soul level of
endless circles balancing each other. There is more available on
present situation realities that Joan is already becoming consciously aware of, feeding from the inner process.

At the present time, the readings are stacked up in such a
manner that they are forcing pressure on the channel to speak

---

*Paul was in the process of making a major change in his karmic path,
through his career, to a much lighter tone.

quickly. Otherwise, the trance automatically switches to a deeper level of feeling that is nonverbal. Suggested is a method of shorthand or a tape recorder.

Vibrations of this endeavor are good. Intents will become clear shortly. There is no fear of strain as long as the entity retains the attitude of joyful exploration of inner space.

The entity is now available for much greater communication in all facets of development—both human and extraterrestrial—the primary reason being that there is more of the entity self focused in on the present endeavor than before.

The entity blesses Joan for allowing source self focus into this wondrously humorous, ever-enlightening world.

Blessings to the scribe. It will get smoother.

▲ ▲ ▲

April 23, 1982
Personal reading (excerpts, not verbatim)
(from the Recorder)

▼

Optimum functioning now involves a focus on the self's physical being as a planet, with the recognition that all parts make up the atmosphere or the vibration for the creative and the psychic work. In terms of optimum functioning, recognize that the physical is the vehicle; the attitude of a loving regard toward it is necessary.

Focus on self strengthening self for the months ahead. Now is the time not so much to reorganize, but to concentrate the being into a laser-like focus that combines the consciousness of every cell of the body in this endeavor. This is the optimum way.

▲ ▲ ▲

April 30, 1982
Personal reading
(from the Recorder)

▼

The keynote of this reading is creative communication, so the personality can see clearly, in every aspect of her daily life, that the major thrust of purpose now is optimum communication between planes and between souls. [It is] to creatively express the personal vibration outward—whether sexually through the physical body, through artwork, or through daily verbal communication with others. Recognize that all this is an expression of being of the source self. All is equal in terms of quality expression. It need not be physically manifest. Every moment of waking and of the dream state can be optimum if the vibration is creative communication.

Pertinent detailed suggestions: For the physical being, it is time to lighten the load—a scary prospect, but possible through drinking large quantities of water with lemon juice. Flushing the system daily with six ounces of fresh vegetable juice combined twice weekly with fresh fruit juice. Focus on protein through higher vibrational sources: less red meat, more seafood (iodine to stimulate the thyroid), green vegetables, and summer fruits. Deep breathing, long walks, and totally letting go. As the body lightens, the feedback rewards will be immediately felt in the sexual sphere.

In terms of the excess energy achieved through this process, it will not be possible to channel it all immediately into constructive creative pursuits per se. So allow sprints, jogging, and running to let go of excess energy during this process.

For the psychic work, it is imperative at this time that the entity, in her development, does not, *does not* push the self or others. Let others come to the entity. Let others come. Let self come to self—a natural flowing process at this time. It is important to work only with those who come freely because of the vibrations involved in the development process.

Like a flower opening. Freely coming, freely going. Freely

giving, freely receiving. No pushing. There is a negative vibration involved for the personality, Joan, in terms of working with tugs of war. At this time, it causes strain on the channel's optimum functioning. It is being released in the dream state now. In the future, this problem should be looked for and taken care of on a daily basis, rather than periodically.

Look around for pushing and resistance and let it go. Keep moving forward. No fighting, no pushing. Smooth, smooth.

Beingness is growing. Self is glowing. Letting go is periodically, haltingly, starting to function as the new pattern. Suggestion for the dream state: work on letting go.

It will be possible for the personality to continue letting go. To become lighter—the load lighter, the functioning clearer. The load lighter, the functioning clearer. That is all.

▲ ▲ ▲

Commentary

Since this reading, and over the last decade, I have worked to let go of all the emotional baggage from this lifetime through an ongoing inventory process of myself. Every year or so, more comes up to let go of, on deeper and deeper levels. At this point, I feel clearer as a channel and as uncolored by personal baggage as I ever have, especially after working in the past year to clear away more karmic patterns that surfaced. But as this reading indicates, the process of letting go is both possible and unending, engendering ever-expanding potentials for clear functioning.

3

THE NIGHTTIME RED ALERT

"This will be a period of letting go, to the extent of a full cycle of the karmic line. . . . Remember that all new levels of consciousness must go through some ripples as they move in."

May 1982
Suzanne present
"I'm going to count from 1 to 10, where you will please focus and do a reading on the present state of the channel."

▼

To achieve the objective distance necessary for this reading, please count to three for what we call the "nighttime red alert." [This was done.]

The key to the present development is that the personality in the plane of the entity [Joan] perceives the potential of latent abilities: being able to handle more on the level of personal responsibility. Viewed from here, the personality is in severe crisis from the fear of letting go of those aspects of physical existence so ingrained in the karmic development, up to this point, as necessary anchors.

There is the fear that letting go of those parts of self projected onto others close to self will leave a void that cannot be filled by self. This is seen clearly from the level of the physical focus. This is true. The void can no longer be filled with self, as self sees self from the ego manifestation. The fear is that the void in the being will be filled with energies that will not allow the personality to experience physical existence as in the past. This is also true.

As the void is filled with Universal Forces (with the personalized soul vibration, of course), the personality's experiences will be fuller. There will be an adjustment period as the being comprehends on many levels, down to the very cells, that the self is not diminished but is being filled to each cell with parts of Universal Forces, personalized with the soul vibration, larger than self, filling self as the channel for work in the creative and communication realms.

It is suggested that the key is to keep existence very simple—simple pleasures, maintaining optimum physical health, simple joys of human communication, connection to nature—and to remember that all new levels of consciousness must go through some ripples as they move in. This period will adjust in four to six weeks and there again will be calm and serenity. This will be a period of letting go—to the extent of a full cycle of the karmic line—from the release of the southern node and a focus realigned toward the northern,* with the recognition that this is the first house of individual development for the Universal Forces to work through as an entity in the plane.

The self is inviolate. It will be enlarged. It will be filled. It will not be lost or depleted. But this process is an evolution that is new. Therefore it involves some alterations in the genetic patterns as well as in the belief systems.

It is suggested to work in the dream state on letting go—letting go, with love, parts of self mirrored in others, as they go on their way and grow. Just as personalities of the entity reincarnated in past reincarnational cycles have gone on their way, it is time to recognize that you can no longer maintain this

---

*This is an esoteric astrological reference to the fact that my karmic direction in this life (my northern node is in the first house approaching zero degrees Aquarius in intercept) is toward individual development through humanitarian pursuits. I also was moving away from a karmic pattern (southern node approaching zero degrees Leo in the seventh house intercepted) of finding power through my relationships. See my astrological chart in the Appendix.

cycle. It is time to close it. It is a new cycle now beginning. That is all.

▲ ▲ ▲

Commentary

At this point in the reading, I experienced the release of all the past lives I was still holding on to. I let them go, with love, and cried.

Visually, this appeared as past personalities of my entity enclosed in a clear plastic bubble, screaming to be free, pounding on the sides of their prison. As I dissolved the bubble, they flew out into space, in all directions, free to develop and explore and create along their own lines—as I am doing now.

At the time of this reading (May 1982) I had decided to quit waitressing by July and live off my savings for the summer, to paint and do readings.

I also began to develop my first psychic therapy techniques, with a few brave souls as guinea pigs. Some of these involved clearing work on the energy and emotional bodies, the untying of karmic knots through past-life regression, accessing soul potential from reincarnational development, and developing channeling skills from the soul-consciousness level and beyond.

Quitting a secure job made me feel like I was jumping off a cliff to see if I could fly. This reading let me know how profound these changes really were.

4

THE COCOON FALLS AWAY

*"The personality is now experiencing very strong feelings of vul-
nerability as all the old barriers, patterns, and structures from
the past and from previous incarnations are no longer there."*

August 20, 1982
Suzanne present

"I'm going to count from 1 to 10, where you will please do a
reading for the channel from the Sympathetic Bridge Recorder,
with a focus on the current point in the continuum, looking forward toward the horizon and focusing on psychic and creative
development."

▼

Every act now expressed through the physical plane,
through the dream state, and through mental processes are all
manifestations of the seed growing within the channel's consciousness. Culminating in the next six weeks, this is truly the
time to end the period of development so far in this life. In the
next six weeks, as the cocoon falls away, this cycle will be a new
birth.

Links are now being made to future development, primarily through connecting with those in whom faith in the purity
of the channel is manifest through much strength in times past.
It is suggested that joy in beingness be kept in the forefront, so
that the process of sloughing off the cocoon's last layers will be
exhilarating, rather than painful or sad. This is moving along.

We see that the channel is ambivalent about this process, and this is causing the body, on the physical level, to manifest resistance to the next stage by throwing off poisons.

Clearly available for the channel's eyes to see, we see that there is only one main tract to be taken. Accepting this now on the most conscious level is the purpose of this reading—for this to be accepted, so that the death and rebirth are spiritually connected on the highest vibratory levels possible.

We are sending through the strengthening energies of faith in the renewal process. It is suggested that the channel keep the energies light and joyful, experiencing beingness as the lightness crystallizes into a new form, lightness and energy without belief structures or old attitudes constricting growth. Enjoy the sun and the wind, eat lightly of the fruits of the earth, paint and deal with others on light channels of energy interchange. Exchange beingness with beingness, without dealing for now with metaphysical philosophies or structural systems.

As this is a time to crystallize the lightness, structures within the light energy coming in are of a new kind than those formed by the mental. They are, in their purest sense, the Creative Forces' eternal validity and faith within itself. Their existence within the being is structure enough for now.

Beingness is precious on all its levels of development. It is suggested that this be the theme for dealing with self and others in this final period. And the work is going well. Blessings to the scribe and to the channel. That is all.

▲ ▲ ▲

Commentary

I did the following reading before a journey home to Chicago—the first in five years—followed by a trip to Los Angeles for a family wedding and to see my maternal grandmother, who was then eighty-three—my first visit to L.A. in twenty-one years.

August 29, 1982
Suzanne present

"I'm going to count from 1 to 10, where you will focus along the line of the Sympathetic Bridge Recorder and do a reading on suggestions for the optimum attitudes of beingness for the coming weeks."

▼

Yes. We are viewing the present personality Joan in a cocoon of her own making, a protection against the vulnerability of the freedom to access flow now available, so its impact will gradually be accepted as manageable and not so immediate in its intensity so as to frighten or halt the new development.

[Slowly and quietly:] This cocoon, developed by the personality through physical problems, is solely a protection against being out there, with the freedom to access the flow and the vulnerability of the new feeling. If acknowledged now, this will recede with residual effects so that, gradually over the next month, the personality will be able to experience the free flow of energies without needing barriers. As the vulnerability in attitudes diminishes, the need for any physical, external cocoons or barriers from the being's new intensity will fall away.

We view the coming travels as a time of possibly great emotional stress. Therefore, the personality has slowed the system down now, being very gentle with the self, so that she will move through the days of travel in a gentle, nonpushing vibration. Send to those relations the quiet knowledge of change in the self in a gentle, nonaggressive, nonjudgmental way, regarding their life-styles and the dichotomy between the personality's life and theirs.

So, while the development's exuberance and intensity will follow after return from these travels, it is suggested that the physical cocoon is now created for the personality to slow down, not to push or be too intense with others on these travels, as they would feel threatened. Rather, very gently exist hour by hour, day by day, in the beingness of the journey and, in quiet knowledge, extend to others that the channel is at peace. All is all right. Also, all is all right with the lives they have chosen. No push-ing, no judgment, no intense qualities of changing anything other than the self. It is suggested the vibration be very gentle, loving, of beingness in the moment, sending out blessings to all those one communicates with, for whatever their paths are.

It is not necessary for the personality to be concerned at this point with the physical symptoms, only to be very gentle with the physical being, with much rest. Also we see hot lemon water with honey, hot liquids flushing the system, citrus, fresh citrus, and sun, if there is no chill involved, and possibly steam with massage.

It is time now to gently acknowledge that the self is going through major changes for the coming second part of existence, and that it is paramount not to push the self or others.

As we are, shall we say, at the control panel, with our fin-gers scanning all the available dials and buttons, we are main-taining the energies of serene flow—no pushing, no more intensity at this time. As we perceive the physical reality focus from our level, the personality is now experiencing strong feel-ings of vulnerability as all the old barriers, patterns, and struc-tures from the past and from previous incarnations are no longer there.

Gently now, the source self of this personality is moving perceptions to a new place, as otherwise the shock of this sense of the new place, without a period of adjustment, would cause too much fear, feelings of being unprotected by ego armor. But in time, this will diminish. This process will be gradual through the fall. We will not say that there won't be times of feeling vulner-able, but this will gradually lessen as the personality becomes accustomed to this new state. Gradually, a new strength will form in feeling protected, with no structures or barriers needed.

We are watching and guiding very carefully at this point, and monitoring as if in intensive care. Each moment's vibra-tions are very special, as the barriers created by the personality are slowly dropped. That is all.

▲ ▲ ▲

Commentary

In retrospect, I can see that the phase of development these two readings address—the cocoon falling away—is significant and universal on several levels.

First, in astrological terms, I was then coming up on my Saturn return, a time to re-evaluate purpose and release old baggage—the parts of life and self that have served their function and are no longer required for the next stage in the journey. This Saturn return cycle happens to everyone in approximately their twenty-ninth year, when Saturn returns to its natal position by transit. The feelings it brings up—vulnerability and the need to let go of old ways—are ultimately positive. Those who go through this first Saturn return by holding on tightly, with ego blinkers obscuring anything new, are due for a period weighted by extra baggage, until the next Saturn return (approximately twenty-nine years later), when they will again have the chance to re-evaluate, though it will be more difficult.

The second reading has information on a physical illness I had at the time—a bad flu. The reading suggested that this illness was a defense to slow me down on the family trip and protect me in my vulnerable state. This is an interesting way to view positively what looks like a malfunction but is really an order from the higher mind.

Being in a weakened state on my journey created a physical cocoon, as my old ego fell away, that softened the intensity of my interactions with my family. That was good; since I was so excited about my transformation and wanted everyone to change with me, I probably would have been annoyingly pushy. The illness slowed me down so that I didn't overwhelm my family, and my physical cocoon served as a protection from their judgment.

5

BALANCE AS A FEELING TONE

"Balance will be reached by expanding the inner and the outer reaches of accessibility in the personal vibratory tone."

September 25, 1982
Suzanne present
"I'm going to count from 1 to 10, where you will please focus on the highest available source energy and do a reading for the channel on the optimum vibratory conditions for the present evolution."

▼

We are here and have been moving into center line position for the past several weeks. We are a group vibrationally connected to the channel's entity as guides of the initiate through time.

We are aware of the pitfalls and way stations of comfort and distraction that the entity, by the vibratory nature, has always found to put on the path. In this case, challenges again have been set up, and with the aid of guides and the channel's sources in the dream state, these challenges will be clearly seen and manifest as way stations set up by the entity as reminders of pitfalls from the past cycle.

Now is a time to obtain the proper vibratory pitch in daily living: willingness to be open to new vibrations as one travels in the world, without limiting daily interactions to those that are secure or comfortable—close friends or close to home—but expanding the ability to handle, utilize, and exchange with far-reaching vibrations. This will enhance resiliency of the vibratory pitch, strengthening its tone for inner psychic and creative work.

That is the challenge now, and it is suggested that much care be given to diet and rest, as the inner and outer realms are stretched further, thus enlarging the scope of the vibrations which the channel can interchange with and reach for in the work ahead.

It is time to look at each new encounter and vibration one meets, even if the interchange is brief. Recognize that each one adds, in a spontaneous, joyous way, to the repertoire of vibrations to be utilized in the work. Not to limit but to stretch, expand, have inner rest, then stretch again, absorb, utilize, then have inner rest again. On a daily basis, work on this balance as a feeling tone, and recognize that this balance with the new mode of operations—reaching out and inner rest—will evolve as the personal vibration is expanded and stretched in the months ahead to the point where, as the entity through the personality experiences changes of human vibrations available in the world, the being will be at rest and at peace.

As the personality retreats into the inner world to find rest and peace through creative and psychic realms, the being will also totally connect with the external world's vibrations. This balance will be reached by expanding the inner and outer reaches of accessibility in the personal vibratory tone.

Recognize that this will come naturally on a daily basis—intense outer and intense inner, intense outer and intense inner. Do not push one or indulge the other, but rather balance until the inner tone is on a line between the two. This will come. The feeling of serenity will be through achieving this balance in tone, not limiting it to either, and not limiting personalities or access for those who seek you out. Openness to the inner and openness to the outer.

This flowing process, to the very core of the being—the flow within the core of the inner and the outer—is the optimum development for the personal vibratory tone of this particular entity on her present path.

▲ ▲ ▲

Commentary

This reading is as applicable today as it was when I received it. As my soul purpose in this life is to achieve balance on all levels—inner/outer, male/female, matter/spirit, mind/heart—striving for balance in my feeling tone has a deep resonance. Through the years since this reading, my striving for balance on a broader spectrum has made me more comfortable and able to function on inner levels of reality, as well as on the physical level. This enhances my ability to work with a greater range of personalities and their patterns of soul development.

6

STATIONS OF INFLUENCE

"While there is a mainline source connection to the personal entity system and the appropriate personal spheres of guides, teachers, and helpers, beyond this, the system is open, just as space is open."

October 4, 1982
Suzanne present

"I'm going to count from 1 to 10, where you will please focus on the highest available channel and do a reading on the development of the channel's stations of influence, with suggestions for optimum interpersonal connections to be made at this time."

▼

Yes. Before the question is asked or considered, all the readings with the channel's hookup are already complete in their probable state. In essence, the readings are in capsule form, dependent on the channel's ability to focus clearly in a given session without debris on the capsule. She can absorb the capsule of the reading, and as clearly as her system is clear, transmit it intact.

Regarding the stations of influence now available to this channel, it is as if she were a planet, like the earth, that revolves on its axis over the space of a sequence that we will call time. She revolves on her axis 360 degrees, so that at any given point, as she revolves (based on the surrounding vibrations, the centering of the physical being, emotional and psychic states, and atmospheric conditions), she can, just as the earth revolves from any given point, perceive different constellations through the seasons. This channel can also, based on seasonal variations and timing, perceive and obtain intact capsules from different constellations or sources of information as she revolves on her own axis and moves through space.

So, while there is a mainline source connection to the personal entity system and the appropriate personal spheres of guides, teachers, and helpers, beyond this, the system is open, just as space is open. While there is the axis based on the revolution of the personal core, the availability through time and space is limitless.

To maintain the balance in the physical plane for the basis of this lifetime's work, we suggest that the stations of influence available to the channel be viewed as one views the solar system from the earth, rather than exploring the outer reaches of space. For space is curved, and through connecting with stations of influence in this solar system or channels connected to the earth plane, it will be possible for this cycle of the Creative Forces' energy to singularly focus on the task of uniting this solar system of energy in consciousness. This rather than expanding too far outside the galaxy —away from the earth's vibration, which is possible, but will not maintain balance for the personality in physical existence.

We are the conglomerate of guides along the main pole of the axis, viewing the stations of influence available. We feel that to maintain stability in the personality for optimum use of psychic abilities for the purposes laid before this entity's journey, focus on gently guiding those in the plane and not on exploring beyond this galaxy. While the personality is in the plane, she is, through creative and psychic work, a guide for others.

We see that it is imperative to remind the personality that while in the coming months there will be certain daily disappointments in the speed at which external gratification may come, this is part of the process. Obtain gratification from external sources based on the inner knowledge that the personality, at any given moment, is exactly where she should be. While it is important to continue making interpersonal connections for support, this is a period where gratifications should be focused on inner sources—through readings, through painting, and through friendships developed.

Once it is accepted and swallowed into the very cells of being that gratification for this lifetime can be obtained from the eternal oneness, externals will fall into place. Not to worry, not to fear about future externals, for that is slowing the process.

We may take questions now.

Suzanne: "Which qualities in a scribe—myself or others who may be the channel's scribe—are the most optimum?"

It is very clear to us that the major qualities that the scribe needs are twofold: an attitude, a primary focus, a vibration of willingness to aid . . . willingness to aid. Secondly, for the channel, the knowledge on an intuitive level that the aid will be returned. That is all. More questions?

Suzanne: "Are there universal readings available now on other stations?"

This station is a serene, benevolent conglomerate now encompassing the channel in a very healing, pleasurable vibration.

▲ ▲ ▲

Commentary

This reading becan̄ ‍ the foundation for my understanding of my role as a psychic guide with infinite access to available channels of influence. It was also a reminder to me that while I could explore channels beyond this solar system,* that was not my primary purpose.

---

*See Part VI, Chapter 6, "From the Other Side of the Universe," done a few months before this reading.

7

BEING FITTED FOR MY FUNNEL CAP, OR IF THE HAT FITS—FUNNEL IT!

"These 'hats' are funnel-shaped energy sockets that . . . transmit along the dividing line between inner and outer."

> *November 28, 1982*
> *Suzanne present*

"I'm going to count from 1 to 10, where you will please focus and, from the channel now waiting to come through you, do a reading on communications between planes and suggested methods for opening up new channels of influence and clearing up static."

▼

[Spoken immediately and loudly:] Yes, we are here, and we have been waiting for the new methods of operations between planes to begin operation today. Whereas before, this open channel system has moved toward her sources for readings, it is now time to balance these journeys. So, rather than her journeying out of the plane to come to us, we have come to her. We have journeyed to the borderline at which she allows herself to maintain operational standards.

On the balance beam of energy between physical focus and nonphysical realities, we have enveloped the physical being of the channel from the top of the head downward with a golden cap of source information directly from us. She has allowed herself to be receptive to this for clear communications with those she will be aiding in the plane.

So her vibrational energy output will be much stronger because she will be closer to them, and she has allowed herself to maintain on the line [between physical and nonphysical realities] so that we may now meet her halfway. This is the next step for allowing those she comes in contact with through the work to feel and believe that there are energies and vibrations and personalities and sources other than the physical, and realities other than the material, that are just as valid.

With this means of channel communication, the energies coming in will be undeniably valid; not ethereal, but just as real as the materially focused personalities she will deal with—although not as personally "I" or ego-oriented, as we are combinations, gestalts, oversouls of larger conglomerates of personalities. One moment.

So it is suggested that the key for the work ahead is for the channel to be open, just as she has been accessible to new vibrations within the plane. To be open for new "hats" that will descend on her in the physical being through readings. These will be, vibrationally, highly charged readings that will be transmuted, and these hats are funnel-shaped energy sockets that she may now wear that transmit along the dividing line between inner and outer.

Rather than traveling along the space-time continuum, it is through energy vibrational levels that these funnel-like hats will allow the vibrational source energies that she once felt as distant to descend and envelop her—without her having to move into the psychic realms at all, just by being open to allowing these new hats to descend on her. They will automatically, comfortably, and protectively fit, allowing her communication to be clearer, as there will be less space in which transmission static can occur.

The strains she has been feeling in her head and neck are due to alterations in the psychic and physiological structure of the nervous system that allow receptivity to this fitting. It has been going on for several days. We are helpers, allowing the fitting of these funnels to be as comfortable as possible. We are comfortable on this balance beam between inner and outer, as we are middlemen for source energies that are now waiting. With the funnel cap firmly in place, we would now like to allow a new channel of influence to come in, with a count from one to five.

[The count was made.]

We would like to open up this reading for questions.

"For the channel Joan, in which ways can she now begin—in daily life and through the dream state—to awaken these connections with personalities, entities, oversouls that are not of the personal ego structures, but are of a greater whole to which we are connected. Have you suggestions?"

It is not suggested that the personality Joan—in her daily life, in communications with others, and in her creative work—be tuning in to other entities or oversouls other than along her mainline structure, as this causes distractions and confusion in the personal vibration. However, in terms of communications between her and her oversoul, this particular funnel cap is being fitted to wear on a daily basis as a comfortable garment for open communications at all times.

Different caps will be available for readings for others, but on a daily basis for life, it is suggested that now the focus be on communication with the higher self: spontaneity and openness in expressing beingness in the moment and two-way communications between the personal vibration from the oversoul and spontaneity expressed in the plane, back toward the oversoul. In this way, the optimum development of strength of the personal vibration's commitment to the work ahead will be established by developing communication with the higher self. It is in a commitment to the self through this particular personality to express the Creative Forces on the vibrational level of the oversoul. It is the commitment to the self to be there in the plane, for self and others, and to recognize that being there is now the commitment to work on.

Being here for self and for others. Being here as fully as possible will allow for the optimum development of the energies to come in from other planes through this channel system at the appropriate times. But again, for now, it is suggested that the cap of this funnel system be of the mainline track of the oversoul of the channel's personality.

▲ ▲ ▲

Commentary

In the years since this reading, I have become accustomed to living on the border between inner and outer realities. The fitting for the funnel caps of energy felt like some weird surgery being performed on my head, but these caps have come to feel natural. In fact, typing this reading for the book reminded me that I had forgotten what it felt like not to have the funnel caps that afford me this access to other realms.

After years of becoming comfortable on the borderline, the time has come to be challenged in a new way and move on. I have spent years stretching further through universal readings and working on my emotional and primal bodies. Current personal readings tell me I can now live simultaneously in both physical and nonphysical realities—no longer balancing on the border, but using my core vibration, within and beyond the plane, as the point of balance.

8

GOING WITH THE FLOW

"This is a new aspect of not needing other human beings for security, as the self's possessions in any sense, but letting go of the definitions of what makes a relationship with another human being."

March 13, 1983
Suzanne present
"I'm going to count from 1 to 10, where you will please focus and do a reading on the present state of affairs, both temporal and spiritual, for the channel."

▼

There is no doubt that the present state of affairs is an accumulation from the reincarnational cycle of karmic debts paid in full. The different stages of development to get to this point are, at their points of clear-seeing, applauding the feeding they have done to reach this interaction, through the entity with the present personality, as the interchanges of energy replenish the whole entity network.

There is some sadness in the personality about way stations that she is overly fond of and yet learning to let go. We see the present sexual relationship as a stepping-stone in the letting-go process. There is no determining factor or need to rush. Just recognize that it is part of letting go on the sexual level, as has already been done on the physical, mental, and emotional. This is a new aspect of not needing other human beings for security, as the self's possessions in any sense, but letting go of the definitions of what makes a relationship with another human being. It is not necessary to define anymore as lover, friend, sponsor, parent, sibling. It is time to start seeing all human interactions in their full range and depth, not solely as the label or definition of what the relationship interchange per se has been in the past.

In viewing the present interchanges with those one meets, deal with crystal-clear gaze to those on the personal, group, and psychic interchange levels. Deal straight across with another soul incarnate in physical form, and see along this line all the dimensions available for interchange—with no labels, no definitions—that this is the next stage in the human interaction system.

Very importantly, we see that this can come to fruition in the coming week with the lover* and with the mother visiting. It is a time to open and let flower the vision in these areas. It will be returned in kind. One moment.

We see the relationships with the healer and the group work going very well up to this point. It is now time to let the emotions flow in with clear-seeing. There is the necessity to allow personal emotions to flow in with Aquarian feelings of compassion and love—to actually feel these. And, as is often true when releasing certain blockages, there will be periods of emotional vulnerability.

But there is a strong support network, and these feelings should be expressed to those who are close, such as the scribe and the sponsor: the feeling of becoming a personality and a soul entity combined on all levels in the plane, including the expanded emotional state this would mean. It is enlarging the heart chakra. To do this, all other channels of energy must also be enlarged to stabilize the system.

We see all is well with the creative work. As for the projected showing of the work,† we see the personality has some

---

*Paul returned unexpectedly the next day, after an eight-month separation.
†I was having my first solo art show two months after this reading.

tunnel vision, in viewing up to the date of the show and no further. In this case, that is well.

For development, many new channels will be coming to relate on all levels—temporal and spiritual. Work only with painting, with the psychic work, and with human interaction at the present level of intensity, and add to these the emotions. How does the channel feel about having the entity so close at hand? And how does this affect the personality Joan in interchanges, to express this for others? There will be a guiding light for the personality and for others who are moving along this path.

Coming to fullness now is a time when the personality can utilize the source energy, combined with all the talents developed through the reincarnational cycle, in this period and for the duration of this existence. It is a fruition of much work and energy, much development gone before. The entity reminds the personality to not hold back because of self-doubt, but rather express these feelings with those who care for the personality, so that self-worth and self-doubt can stabilize at a new level, based on the new intensity of the depth of the flow.

It is a time now when, in viewing the panorama, the personality is getting ready to step off a ledge and see that she continues along the same panorama with no earth beneath—infinite above and infinite below. Walking along the path, off the ledge, and viewing infinity in all directions—front, behind, upward, and beneath—and not losing or straying one step in the personal dance.

Blessings from the entity to the channel and to the scribe.

▲ ▲ ▲

9

NEW LEVELS OF EXPANSION

"The expansion from the energies channeled in through these changes will enlarge the spectrum for the personality's growth in beingness for the duration of this incarnation."

November 30, 1983
Sophia present
"I'm going to count from 1 to 10, where you will please focus on the highest available channel of clear-seeing and do a reading of the channel's choice."

▼

Yes. Energies are now aligning with this channel system that are gestalts of such immense creative source energy that it is now possible for us to channel in this information: There is a very high probability for the channel to expand through all dimensions within the personality presently incarnate, Joan, and along the whole channel system, as the entity concurrently expands.

At this point, we see that painting, work on the manuscript, and group meetings are now the primary structure for the expansion process. And recognize, while these three areas of focus and outlet for the personal energy are the structure for the expansion, that they are not the areas where the center core of this expansion will occur. They are the structure.

Utilization of the energies now available for expansion in the plane will occur daily on a conscious level, if the personality

233

now chooses to allow certain changes in daily routine. The expansion from the energies channeled in through these changes will enlarge the spectrum for the personality's growth in beingness for the duration of this incarnation.

These changes are: First, that one hour be set aside each day to meditate and channel these energies, to become consciously aware of the expansion process as it is ongoing. Second, allow more personalities into the psychic arena, doing psychic-energy exercises one-to-one and readings on various subjects of interest to both—not for the manuscript but for the expansion process and to feel more comfortable utilizing the channel system on a daily basis. With meditation and the expansion of psychic contacts, the channeling in of this energy will come. Recognize also that painting, the manuscript work, and the meetings are the structure that will allow this expansion in the psychic area to occur.

This is a probability that is aligning now because the personality has reached a plateau in her development, stabilized at a point of comfort, where the next level of expansion in the psychic arena can occur. This will naturally integrate and feed into the personality structure and will be the project evolving over the next six months. It will enlarge the perceptions in the moment and enable the personality to deal more expansively in the area of service, with a wider range of vibratory tones. Allowing this energy in through this period is enlarging the vibratory accessibility. One moment.

We will say in closing that all the work in the psychic area and in painting, ongoing and to date, is the strongest the personality has yet experienced. While consciously recognizing this strength and validity, also innately planted is the seed of complacency. And that is also why this message is being given now: Ever recognize that, as new levels of creative and psychic strength become part of the structure, new levels of expansion can also be explored.

We send blessings to the personality present and the channel, and a reminder to the channel that the validity of the reality of the energy now aligning is as secure a source for nurturing as the groceries that she stocked up on today, and of much longer duration.

▲ ▲ ▲

Commentary

This reading recalls the process of expansion I go through repeatedly. At each new level, complacency can arise from my unwillingness to move away from a comfortable plateau. In each expansion, I work to attain new levels of strength and energy, co-creative and psychic, that integrate over time and give me a foundation from which to move on.

It usually takes the internal nudge from a reading and the impetus from external events to move me off a plateau. Each time I think I've done enough work, I am amazed when my growth speed picks up again. Sometimes the process is exciting, at others exhausting. But once I surrender to the new level moving in, I feel exhilarated and empowered by this process that truly never ends.

10

THE NATURE OF THIS CHANNEL SYSTEM, WITH SOME UNIVERSAL DEFINITIONS

"The soul is the personalized God-energy of each entity, just as the entity is the personalized Higher Power of each personality."

December 29, 1983
Sophia present

"I'm going to count from 1 to 10, where you will please focus on the channel now waiting and do a reading of the channel's choice."

▼

Yes. The personality [Joan] was questioning herself last night about the nature of the channel system and its purposes.

Several channels of the system, labeled with names through the years, passed through the personality's mind, such as: Santos, the spirit of joy; Quantos, the male counterpart of Santos, who refers to Santos as his cousin, whose function is keeping track. Also other channels of influence, such as the Compassionate Hot Wire at the core of being, gestalts of source energy from further out in the ethers that have never been incarnate, and various others that have so labeled themselves.

Recognize that the labels given to these various channels through the course of these readings have been solely for the convenience of the personality Joan, to understand the vibratory nature of the channel's message to those in the earth plane.

However, it is time to recognize that these particular channels that have named themselves for the sake of convenience (with names based on the information's vibratory tone) are not static entities in any way. These sources, these guides, these gestalts constantly shift, expand, and explore on their own. Only in the reading's given moment is the particular energy of that channel ever available in that exact way.

As an example, let us say that the channel wishes to do a reading from the Sympathetic Bridge Recorder in the Hall of Records. Based on who the information is for and the vibration of the question, this is what will happen: Certain energies, certain discarnate personalities, and certain guides will be drawn together to channel in the appropriate information aligned along the track of the Recorder.

It is as if one were giving a tea party in the personality present Sophia's home, and you would say: "What is it like in Sophia's home?" And the answer is, of course, that it would depend on her mood, who she invites, the atmosphere and vibration of the day, and all of her guests. It is so with the channel system and the guides along it: constantly variable, based on desire and intent of the information combined with the personalities present, incarnate and not.

In terms of what we mean by the entity, the personality, and the soul in these readings, we would say first that the channel now speaking is along the line of the spirit of Quantos, who keeps track, and the vibration of this energy is primarily male. An entity is the conglomeration and the combined consciousness of multiple personalities that have explored both the physical plane through the reincarnational cycle and other spheres of activity—other spaces, planets, and energy vibrations—for development. The entity combines the knowledge acquired through the various personalities' development into a combined gestalt of consciousness.

When we speak of the personality's entity being on hand with the personality, it is that the personality has allowed an openness where the personal Higher Power—the entity—can fuel them and feed them with the greater knowledge and energy of which they are an integral part. From the personality, as an integral part of the entity (which is the consciousness of all explorations and all personalities within the entity system), we move to the definition of the soul.

The soul is the combination of the entity system with the consciousness of energy of the source from which the soul was born, the entity was born, the personality was born. The soul contains the entity that contains the personality. It is the entity system and more. It is the Godhead within each being. It is the infinite creative variable with its unique vibratory tone that creates the consciousness and desire for growth and exploration that forms the focus that allows the entity to consciously motivate and create personalities in time and space. The soul is the personalized God-energy of each entity, just as the entity is the personalized Higher Power of each personality. Therefore, the entity is the mediator between each personality in the plane and their original creative source energy—their soul.

The entity is the combined knowledge of all the explorations that the soul has undertaken in its creative existence through infinity, and its consciousness is not focused in any particular direction. It just is. The entity focuses in multiple directions, continuously expanding, creating, and growing within time and space and beyond. One moment.

In closing, we would like to make appointments in time and space through this channel system, with a deeper understanding of the operations of such, on various topics for the work now in progress. First, for the information desired on health and healing at this time of the race, the optimum channel of influence is along the track of Santos. Upon request, Santos will draw to its line all the necessary entities, guides, energies, and combined wisdom for the optimum reading.

For a reading on various diseases of the mind, labeled in this case as madness or insanity, it is suggested that the channel system align along the Sympathetic Bridge Recorder for a broader picture of the various focuses in which mankind has allowed himself to develop, explore, and define through history. One moment.

We are leaving [said distantly] the focus of this channel

system, as it is aligning with energies from gestalts that are from higher vibrational sources. For the well-being of this channel system, this alignment is centering the channel, with the vibration and the remembrance of the [inaudible]. We will open it up now, suggesting first a moment's pause. We are aligned now to channel information.

▲ ▲ ▲

Commentary

Though I always knew intuitively that channels were named by function for convenience, this reading articulated the fluid nature of the source energies from which I read. I could then stop trying to explain them with such rock-solid labels.

The definition of the personality as the focused part of the entity in an incarnation, the entity as the part of the soul focused on the reincarnational process, and the soul as the connecting link with All That Is also helped clarify for me terms whose boundaries were a bit nebulous, and after this reading I can see why. Because just as my various source channels flow into each other, so do these various parts of being. It reminds me of one of those dolls that open to reveal a sequence of smaller dolls inside. The last and smallest one doesn't open, but one can still feel in the process of the opening the movement of infinity.

11

CLEARING THE DECKS

"Need is not the issue here, desire is not the issue here, fear is not the issue here. The issue here is freedom in aloneness, openness without vulnerability in the negative sense, and integrity of be-ingness based on this open flow."

February 7, 1984
Sophia present

"I'm going to count from 1 to 10, where you will please focus on the highest available channel of clear-seeing and do a reading on what's happening right now with Joan."

▼

In essence, the personality Joan has finally given herself permission to expand, developmentally and vibrationally, to her furthest possible potential. The final karmic remnants, the last vestiges of the physical reality structure of childhood, have now fallen away.* Now the personality feels free on the deepest level to move on, to develop her highest potential, with no other vestiges of past entanglements to hold her back.

It is as if she has fallen through what has always appeared to be a firm structure, fallen through the trap door that she has created for herself. Falling through has caused disorientation, now past. The feeling is that beyond the trap door exists infinite space, infinite freedom. The need here is to develop inner secu-

---

*At this point in the reading, I was weeping, feeling a great sense of loss.

rity, as the previous structures—the foundations, the floor—that formed the security are no longer operative, but limiting.

So then, with the recognition that the personality has created the trap door and chosen to go through it, there needs to be a period now—four to six weeks—of working on the inner foundations for security based on clear-seeing of the path ahead, as the potentials are now developing at a rapid rate. In all the major areas of focus, the development of potentials will be the foundations for inner security.

Security will be developed and maintained within the being for the remainder of this lifetime, starting now.

▲ ▲ ▲

June 4, 1884
Sophia present
"I'm going to count from 1 to 10, where you will please stabilize along the mainline of this channel's entity system and do a reading on the nature of the present personal development, with suggestions for optimum stabilization in the coming months."

▼

[Very loudly:] The personality Joan is clearing the decks for freedom of being now with personal integrity, so that the work ahead will be joyful and the playfulness worthwhile.

Clearing the decks now on the deepest level of karmic interactions, which in this case is the emotional. The clearing here and the acceptance of such will leave the personality feeling freer in this incarnation, with less personal bondage than ever before. It is new and vulnerable to be clear in this way.

For the coming months: the house in order, then the physical being in order, then the mind in order, through mindfulness, then the soul in order through meditation. Playfulness in taking, through the fall, two days a week for outdoor sports. Parks, the country, the ocean, beaches, special [longer] walks with Luna [my dog] twice a week, as a necessary structure for the freedom of beingness.

From this all else will flow. The focus is on strengthening the ability to be comfortably centered with no emotional loose ends. All clear, all free-flowing, nothing left unsaid, nothing left unthought or unexpressed. All clear for the work and the play ahead.

First the home, then the physical, then the mental, then the soul. On a daily basis now, all energy interactions free-flowing. Need is not the issue here, desire is not the issue here, fear is not the issue here. The issue here is freedom in aloneness, openness without vulnerability in the negative sense, and integrity of beingness based on this open flow. Any questions?

"What about Joan's dizzy spells?"

The dizzy spells are a symbolic manifestation, as if the personality were a gyroscope thrown into the ocean, wrapped around with ropes of emotional entanglement. As the ropes unwind, the gyroscope spins in the water.*

These will dissipate quickly if the personality chooses to take the top off the gyroscope and swim away, and let the ropes' entanglements play with the gyroscope at their will. The personal power of this personality is in letting go with compassion by leaving the gyroscope there as a physical, external image of the personality to unwind, while the inner being is free to swim away. The unwindings are causing the dizziness. Not to fear, not to worry. Just swim free and align with the entity, to remind and aid.

It is not physically manifest through the paternal side for nothing.† The emotional bonds that pull the father are continuous, because he is trapped inside his gyroscope. The escape hatch is easy to open, but then one must *be* open.

▲ ▲ ▲

---

*Two months before this, I had made a break from Paul that was to last for three years.
†My father had dizzy spells from inner ear imbalances.

July 31, 1984
Sophia present

"I'm going to count from 1 to 10, where you will please align along the focus of the conglomerate of all major sources of energy available for a reading on the present state of development of the channel Joan, on all levels."

▼

What we are viewing now is the channel's ability to synthesize disparate sources of energy into information available to input into the plane. Of interest to us is the apparent ability now developing for the openness of this channel system. As with many channels in the plane, now and from the past, it is not just the channel's ability to align for information with one or two sources of energy or one or two discarnate personalities on the line of the channel reading, as is the case with this channel system. We also note the expansive abilities and flexibility of this particular channel to utilize many different vibrational points of view, perceptions from different points of influence in the universe, into a combined whole.

If one were to look at, for example, a computerized synthesizer of music, where some mediums channel one personality and some psychics are able to channel several different tones, this particular channel is able to utilize whatever tones or sounds are needed for any informational mode that is requested. While doing personal readings for those who come to her, this is not necessarily as when channeling information on a universal basis. It is the most optimum hookup now available to all types of energy.

The split that the personality has been feeling over the last week or so is due to the mechanisms of ongoing internal change on the electrical circuitry level. This is causing some disconcerting feelings and thoughts as to what the true desires for beingness are now, for there is a need to spend more time alone to get in touch with these energies and become comfortable with channeling them moment to moment—whether for information or merely feeling them flow through the being.

While the desires of the personality's old nature were to be amongst others on a daily basis, to balance and integrate this new development there needs to be a balance between time alone and time with others. Because of the personality's past desires, this causes some confusion as to this new, alien stage of development, causing feelings of imbalance as to which stepping-stone she is on.

Actually, she is not on any stepping-stone at the moment. The point of development she is now at has nothing to do with direct connections to the earth plane, but with connections to the Universal Forces, the ethers and the energy sources that she is allowing herself to align with now as a daily mode of living. So her present point of development is not one that can be analyzed or thought out clearly in physical terms, for the movement is not so much to higher levels of consciousness. It has nothing to do with levels of consciousness, but rather with the levels of beingness where this energy can reside through the channel on a daily basis.

It is enlarging the physical and neurological systems to comfortably contain this energy for the work ahead. There will come a stage with the need to balance this out in more physical terms, but this will not come until the fall. In this period, then, it is important for the personality's comfort not to resist these energies or the need for aloneness because they are new, but rather to recognize that the go-ahead signal was given by the entity system, as the personality has committed herself and chosen this path, and the momentum is multiplying.

Through this period, it is important not to fear that connections with others are falling to the wayside, for there will always be connections on all levels with the personality in the plane, as she so desires. However, as this energy becomes stabilized by the fall, they will be of a different nature.

It can be said, then, that the personality's dealings in personal relationships will evolve to a point where interactions, even in the most intimate relationships, will become much less on the personality level and more on the entity or universal level of communication. This is an integral part of the rebalancing that will occur for the personality to utilize these energies—not just through her work, but in her daily life. The physical symptoms involved [a sore hip] were only utilized as a very light knock over the head, so that this reading could occur.

You have a question?

"Yes. Can you give the proper information now to clear up, once and for all, Joan's negative reaction to whistling?"*

One moment. What we get is the primary disturbance in this connection. It is from an alternate reality—not past and not future, in terms of civilization or history, but rather in a personality connected vibrationally to the present one. An alternate reality, shall we say, utilizing futuristic modes of technology. In that alternate life, the personality chose not to abide by the autocratic rules of the state and was subjected to a torture that involved high-pitched sound in a chamber. This high-pitched sound was utilized until the mind cracked and the life terminated. [In trance, the channel experienced again the final moments of that life and wept.]

Recognize that this is not a life directly from the reincarnational line in the earth plane, but an alternate reality in which force was used to deny internal freedom of movement and individual free will. It is suggested that the personality turn this memory around, so that the whistling triggers the reminder that in *this* reality the personality *is* free to act based on free will. Rather than utilizing the whistling sound as a neurological stimulus toward breakdown, utilize it at a distance as a reminder that she is now free, and the sound in this reality can no longer harm her—to say, when she hears the sound, "I am free."

▲ ▲ ▲

---

*Over the years I had developed a severe aversion to whistling, the sound of which caused me pain in the head.

Commentary

Since the readings in this section were channeled, I have been consciously integrating them all and have experienced an exponential, continuous expansion of psychic abilities. The readings describe each developmental stage, clarifying each phase as I moved through it. I hope they are helpful for anyone who is beginning to develop psychically. I decided to include so many readings about my development as a psychic because the question I am most often asked is, "How did you get this way?" I plan to continue to chart my psychic development since 1984 in my next book, *Soul Flow: Psychic Living for the Third Millennium.*

Evolution never stops. We all have infinite depth and cocreative potential. There are the inevitable rocky periods, but the rewards have always been well worth it. I often feel like the "evolutionary guinea pig" or "mutant" that some of my readings have called me. But I have grown comfortable with this almost constant stretching of my being. It's certainly never boring and, on the deepest level, I know it is the direction toward which I have continuously been evolving.

Part VI

CHANNELS OF INFLUENCE

INTRODUCTION

When I was still working with automatic writing in the earliest days of my development, I received readings from many different channels of influence—some labeled by function, some not. After I received specific readings (included in Part V) on my own psychic development in the early 1980s, I began to understand that a channel system is like a radio receiver, with access to an infinite range of bands.

After that realization, I no longer needed the reassurance of labeled channels, and for the period when I felt all my channels merge into larger gestalts of Source energy, I simply instructed whoever was conducting to direct me to "all the channels that be." Since this intermediate period of merging, I now go to whatever available channels are optimum for a reading. Depending on the questions asked, I have sometimes felt simultaneous or consecutive sources coming through.

Included here are a sampling of channels of influence from the early days, giving a flavor of their different vibrations. In the first chapter are excerpts from the automatic writings, and although I have not heard from these channels again by name, I have always felt them to be a part of the channel system I draw on.

1

EXCERPTS FROM AUTOMATIC WRITINGS

"Consolidation is an art, just as expansion is. [It is] the ability to expand and crystallize at each step upward. . . . You must be willing to retain your identity while allowing it to expand and contain within/without, with those to whom you will communicate."

January 31, 1976

▼

The earth is connected internally to the five points attached through the center on a thread of blue. When you feel yourself outlined in blue, it is you and the earth resting peaceably together. From this framework, it is then possible to conquer the infinite variety of available subterfuges at their leisure—but not at yours.

The test of assurance is to recognize the ring of peace surrounding and enfolding you and to sing out the praises of all your HIGHER PARTS as they combine to journey through all space—all time—as the earth is within you, and enfolding you—[then] LEAP—and catch a ride going your REAL WAY HOME.

Reactions to the infinite variety of existence possible within the plane range from whirling dervishes, like Sean the Pauper,* to gargantuan leaps into the symbolic, like Houdini.

---

*A friend who, with all good intentions, moved so fast with so little focus that he was always broke.

Castes of souls reaching for a means of expression often revert to symbolic patterns of behavior truly reflecting the inner state of mind, or they revert to past states of indecision. Concentration on patterns will evoke the secrets of such behavior.

To reach the ring of blue is not easy for those who don't want to be at peace. For being at peace with NOW's existence means a time for inner movement, rather than outer, and doing the dance routinely or monotonously is a fear reaction to inner peace leading to inner journeys.

If one has a nickel, then to exclaim, "Oh Lord, what am I to do? I only have a nickel," will extend itself out in many directions. Say rather, "Thank ALL, for there is ME and I am here NOW"; then the nickel in its absorption will multiply into its proper state.

Consequences of the dance are to turn the music inward. For if one hears it only at a distance from without, one might finally feel the music moving in the same way. For the music never stops. Only the musician changes. And when the musician and the dancer become one, then the ring of blue can descend and it is time for the inner dance . . . of fire.

The eternal struggle for redemption from the plane is like knocking at heaven's door every day. Finally, the door opens and you are looking in a mirror. Some people do not like to look in mirrors very often, and some people dine on other people's food. This too is truly a pattern of self-denial and an indulgence in mediocre experience in the plane. Your earth should be felt as a protective seal from which you may travel and partake at will.

If one is thirsty and looks down a well, one will see his own reflection. You cannot grasp someone who is afraid, twist their face into the light, and say, "There now. Look into the mirror." One can only reflect the inner peace that will set others longing for what you have. And you have—yourself—a true love that never withers. The mirror is there for all those who will only look. Peeking is a start and to be encouraged, but never twist someone forcibly to look. It must be an individual choice—of readiness, of realization that something is missing.

One day, my friends, the earth will be a mirror of solid see-through souls.

Messengers of the Blue Line

April 2, 1977

▼

Revolving doors of the mind flicker past your eyes—briefly, spontaneously—as seconds unfold into your life's being. Why a revolving door? So that many opportunities can come into existence at once, frequented by visitors of exterior planets of the mind/soul.

Adventure through these doors. They are transparent for those who wish to see through them, and the echo of your name will be found to the calling of other parts of you. For your soul lingers like a star, pinpointed and exalted betwixt the tower of mind over matter, and will not allow these echoes it so lovingly directs toward you to be neglected forever.

Frolic through eons of moments
captivated by the existence of
a flower called Loa-ai
replenished by the dew
of tears of joy
squeezed from essence of love
upon
the ride of the twins
Announce your being's name proudly

Loa-ai
I call to you.

Echoes

▲ ▲ ▲

Late summer, 1977

▼

Physical anatomy is but a construct of psychic anatomy, the realization that as we form a system of souls interlocking on a more ethereal level than the genetic one, we immerse ourselves in this psychic/genetically constructed system as a means of soul races. From this, physical genetic patterns are born.

The anatomy of the different soul races can be discussed, based on the patterns which come out of them, for an inner intuitive bridge of beginnings to be understood.

Synestry of ancestral urges into a composite picture of corporeal structure can allow tracings of soul trees much likened to their physical offspring of physical ancestral trees. To compare such a psychic lineage is important—not for names or dates or places, for these are only of passing interest in a physical sense. If this study is to be delved into, there must first be an understanding that the nature of this work is to round out the soul—its patterns, potentials, previous and future goals, and operational standards.

There must first be the creation of a certain intensity of purpose on your parts if this study is to be done in an objective manner—at least as objective as can be seen from our particular part of the tree.

To satisfy moribund curiosity, let me humbly announce that my lineage is one from which you are twentieth-century offshoots. We are fondly known to our relatives as the Condensers of the Ultimate. Echoes, Messengers of the Blue Line, and a few of the others are psychic constructs of various channels of influence on this tree.

Consolidation is an art, just as expansion is. And the ability to expand and crystallize at each step upward is the motivating force to success in this endeavor.

Concentration must be given to the idea that without Jim as channel stabilizer, you would be tempted to maintain communications at levels much lower than your ultimate potential.

Saturation of desire with belief in your ability to receive this information is penultimate. You must be willing to retain your identity while allowing it to expand and contain within/ without, with those to whom you will communicate.

▲ ▲ ▲

Commentary

Unfortunately for the Condensers of the Ultimate, who indicated in this reading that they wanted me to channel a book on soul families, I was not yet ready to commit to such an endeavor.

It angered me to hear that without Jim I would tend to channel at levels below my potential. A year later, with this challenge still ringing in my ears, I put channeling on the shelf and went to Europe, partly to escape the feeling of psychic dependency on Jim. There I went to art school and tried a more normal existence with my then boyfriend, Donovan.

By 1981, when I was finally ready to start channeling again, with Suzanne as my scribe/conductor (and with the impetus from my higher self in the form of a physically debilitating condition—migraines and a swollen leg), I had developed enough inner strength to channel without Jim, without fear.

But as I write, seventeen years after this reading, I still find that doing personal and universal readings with Jim as my conductor and channel stabilizer stretches me more than would be possible on my own or with anyone else to date.

2

THE CREATIVE OCTOPUS

"As I speak, I feel other parts of me reaching in new directions, seeding to parts I have no conception of yet."

May 7, 1982
Suzanne present
"I'm going to count from 1 to 10, where you will please focus your consciousness through the next channel along the line of the present soul development and do a reading on a topic of the channel's choice—to stretch the psychic muscles and strengthen bonds along the web."

▼

For you, I choose to reflect my being visually. I have red eyes; my facial structure is interlocking rainbows. My consciousness frolics with squirrels, and I like sending seeds into children's minds so that their crayons look like rocket ships to them. Sometimes I feel like a creative octopus, but in a very friendly sort of way, because my tentacles pulse outward much more brightly. Using color, the ink that seeds your reality is that of spontaneous joy through play.

I also greatly respect those who explore beyond my realm, but [I] recognize and feel serenely secure in my position in the universe as a seeder of joy through the earth. I love seeding trees and flowers and playing with the creatures of the earth who do not have ego consciousness as disciplined as human

255

consciousness, and I enjoy seeding spontaneity in the young. I also have spent much time on the water, and part of my distant cousin's (in the plane now as Joan) longing to be near water is from me. I send her two strands, three strands of blue seeding ink . . . indigo . . . seeding cells of the brain . . . seeding through the being.

I love the earth plane dearly. As I speak, I feel other parts of me reaching in new directions, seeding to parts I have no conception of yet. I am another development along the future direct line of the present personality. I am not linked directly to the Recorder but, through the personality, I am linked. I am linked to others beyond and surrounding me. I am the center line through which the necessary vibrations from the Universal Forces will flow into the present personality for optimum development. Much seeding is happening now.

▲ ▲ ▲

Commentary

The powerful visual image that accompanied this reading inspired one of my paintings. This channel felt like my connection to playfulness, creativity, nature, and my capacity for joy, at times on simultaneous multiple levels and always in vivid colors.

3

SANTOS, THE SPIRIT OF JOY

*"Our function is to infuse the growth process not so much with
security or insecurity, self or nonself, duty along the path or no-
path, but rather in the steps of each moment through space, with
the connectedness of All in each moment."*

August 6, 1982
Suzanne present
"I'm going to count from 1 to 10, where you will please focus
and do a reading of the channel's choice."

▼

I am a channel through which passes much joy in being. I
have been through this line system of communications, briefly,
before. At the time, I sent greetings and called myself Santos.
We are here to express to you, and to the channel, the importance in present development of the joy of spontaneity, while
the shift is taking place.

For the optimum channels to open in the present development, we consider that the vibration of the endeavor on a minute-to-minute, day-by-day basis be one of openness and
willingness to experience joy in the spontaneous connection of
beingness in physical existence. This will allow a vibration on
all levels that was so often lacking in this development, specifically for the channel now speaking—not only for the self and
connection to the Source but also as a bridge for others on this
path.

It has always been our purpose to feed from our way station of influence into the physical plane and the appropriate spheres connected to it the vibrations we feel of the joy of the eternal moment's memory in the present moment. And the ever-expanding consciousness within the self of All That Is widens the channels for growth along paths that have never been felt before with this depth of consciousness.

So rather than a sense of purpose or duty only, experience the most minute sensations of beingness through whatever daily existence brings—the breeze, walking, talking—from beingness alone, creating on all levels, carrying within the seed of this vibration the joy that is contained within each soul. But unfortunately, through the development of the ego structure, the seed of this vibration is enclosed, encased so deeply within the being that seldom is it felt, except as mere glimmers.

In this opening now occurring, it is possible for the seed to birth on a living continuum with personal development so that it will become, as the channel becomes, more than a seed potential. It will become, in its creative thrust outward, as a full blossoming flower—experiencing inner beingness again, balanced with outer beingness. Inner and outer will be balanced with joy in recognition of the fullness of the moment, connected to the past and future by silver threads. But never before in this channel's consciousness was/is the present moment felt with so much joy.

This will automatically add new dimensions to the shift taking place and should be considered not as subsidiary, but rather as adding to the fullness of the shift on a personal level. This will allow it to be a time-space of incredible inner perceptions, of inner and outer love. And in experiencing the full intensity of the positive nature of any given moment, the only moment— [Reading was interrupted by outside noise.] One moment. Is it possible to close the window?

"Certainly."

Thank you. One moment.
There are silver threads being connected here. This being-

ness, this vibration, if it is developed and cultivated now through this period of growth, will be carried with the channel for the entirety of this lifetime as a foundation for spreading the joy and spontaneity of the shift in others.

Whereas the personal path of growth is, of course, of primary importance in connecting to the source self in the vibration on its universal level, we feel our function is to infuse the growth process not so much with security or insecurity, self or nonself, duty along the path or no-path, but rather in the steps of each moment through space, with the connectedness of All in each moment. For if the personal path is, at this point, the major focus without this vibration, it is limited in its potential as a channel for others.

On the level at which we are communicating now, we are being interfered with by the Saturnian aspects of the belief structure, as they are, shall we say, threatened by our vibration that on some levels invalidates their necessity as structures within the being and guides on the new journey.

As far as we can see, the channel's perceptions are split, so we will close with the statement that in this case, the lighter the load of the belief structure, the more will flow toward the personality. Through spontaneity in existence as the belief structure, the personality's load is lightened. The less belief structure, the more available space to allow energy, events, and connections to flow in. That is all.

▲ ▲ ▲

Commentary

The idea of "sweetening" the shift from the physical to the nonphysical dimension with joy in each moment has always been a motivating force in my own development and in my work with others.

Up to this point, my approach to life and growth was controlled and rigid, without much spontaneity. During this reading, I became split between the old order—of control through my personality's Saturnian aspects—and the new spontaneity and joy that was flowing in.

Since then, Santos's vibration of joy has been integrating into my life, gaining more depth with each passing year. I can now truly say that the primary vibration that I live from is one of joy in beingness, infusing every moment . . . when I allow it.

4

THE LEMURIANS

"Sometimes, as we sit in council, we must laugh because, as we project our probabilities through the alignment of the points [through time], we can feel them rushing back toward us from the backs of our consciousness."

November 18, 1982
Jim and Suzanne present
"I'm going to count from 1 to 10, where you will please focus and do a reading from the highest available channel* on new directions—both mass and personal."

▼

Yes. Could we have the lights down, please? Thank you. The place from which this reading comes is illuminated by its own inner light and—to allow the channel to absorb the vibration of these environs completely—externals are distracting. One moment.

We are viewing a panorama of points in the probable histories and futures of the race that align themselves with the present moment. Of course, no present moment in its corporeal existence re-enacts exactly along the line, but there are connections and alignments now being noted in the possible developments.

---

*I identified the source of this channel as the Lemurians, members of a pre-Atlantean civilization.

We see, in the early and pre-Atlantean experiments, a small group who experienced, to a great measure, the sensations of existing in exterior, physical terms while experiencing inner reality simultaneously. This of course enlarged possible perceptions in the plane of the expansiveness of time as the eternal moment. This experiment is aligning—along the present path and with the present company—because a point has been reached where the development of curiosity, exploration in the plane, and the development of ego structure have allowed again for experience at a new depth of what this small band once did: the simultaneousness of all existence in the present moment.

From a larger viewpoint, in that there is more depth to the physical vibration of existing with inner and outer, the inner dimensions, in balancing, will also have a broader range. This is along the same lines of expansion, but it is the next step projected from that small band to this moment, as they themselves recognize that they have gone as far as they could without developing further into the plane. This point has been reached now for rebalancing and re-aligning. One moment.

We are now at a midpoint between that small band and this one. However, we will attempt to move to them, as they wish to speak directly.*

Yes. We have projected and seen this development and we are very excited to experience, through your present, emotions of physical depth that did not exist in our present except in their projected state. We are sending you the skills and abilities that we have so highly cherished and developed to eternally balance inner and outer, the flows in and the flows out, as spontaneous as the waves or tides. All of your striving and your

---

*At this point in the reading, my perspective in trance switched from a mode of witnessing the Lemurians to experiencing directly through their consciousness.

work toward developing higher consciousness is again to return to our point, having incorporated the depth of experience in the plane that has developed through the millennium.

As we sit here in council, we are feeling new sensations as the alignment of the panorama opens. And while we have seen and projected this alignment and this occurrence, for us this is also very new: to experience this connection so far into our projected future on an experience/sensation level of physical depth that we have only foreseen. We are now humming with it.

When we speak of the full cycle, of course there are degrees along the alignment of this development. But in its full cycle, all depths, all experiences, and all sensations of perception are connected as one, along one thread.

We wish to pass on to you one of our favorite exercises—what we call the dance of the inner and outer. In it, we engage in the feeling flow at the same time that we physically feel our presence here through vibrations and in the physical being. It is aligned to the individual tone in terms of the movements, and they flow also as regulated along the individual tone. But the connections through this not only combine the inner and outer but also align the understanding of our uniqueness to each other as we dance.

We are getting the signal from the midpoint that the connections maintained now as a triangular basis are flickering. We will take questions if we can.

Jim: "What can be done at this time to stimulate and balance the flow, cooperating and integrating creatively between these two energy poles?"

You see, for us the emotions, in the human physical sense, were in a latent state, and we created our environment through the mental, fed by the inner great mind. In terms of creativity, we moved in a way, inspired, of course, by love. But for us it was—and is—a building structure of the mind. And as the emotions developed along our line with ego consciousness, perhaps our open communication with the inner great mind began to break down.

For our present communication with you, we send you the knowledge of our experience of mind as the builder of the external structure of physical reality based on our knowledge, from whence we came, of the greater inner mind's structure and innate order in the connectedness of the whole. From you, we feel the vibration of many emotional substructures that were only seeds projected as probabilities at our councils.

It is suggested that we interchange our knowledge. This will widen our understanding of our functions and align us for interchange in the future. It will combine our experience with mind and a loving regard for our connectedness as the basis for forming our reality and how, in forming your present-day environment, you have incorporated emotional validities into your belief structures. So that we may rebalance the strengths and weaknesses of these systems as we move forward to a projected third point, we hope for an equilibrium combining the best of the evolutionary process now ongoing in the consciousness of the race.

While we do not yet completely understand all your emotions, we recognize that while they have developed in the race very slowly through the ages, they are now ingrained as part of the structure that we need to deal with for realigning. This is accepted. We always knew, as we watched each of our generations move further from our sources, that there would be unexpected developments of this nature. Anything else?

Suzanne: "Is this alignment in its final stages, or are we at a point in the alignment that will continue further?"

Let us say that in each stage of alignment through phases of the earth's development—the Atlantean, the Egyptian, the Far Eastern, the Indian, and several others—we have communicated our connections and development on points along the way that are unique, as you are. When we express our communications through you toward a future, recognize that we do not know where the midpoint lies—only that we scan the panorama as the points line up. It is, in its probable state, a completed infinite chain of points. Where is the final? Where is the beginning? And where is the midpoint on an infinite chain of connectedness?

Sometimes, as we sit in council, we must laugh because, as we project our probabilities through the alignment of the points [through time], we can feel them rushing back toward us from the backs of our consciousness.

As we move back toward you now, at each count we will absorb again the vibrations of major points, bringing and aligning them through your physical present. That is all.

▲ ▲ ▲

Commentary

At each point in the count back from this reading, I experienced different phases of the earth's history, connected through my entity to the Lemurians and to the present. I have since incorporated these points into a series of paintings called the Panorama Series.

So far, the seven paintings in this series are: *In the Beginning* (pre-Lemurian), *The Lemurians* (in council), *The Height of Atlantis*, *The Deluge* (the end of Atlantis), *The Living Light* (Egypt), *In the Garden by the River* (India), and *Dragon Dance* (Far East).

My sense of the level of consciousness at which the Lemurians lived is much less immersed in the physical plane and more directly connected to spirit. Because they didn't develop fully separate ego identities, they could more easily stay connected to what they call the "inner great mind."

They seem to suggest that while we as a race have immersed ourselves more deeply in matter through the millennium, there have been some positive new developments in the area of the emotions as a deeper and more sensory-experiential response to the physical plane than the mental alone.

But they also suggest that as our experience of physical depth has increased so much over time, the next step in returning to their state of exquisite balance between inner and outer will allow us a range of experience beyond theirs. Balancing this physical depth would also allow us a greater range of experience on inner levels. They perceive that our development of ego consciousness as separate entities broke down our open communication with the inner great mind. Thus, breaking down the ego structure would allow us to reconnect on this level and line up along the points of time, in balance once again with the Lemurians.

During this reading and at times since, my experience of the dance of inner and outer has been felt as an exquisitely timeless balance between inner and outer realities in an eternal moment, without the loss of my own unique core tone. When I think of the Lemurians in council or look at my painting of them, I can't help but smile.

5

THE EXPERIENCER AND THE SOURCE ENERGY FEEDING STATION

"We are a feeding station, not just for travelers within the system of space-time earth vibrations, but we also send through other systems and realities that do not deal at all with space-time coordinates."

August 13, 1982
Suzanne present
"I'm going to count from 1 to 10, where you will please focus on the Sympathetic Bridge Recorder and do a reading."

▼

The way to me has been pointed out by the Recorder. I am in the records, so to speak, not as a viewer or recorder along the skein of time and space. Rather, I am in it more directly as an experiencer, as events and flows of energy pass through me. I can, as I choose, plunge myself into the midst of an epic battle at sea, or into the shadows of the curtain in the king's throne room, or into the chambers of the initiates in the temple, feeling the time of the mass nature of events through the vibrations of the souls involved.

As I move and directly experience the flow of events in the present physically focused space-time continuum of the channel and her associates, I feel this time as a coming together of several skeins of unraveling events. They are developments in the evolution of the ego balanced with the inner realms, to achieve within the space-time continuum a consolidation of various elements along the three main lines, merging toward a point which will culminate in a new vibration of beingness for the channel, at the age of forty-five.

At this time, we see it as our function to experience in their fullness all the levels possible within physical events, combining with soul vibrations and intents; that the present period in development now being enacted by our connections is preliminary to the next three months' explorations. This will be to experience stretching the sensory muscles along the psychic strain—to experience existence, events, and energy.

On this level, we have achieved connections in the flow we are in, and we are connected now through this channel reading to experience the same flow through space and time within the physical focus. This is momentous for development in that the feelings experienced in time will be able to be transferred through vibrations to others and be expressed through creativity.

It is a sense mechanism that all souls, between incarnations, can hook into at various points along their journeys. It is for us, as we are here always in the flow being experienced within the physical focus. For us, it is opening up new levels through which our energy can flow.

There is a channel, so to speak, waiting to say a few words. Count upward to five to reach it. Thank you.

[This was done.]

We are the source energy at the outer reaches of the earth's magnetic vibration. We are the source energy that is sending the necessary generative power to make the connection between the experiencer and the channel.

It has been and will continue to be our function to be the source energy to souls along their journey, feeding the necessary circuitry for experiencing levels of being without utilizing the space-time focus.

In its most direct line, this is truly the clearest sensory perception available for souls still in the earth vibration cycle for experiencing oneness along the grid.

We are, for your benefit, a brightly lit segment that has

combined its forces along the grid in an interlocking pattern or force field to send this vibration along the circuitry. We are also a feeding station, not just for travelers within the system of space-time earth vibrations, but we also send through other systems and realities that do not deal at all with space-time coordinates. To those available to experience new dimensions, we send messages of our functions so that they may understand the various dimensions within reality that can be experienced within the interlocking framework of the grid.

These are levels that experience their beingness, their creativity, with no sense of structure in their energy. We send you messages from these explorers also—as through this channel system, through us, and the experiencer, they experience some concept of structure—to appreciate new levels of perception for them.

Moving back now from this source and carrying the experiencer as directly as possible into the physical focus, we are pulsing much interconnectedness to loosen the grip on structure in this space, so that the experiencer can move into the circuitry. Three to one, very slowly please.

▲ ▲ ▲

Commentary

My level of consciousness as the experiencer has continued to evolve since this reading, which tells me that it will continue to move in, culminating in a new vibration of beingness for me in 1998, at age forty-five.

Interestingly, the source feeding station, a generator of energy, came through in a reading again in 1992, letting me know that it is now moving in at this stage of my development, which has been picking up speed over the last half of 1993. Working with numerous clients has enhanced my capacity to generate energy, to the point where I can now add generator functions to my channel capabilities.

June 23, 1984
Sophia present
"I'm going to count from 1 to 10, where you will please focus on the highest available channel of energy and go with the flow."*

▼

There is no life on earth that is not first reflected from the heavens. This is going to the source now. [At this point, I felt encompassed for several minutes by intense source energy.]

Picture a giant sun: source, star, generator . . . from which emanate infinite rays, each one a soul.

Picture now the two rays in this room directly connected, surrounded, regenerated, and contained by this source, no distance between.

If one thinks that rebirthing or primal scream is going to the source, picture that as one small pebble in the sea from the reconnection to this source.

From your deepest longing of desire to become—use your own image—from the deepest part of being toward your greatest potentials here, let your energies meld and infuse toward this creation.

[Long pause.] This energy is for transforming and becoming. It is not for doing, but for being.

Picture the self, as you know it, dying in this moment, feeling unconditional acceptance in the moment and fulfillment of purpose in the moment. And in this same moment, in the fullness of this energy, picture a rebirth of each cell of being—potential intensely contained within each cell, ready to ignite as a catalyst for becoming yourself, like a sun—source, not from the rays, but from the center.

We of this source-light recognize that this alignment is the final purpose of all earthly cycles. Carry this source-light within you now, and see that the journey is always where one is.

---

*This is a psychic exercise for expansion that, while given in a later reading, aligns vibrationally with the last one.

Just remember: There is nowhere to go and nothing to do. Just be, becoming more here. There is no there. It is all here. There is no journey, only clearer vision.

This is a source energy that the channel system does not wish to disengage from now on any level. There is nowhere else she would rather be.

Does ground control feel the source energy directly, or is there any question or desire for hands-on work? Your choice.

"Yes. Hands-on work, please."

Give it a few moments then.

▲ ▲ ▲

[This reading/exercise concluded with a direct energy session for Sophia, with me as the generator-channel of this source energy.]

6

FROM THE OTHER SIDE OF THE UNIVERSE

"We acknowledge that, for evolution, the only direct line of communication is through the hearts and minds of individuals."

July 19, 1982
Suzanne present
"I'm going to count from 1 to 12, where you will please focus and, from the gestalt of source energies now seeding the plane, do a reading for the evolution of consciousness."

▼

If, figuratively, one were to take a knife and slice through the universe, dividing the vibrations focused on physical development from those in the other half focused on other spheres of development, it is very clear that we would be in the half of the universe on the other side from the physical dividing line. However, we have, so to speak, skipped through this division, as a thread pulling together a schism, as the energies have become more immersed in matter and less ethereal. We are from the other half but are connected by threads to this half and have entered this half of the grid. We are, of course, very near the boundaries, but we are sending out feelers in all directions, pulling in energy from behind us, from whence we came, and sending it toward you to reconnect and strengthen the bonds of the knowledge of consciousness, before physical existence was even imagined.

It is interesting that those discarnate entities along your "Hot Wire" have picked us up,* connecting us through them to your voice, because these golden entities have never lost their memory of our function and have allowed us immediate understanding and access to the present development of the race with a compassion which we, under our own guidance, would not necessarily attain on first encounter with all this scurrying around.

[At this point, I was perceiving the earth plane's activities from this distant channel's telescoping perspective, which made humans look like little, scurrying creatures.]

There are very few power stations in the plane that are aware or conscious of their ultimate function. We acknowledge that, for evolution, the only direct line of communication is *through the hearts and minds of individuals of the race.* These are the builders, the creators of energies that feed the universe. Only through igniting once again these sparks of remembrance of our system—feeding, seeding, and continually creating—can the essence of the true nature of our functions be understood.

There is no ultimate purpose for the Creative Forces in the plane, except for the consciousness [of humankind] to acknowledge connection with the Creative Forces as co-creators, using the plane as a new means to express universal energies. All creative endeavors, all human interaction, all love of nature and beauty and interpersonal connection are ultimately means to the end of universal consciousness along the grid through all dimensions.

The fish that swim in the oceans recognize that they co-exist with the ocean, with their fellow travelers, and with the substance that makes them the same as that around them, only with a different consciousness in the cells. To a large extent, the race has lost this concept of the oneness of all energy, except in the deepest subconscious and in dreams. We have more understanding of the vibrations and consciousness of the earth itself

---

*See the next chapter for a reading from the Compassionate Hot Wire.

as an environment and a planet, of its nature and its love for itself and its creatures, than for humans with one another.

At this point, our main purpose is to rebalance the vibratory structure of the universe through seeding to the race, by whatever means we can, with the aid of the Compassionate Hot Wire, through whatever power stations we can, through whatever dream states we can infuse—with the knowledge again, the consciousness that we are all in this. The endeavor of the race to achieve a balance between inner and outer is an artificial boundary, just as the split in the universe is an artificial symbol. There is a probability that the luminous beings will walk in the plane.

We have never been incarnate in the plane, but we foresee that, to aid as a catalyst, we are seeding the new generations. We are also learning new lessons about creativity through existing structures, as opposed to creating structures.

We will meet again along these lines, and this channel is good for both of us. That is all.

▲ ▲ ▲

Commentary

The energy and tone of this reading were the most remote from the human vibrational system that I have elected to channel so far, although some others have come close. I believe that these source energies—which have never been incarnate in the earth plane's reincarnational system and have only recently been pulled into earth's vibratory range by the increasing density of the planet's vibration—are as close to what I would call "aliens," in New Age vernacular, as you can get.

Therefore, I define aliens as source energies or souls who have evolved more through other planetary systems or realities not vibrationally similar to souls primarily engaged in the earth plane's reincarnational process. But they are, nonetheless, made up of the exact same creative source energy that fuels the universe and sustains us all. While our human vibrations may at first be somewhat alien to them too, we are all swimming in the same cosmic ocean with co-creative potentials, and all made of the same God stuff.

Many of my clients, as part of their soul experience, have had at least some "alien" development in other planes. Those entities with strong memories of alien lives—whether conscious or subconscious—tend to be less comfortable being fully in their physical bodies, in the density of the physical plane, and with human emotions. But these lessons are exactly what such souls are here to experience and integrate into their soul repertoire. In essence, then, we are all aliens to some degree— and, as always, there is ultimately no separation.

Part VII

READINGS FOR THE COMING AGE

1

THE COMPASSIONATE HOT WIRE

"As each individual is able to consciously utilize this circuitry in daily dealings, the ramifications will be multiplied. This will position the race in a more positive light for potential survival."

June 7, 1982
Suzanne present
"I'm going to count from 10 to 1, where you will please focus on the deepest available emotional core from your greater being and do a reading."*

▼

[Two-minute pause.] Rather than a core, I am experiencing a very hot wire current that runs through all entities, connecting us all on an emotional intensity level. It is a hot wire current, a golden, highly electrical flow.

We who are here with you tonight are a combined source battery of senders and receivers of the impulses that connect mankind and the Creative Forces. These impulses are always available, are always open to send and receive on the circuits along which this reading is being done. The blocks and knots that stop these impulses of the Creative Forces from feeding individually and en masse to the race are due to the race's choice

---

*Due to electrical wiring difficulties, some of the recording of this reading was not audible.

to develop in the physical to a point that has not been incorporated or affiliated with histories or probable future plans.*

The circuits are always open, sending and receiving. On this level of the Creative Forces, the connection, one way or another, always gets through. It is what keeps you all from killing each other. At this point, it is suggested to aid in realigning the circuitry so that more of the Creative Forces' compassion and connection with the race is utilized for the evolution of consciousness.

The circuitry now being experienced is to be sent out daily from the channel, through the work with others and the creative work. It is to be passed on vibrationally with the conscious recognition that it is open. The circuitry is sending and receiving. As each individual is able to consciously utilize this circuitry in daily dealings, the ramifications will be multiplied. This will position the race in a more positive light for potential survival.

There is a concentration of forces ringing in its power, its focus, and its energy—not previously focused into the earth plane but now aligned for this purpose. It is a gestalt of many, many major sources now aligning to feed the plane with the seeds now being planted. The limitations are within each individual self only. From our perspective, there are none. We are dealing only with your perspective of your own limitations. Again, from our perspective, we do not deal with this concept.

If you choose to limit yourselves and your focus to the physical being to be one among your fellows, recognize that you are not helping them or yourselves. By being a receptor for this energy and utilizing it so others receive it from you, you are helping them in a way that being their playmate, in their limited focus, could never do. The rewards are in knowing that this is the next step.

[Long pause.] Who is the sender and who is the receptor?

---

*Two minutes from this point in the reading were not audible.

You see, we are both for each other. We cannot let you, watch you, allow you to destroy yourselves or detach from the Creative Forces. You are within us and we are within you; we are a part of each other. We cannot cut off our own wandering limbs.

Anything to ask?

"Yes. Why did our race choose to go so deeply into the physical plane?"

This is a very interesting question because, of course, there was never a conscious choice made on any level. As the race's curiosity developed with its other capacities, the physical plane itself developed more levels and depths to explore. Just as we continually explore new levels, new levels are being explored in the physical plane in how much of the Creative Forces are able to move through it, while still in the physical vessels.

How much heavier can contain how much lighter . . . it is a continual process that, infinitely, will be a full cycle.

It is suggested that the channel be counted from 1 to 3, with the circuitry intact within the system, outlining it with the conscious knowledge of its vibration. And we will continue to be with you in the dream state. [Inaudible] . . . love . . .

▲ ▲ ▲

Commentary

Since this reading, I have been integrating what I call the Compassionate Hot Wire into my daily life and my work with clients. As it moves through my energy body, it feels almost like a higher octave of my nervous system, centered and resonating from the crown chakra and through the heart chakra.

With psychic therapy clients, when we focus on clearing and strengthening the energy body and chakra system, I use hands-on work to activate the Hot Wire in their electrical system. With clients who come for readings and are working on heart level development, I teach them a self-love meditation using a mirror and affirmations to help them center an ongoing consciousness of this level of experiential compassion. Over time, this hopefully permeates the vibration through which they move in the physical plane, as it has mine.

2

SURVIVORS AT HEART

*"Only in the individual in a given moment can the flowering of
faith in mankind's potential for peace, compassion, and brotherhood take a leap forward."*

December 5, 1983
Gari present

"I'm going to count from 12 to 1, where you will please focus
along the Compassionate Hot Wire at the core of being and do a
reading of the channel's choice."

▼

There is no doubt that, by the nature of the experiment in
progress along the skein of time and space in which this particular probability of the human race is evolving, and based on the
rapidity with which current events are moving, it is of tan-
tamount importance that the concept of consciousness evolve
faster now.

Recognize on the deepest level that the human race is
made of survivors, whether physically incarnate or not. The
concept of survivors—as it is currently used in its limited physical focus—connotes a clear lack of faith in the eternal nature of
the soul.

For the most positive vibration to infuse the earth plane for
the trials and tests and challenges of the remainder of this century, it is imperative that the vibration of man's consciousness
be tuned to faith in the eternal nature of the race as it evolves:

faith that the race will continue along the lines of the present experiment and that evolution in hearts and minds is latent, that the seed is there and it will flower.

It is not so much a question of whether there is still time for this, whether now is the time, or what will happen in the future if consciousness does not evolve now. Rather, it is for each individual to accept the responsibility for the small piece in the puzzle of mass consciousness for which he holds responsibility. And recognize that only on this level of personal power and responsibility can the evolution of consciousness toward faith in the race's eternal nature be developed through souls, established, and nurtured.

It is so important to emphasize, not to avoid or negate the current nature of the mass arena, but to recognize that only in the individual in a given moment can the flowering of faith in mankind's potential for peace, compassion, and brotherhood take a leap forward.

It is not to look into the future, but rather to *be* fully in the present moment. On the deepest levels of reality, without the blinkers of ego consciousness, the given moment is all there is. It is the only moment. It is the eternal moment. The past and the future are contained within it. Accepting this, it will be possible to affect the hearts and minds of the individual and en masse, seeding through faith to the masses into the subconscious in the dream state, to shift the vibratory nature of the experiment now in progress.

Recognize that violent events, political and otherwise, are not all that is going on in the world. It is one manifestation, yes, fueling and multiplying negativity outward as it is absorbed by the masses in terms of loss of faith. Rather, look at these events and say not, "Is there still time?" but rather, "What can I do in the present moment?" What one individual can do in the present moment is detach from the negative vibrations of the experiment's dark side and choose to surround the being with the protective light of All That Is. Through faith and consciousness, one can radiate outward into the ethers the positive nature of

All That Is expressed by the Creative Forces along the Compassionate Hot Wire that is contained within each entity.

It is in saying on a daily basis "I care" and in acting based on this statement. It is not in looking at the negative side of events nor the positive side either, except for inspiration, but in bringing it down to the individual and recognizing that each individual consciousness acting along compassionate, positive lines within causes a ripple effect outward in all directions. That affects the mass nature of beingness in the plane.

▲ ▲ ▲

Commentary

This reading ended with a personal message for Gari and one for me, which follows. Mine was labeled "For personal use only." But that was in 1983. Though making my personal reading public would have made me uncomfortable then, it doesn't now. I include it because it might clarify, for interested readers, the source of my channel system.

▼

"Is there a message for the channel?"

We will just say, in reference to the ongoing manuscript and readings such as these, that—this is information for personal use only—the personality, as an expression of the entity, is a co-partner in all these endeavors. These readings could not occur without her acceptance of the responsibilities involved on the deepest levels of being, before entry into the plane.

However, because of the present development of the personality Joan, there is a need to separate the personality from the channel system as a conscious source for the information channeled in, and to keep these separate in terms of responsibility. For the personality and the well-being of this channel system, it is imperative that the personality lead a balanced life—physically, mentally, and emotionally—for the stability of the tone of these readings to reach as many humans' consciousness as possible, in terms of variety of vibrational tone. That is why the separation of conscious responsibility is involved.

But in essence, the entity is a co-partner in channeling this information, and the tone of the information is set by the entity through the channel system. The compassionate tone of these readings would not be possible exactly as they are through another medium. The channel system has been developed to take responsibility for the purposes of this information along this particular tone. Blessings to the personality present and to the channel system.

▲ ▲ ▲

3

WE ARE ALL APPLES

"In the new definition of karma, pass on the recognition to all others one meets in the plane that we are all connected to one large source energy, or tree—we are all apples on it."

May 10, 1983
Gari present
"I'm going to count from 1 to 10, where you will please focus and do a reading from the channel now waiting on a subject of the channel's choice."

▼

There is no need for human beings now in the plane to be as fearful—in their lives and en masse—of so many things. Along this line of the evolution of consciousness, it narrows the focus to the ego that has become the definition of responsibility in daily life.

To make an analogy (which in the future may not seem as absurd as it has in the past, as it may sound now for the general populace), it is like an apple on a tree. It is as if this apple on a tree full of apples had the consciousness to think, verbalize its thoughts, and its thinking was focused solely on itself. Its blossoming, its ripening, its future, and its fall happen without feeling or thinking of the connection between it and all the other apples on the tree.

Thinking of the tree only as it affects this particular apple, it does not recognize that the source energy and nourishment that flows to it grows from the tree—through the roots, from the earth—and also affects all the other apples. It is the same nourishment and, while its placement on the tree may allow it to receive more light and more nourishment, it is still connected to its brother apples, even those on the lower branches that do not receive enough nourishment and fall off before they have reached fullness. In some ways, it is *because* of this that some apples do not reach fullness. It is then the responsibility of those apples who do to be aware of the gift given them.

In the human realm, those personalities, because of various factors in the reincarnational cycle, who have the potential in a lifetime to have the fullness and ripeness of a mature apple can recognize it as a gift. The responsibility lies in knowing, in seeing, and in communicating daily with those who, for whatever reasons, are not in a position to receive full nourishment.

There is a commitment and a responsibility here to channel some of the nourishment and the energy and the fullness that they have to their fellows. Not just to clasp tightly to their fullness and in fear draw back from those who have not, but to see that it is a gift that can be channeled, even in small measure if in no other way, in the knowing that it is a gift to be channeled.

The fear here is that there might be a diminishing, even in knowing and accepting this responsibility. Rather, in the new definition of karma, pass on the recognition to all others one meets in the plane that we are all connected to one large energy source, or tree—we are all apples on it. We are all connected because we are all fueled by the same energy, which, in this case, has its roots through the earth.

There have always been such concepts as ancestral trees. In nationalistic terms, one may perceive one's countrymen as connected to the same tree. What we suggest now, for the evolution of consciousness, is broadening this concept to all inhabitants of the earth plane. We are all fueled by the same source through the same roots and, as such, all connected through the earth from sources far beyond it that created it. It is toward this concept that the race will be moving in the future, if the experiment now in progress is to continue.

There are lines of power moving into the plane now, lines upon lines upon lines, entering personalities with flickers of this recognition of which we have been speaking. In daily life and in viewing with the clear-seeing of the channel, this will become steadily more apparent in the coming weeks, as new connections are made for future work in all areas. It is now time for the channel to come out into the world, to be open to all varieties of apple, and to see clearly the potential for sending out nourishment in whatever directions are open and available.

Recognize that the nourishment, the energy, and the fullness that she experiences daily, while well-earned through the reincarnational cycle, are also a gift to be passed on to others daily—serenely and generously. By allowing this process to flower through the spring, the summer will bear fruits not seen before in this lifetime or this personality's lifetimes—new fruits, both inner and outer, of peace and contentment, as she aligns along new power lines. It is her direction along the same path she is on now, but aligned with power stations of influence, sending in much more energy and nourishment, as long as she remembers to channel them to others daily and not to utilize them solely for personal growth.

▲ ▲ ▲

Commentary

This reading fit easily into my belief system as a theoretical model. Over the years, this interconnectedness has been incorporated into my psychic work with clients, expanding my ability to work from a nonjudgmental, nondiscriminating heart level mode.

In my personal life, I can also practice this principle of nourishing other parts of my greater being as they are expressed through other entities I have allowed into my life. The

key word here is "allowed," because I tend to be more discriminating about who I invite into my life as friends. I have
accepted this point in my development; there are only so many
hours in the day, so I only have room for so many people in my
life.

But to compensate for this realistic limitation, I try, in the
way I channel my energies out into the world, to operate with
this principle of interconnectedness. The challenge is to maintain this nondiscrimination as I view those around me. As long
as I keep my ego out of the way, I can channel energies out on
the heart level to all those I see—without taking them all home
with me.

4

THE FUTURE DIRECTION OF THE EMOTIONAL REPERTOIRE

"It is no longer enough to evolve for the self alone. . . . Each glimmer of light one receives is a gift to be given to others."

> *January 16, 1983*
> *Suzanne and Nora present*

"I'm going to count from 1 to 10, where you will please focus on the light in your funnel system and do a reading on the nature and root causes of the emotional repertoire the human race has developed, and the optimum direction for future development of the emotions."

▼

Yes. Just as there is for the race—en masse in the physical plane—a finite number of variations on the roles in the repertoire of personalities, just so has there developed an emotional network system, a repertoire of available emotions. And just as the archetypal roles are finite in number, depth, intensity, and uniqueness, this is also the case with the emotional repertoire system.

Where the intensity and extreme nature of certain emotions have been developed and expressed by individuals, enlarging and expanding a particular emotional reaction system, in cases of violent emotions, as with certain personalities such as Hitler, the depth of the vibration has been incorporated en masse into the human potential system.

In the universal consciousness of mankind, these depths of emotion have been explored by some personalities for the race as a whole, enlarging the system and the depth of immersion into the plane through emotions, causing fear of disconnection [to Source energy]. But by manifesting these emotions in physical reality, others need not go as far in developing their emotional repertoire. We use the case of Hitler as an example first because, as we view mankind's direction and present stage of emotional development, there is a crucial time coming in the direction of the race as to the feeling tone of physical existence for the coming age. In the higher consciousness of the gestalt of souls involved in the physical reincarnational system of All That Is, there is now the knowledge that the race has played out the depth of the emotional repertoire to date, immersed as far into the physical plane as possible without cutting off all light. At this point, the light coming into the plane, in general, comes from the consciousness and knowledge of the souls connected to All That Is that are not incarnate. Here and there, the kindling of the mirrors of the light backward is beginning to be expressed in the consciousness of personalities. This is of vital importance for the continuation of the experiment now in progress.

We would suggest then, for the soul consciousness in all those personalities who now feel the light coming in and can mirror it back from whence it came, to start turning this lighted mirror of consciousness to others, rather than reflecting it back in terms of personal soul growth. For unless this mirror is transferred to others in the plane who have closed their blinker systems to this light, the development of the fear mechanism in the emotional network system will cause the experiment to not continue along its present development but alter radically, unless this mirror of lighted souls is begun now, in the New Age coming, in the next hundred years.

It is time for this message because it is no longer sufficient for personalities in the plane to develop themselves and their connections to All That Is to the highest level—to develop personal consciousness, the joy of being, the emotional repertoire to its optimum vibratory tone—for the self alone. Rather, in each glimmer of light coming into the being as the inner growth process allows more light in, rather than just mirror it back, we see it as imperative that each glimmer of light be given to others. Because of the vibratory nature of the race's emotional consciousness, they cannot now receive it directly from within, but can still receive it from others.

So then the new direction for souls experiencing the light and joy of being as they move through their personal, evolving dance is to reflect the light outward to others and recognize that it is no longer enough to evolve for the self and for the personal source battery alone. Recognize that, for the experiment of this race, in this time, on this track to continue, not just the optimum but *the only available direction* for the continuation of this probability is to mirror the light to all those one comes in contact with in daily life. Recognize that each glimmer of light one receives, as the gift of one's own inner growth, is a gift to be given to others.

The message is: Be a channel of this light to others so that their Compassionate Hot Wire systems can be reactivated by those now compassionately active with this light. This is a crucial point from the gestalt of souls connected to the reincarnational process, as the pulsing light is not being received by enough incarnate personalities to maintain the direction of the emotional repertoire system toward joy in the evolution of consciousness, rather than other alternatives.

The key in transferring this light to others is through the Compassionate Hot Wire system involving the heart chakra, so that in all dealings, the consciousness of this light will reactivate this channel in others and counteract the fear of disconnection that leads to the overdevelopment of ego. On the balance beam of inner and outer, this has gone as far as souls outside the plane can maintain and still allow light in—the light of compassion as one walks through the days of one's existence—triggering here, triggering there. It is in seeing and in sending and in being. It is not in thinking or in words.

The question of development of the ego structure and of

the emotional repertoire system has reached a point of depth in terms of a negative, grasping connection to the earth plane. Through the recognition of the light again, the spirit of Santos [joy] is available as the optimum vibration in the emotional repertoire for the coming Aquarian Age. We may take questions.

Nora: "What gives our brain this light reception?

In this time, this probable reality, the human race has overdeveloped the rational ego, which has developed the emotional repertoire connected to the earth plane in a darkly negative way. Vibrationally, the mind/ego structure has overdeveloped, so immersed in matter that while light is filtering in, affecting the emotional structures, it is, shall we say, overbalanced darkly around the heart so that the light comes in and the mind/ego darkens it within the being before it can be communicated to others in joy.

In this process, on the down side of reincarnational development into the depths of physical existence, the light filters in. But in those beings who are developed along the outer depths of emotions explored by other personalities, the vibration of the mind/ego does not allow light to flow through the being or outward. It is blocked by the blinkers of the mind/ego structure. More questions?

Suzanne: "Is it possible that, through this compassionate connection with others incarnate in the plane, we may become aware of the connectedness that does exist, and therefore raise the vibrational tone of existence in all facets of society?"

The key here is through the compassionate vibration. Allow the light in, share this light with others, for it will be easier for them to receive it from others in the plane because of their blinkers, overdeveloped by the mind/ego system. It will be easier to raise the vibration of the emotional repertoire system by sharing this light through the Compassionate Hot Wire vibration we all have—triggering this in others. For they can receive it from those who consciously see it, feel it and receive it from All That Is, whereas when it comes in as a direct channel themselves, it is dampened.

So then, raise the vibration of existence now. The gestalt of souls along the hot wire is sending it equally to all souls incarnate in the plane. But their consciousness recognizes that the light is dampened in so many that, for those in whom it is not, the message is not to reflect the light back as conscious recognition of your growth within being. Rather, reflect it to others, for they can receive it through you, and not directly from us at this stage. That is the message. More questions?

Suzanne: "Can the scribe ask a question for the channel?"

Yes.

"In the work the channel is now involved in—painting and work with spiritual groups—do you have some suggestion to facilitate or increase this filtering of light to others she comes in contact with and the people she can bring into these groups?"

We would only say to record for the channel the memory of this time: as she moves through her group activities, her personal activities, and her creative/psychic activities, that she bear in mind at all times as she views the panorama she is in the future self she is becoming, and not the ego cloak she is still wearing. So, vibrationally, her view and her words are based on the compassionate being she is moving toward, as the cloak gradually becomes lighter. With this vibration—in seeing and in words and in actions—all will be well.

Suzanne: "Can you suggest some way in which I can mirror the light of compassion to others or those whom I fear?"

The fear comes from not feeling and understanding. Those feelings are parts of the self mirrored in others that you do not have to personally express in being this time. It is [spoken very strongly] *your choice* to stabilize the vibration of personal existence on the compassionate level with the self. Then the next step for you will be mirroring. For now, the fear is in not understanding that what you see in others as mirrors of self is only possible if it is your choice to stabilize the vibration.

Blessings to the guest and the scribe.

▲ ▲ ▲

Commentary

In notes made just after this reading, I wrote, "The energy entering the room through me was the most overflowing and powerful ever felt." The reading very succinctly describes the emotional changes necessary for the race: making humanitarian connections and concerns a priority as we move into the Aquarian Age.

Regarding the reading's personal message, I get shivers every time I hear that I am to record that time as a memory as I move toward my future self. That's because, as that future self now, I am aware of the absolute priority of channeling light on a compassionate heart level to others. Then it seemed like a good idea theoretically, but it was quite a stretch as a personal priority (which refers directly to the next reading). On my recent trip to Egypt with Jim in the winter of 1994, the image they had shown me of my future self crystallized, from an awareness to part of my being. It no longer feels like a perception I choose, but an understanding that comes from all the experience and knowledge I have gathered up to this point.

5

EQUILIBRIUM BETWEEN INNER AND OUTER

"It is within the realm of existence to affect and alter the course of civilization."

March 20, 1983
Cathy present
"I'm going to count from 1 to 10, where you will please focus on the channel now waiting and do a reading on a subject of the channel's choice."

▼

There is a time coming where it will again be possible for more personalities in the plane to achieve a state of equilibrium between inner and outer, between the personality and the source entity. Aligning now are certain electrical configurations (the closest term we may use) in the ethers of the earth plane, to allow for an integration on levels much more minute than cellular that will bridge the synapse between inner and outer. The time is now coming when there will be personalities walking in the plane, viewing the world, and taking action in physical matter with a vision of the entity close at hand. It is not in any sense a denial of selfhood, but rather an enlargement of the very concepts from which humanness springs.

The motivation behind the electrical charge now entering the plane, allowing for this synapse between inner and outer to be bridged easily, is [very loudly] the intent of the souls of the guardians of the earth plane to infiltrate, by whatever means, the consciousness of the hearts and minds of the race.

It has been decided by the councils of souls that ring in and oversee the development of the Creative Forces in the experiment now in progress to allow, through this electrical synapse, more personalities to enlarge their vision of what is available and what can be done while in physical form. This we see happening in a network of personalities surrounding this and other channels. These networks will expand outward, connecting electrically and magnetically to others in whom this type of communication between inner and outer is feasible.

It is to reinforce within those personalities in whom this leap of consciousness is possible that it is within the realm of existence to be able to affect and alter the course of civilization. Only by this influx of entity consciousness into the very personalities of those now living can this direction alter the probabilities allowed for the continuation of this line of the experiment.

The key here will be through communication with others in the plane and in the dream state, not just in knowing and feeling, but in verbal communications that spring from knowing and feeling. It is essential to see that the evolving selfhood, ever becoming, can enlarge with the electromagnetic energy now coming in within personalities. That way, the concept of selfhood is enlarged to encompass the idea that the source energy from whence each personality springs has a mediator between All That Is and the personality. This mediator—the entity—who has overseen and directed reincarnational activities, is now available for access and input to increase the availability of the Creative Forces more fully through the personalities who are willing and able to allow their blinkers of physical focus to be lifted.

This will indeed change all concepts of what living in the plane has been about, such as being comfortably ensconced within a familiar network and biological urges and the view toward developing self through what one is doing, rather than what one is. These concepts are strangling civilization, switching tracks, and evolving consciousness into a more survival-oriented vibration.

It is now a time when there is not enough energy coming into the plane through personalities themselves, and the connections felt with nature have been depleted due to the development of urban centers with so many personalities cut off from the consciousness that, down to their cellular makeup, they are one with the earth. Therefore, the source energies at this end have made this electromagnetic energy available to bring the mediators closer in, to allow the channels to widen so that there will be more generators in the plane. They are generating knowledge and energy through communication in daily life that there is more possible in the physical plane than what has been available and accomplished to date. There is much more available to be done. It is only the limited concepts of what a human being is capable of in a given lifetime that has allowed this stagnation to occur and has closed off the potential for clear-seeing from personalities alone.

There is much now happening internally to the channel's structures to enlarge the available channel for energy inputs. We are experiencing, shall we say, too much information from too many sources, arriving at too small a channel to input directly. We would suggest that the channel rest much, eat very lightly, and find fresh air and enjoyment as the process continues through the structures of the being, as the channels are being widened for more information. The message coming in for this reading is combined from several gestalts of souls ringing in the guardianship of the earth plane. It is, in its intensity and multiplicity of messages, very, very concentrated energy.

We send blessings to the channel, peace, and rest.

▲ ▲ ▲

Commentary

A note made at the time of this reading indicates that I had overdone energy work in the previous week and was at a very low ebb before the reading.

More and more in the years since this series of readings, I have done the necessary work, though at times reluctantly or with ego resistance out of fear, to integrate my source entity with my personality so that they are one, acting in and experiencing physical reality simultaneously, moment by moment. I am now at a point where this is normal and comfortable, and I have developed psychic therapy techniques to facilitate making this mode normal for my clients.

It is important to recall when these ideas seemed like a stretch. If I don't keep this memory fresh, that will make it difficult for me to empathize and communicate with those I work with who experience the same resistance from fear of the annihilation of the "little self," or ego. This comes from not understanding, before getting a taste of this expanded sense of selfhood, that nothing essential is ever lost, but everything, in terms of consciousness, is gained.

6

EXPANDING THE CONCEPT OF HUMANNESS

"Ultimately, each being in the plane is only as evolved toward unconditional connection with All That Is as the weakest link in the chain."

December 6, 1984
Sophia present
"I'm going to count from 1 to 10, where you will please focus on all the channels that be and do a reading on expanding the concept of humanness."

▼

To begin with, let us just say that even with our hookups to the Universal Mind, we do not know how the evolution of the human race—the experiment now in progress—will unwind itself through time. There are many probabilities at play here, some based on original patterns for evolution through incarnation from the various races of consciousness as they moved in and evolved—in the plane and not in the plane. But there are also probabilities based on the patterns evolved to date, mutant strains of consciousness feeding into the whole, original patterns that could not have been predicted from the beginning of the experiment.

In general, by the consensus of those of us here, we would like to focus on integrating the strands of the mainline probabilities for the optimum evolution of the race in its unwinding and ultimate purpose, as connected to the universal plan and All That Is.

The next step is to seed these new concepts based on universal principles into the race. The link is between the Universal Mind as it connects to the circuitry of every being, through the higher mind of the entity linkup, to the personality now incarnate. It is phrasing the words to ignite and catalyze the circuitry, subtly altering vibrational tones of the thinking process about beingness—in the plane and not in the plane.

The primary perception that needs to be integrated into the concept of humanness is the true reality that each being is ultimately in the plane for one primary purpose. Disregarding all the ways of getting to it—such as reincarnational cycles and various developments along karmic, soul family, and sexual strains—the primary purpose is unconditional connection, through consciousness, feelings, the senses, and the heart, to All That Is with no differentiation. This is the primary purpose.

As a means to this end, there needs to be a recognition that, ultimately, each being in the plane is only as evolved toward unconditional connection with All That Is as the weakest link in the chain. This then leads us to the next planting of the seed in the expanding concept of humanness, in terms of evolution toward connection on all levels. That is the need and the desire to be of service to others. At whatever capacity, whatever vibrational tone, this is potentially within the capacity of each being in the plane.

The next step toward connection of consciousness to All That Is is to recognize that this connection will never be complete until the weakest link is raised to this level of connectedness. This necessitates the desire within each being to activate the core vibration of service to others—cutting across all judgmental boundaries and prejudices as to sex, race, nationality, class, and any perceptual stigmas, in terms of quality, mental capacity, etc. Also aligning is the need for all entities to ally themselves with the purpose best suited to their capacities, connected to the primary purpose and service, basing this on talents and gifts developed.

We see that the keys for the evolving of the race, from the mind/ego focus to raising the level of the vibratory tone to a more spiritual connection to All That Is, will be possible if the seed is planted of service to others, to raise the vibratory tone from the mind/ego focus in the material plane to the primary purpose of connection on all levels.

The clearinghouse will be through giving of self in service—whether through creative, communication, or administrative realms, production or entertainment realms, teaching, guiding, and healing realms or through the propagation of the race as physical vessels for the nurturing of the young. All are equally valid capabilities developed through service to the whole.

The key in the coming age will be to enlarge consciousness to perceive the connection between every being in the plane and All That Is. When viewing panoramically the seeming chaos of the world today, we admit this is a very difficult proposition. However, each individual needs to take responsibility for his perception of reality, raising it to higher levels of connectedness to All That Is and seeing in daily life the great challenge involved in maintaining this perception—no matter what.

It is raising the level of perception to a midpoint between the universal mind and the consciousness of the race as it now stands that will align it for more optimum future development as beings and channels of Universal Light. As it evolves, this process generates the creativity of All That Is, creating new universes from this concentrated way station of influence here on earth. Just as each in the plane has always been fed, feeding All That Is, continually generating as co-creators back to the source, so the source creates each individual uniquely toned to create the whole—each piece with an essential place within the scheme of the whole. And so it is. We will open it up now.

"Is there any message for Joan?"

Keep in mind through this period that the information just given in the universal reading also applies to her directly, in terms of primary purpose and actions. If she is willing to generate energy in the areas where her talents are developed, the fruits of the labors will be returned in the emotional area,* on higher levels, contained within the commitments made [to be of service] that are not within the imagination of the personality . . . yet.

The bridge here will be through commitment to the work, focused on the capacities developing to be of service with the psychic work, the book, and the creative work. This focus will generate the optimum fulfillment for this lifetime. It is not necessary to believe it, just to maintain the faith.

---

*I was crying as I spoke this.

7

ON THE THRESHOLD

*"The more energy each soul puts out in its own unique way to
light and nourish these seeds, the more hope there will be of conscious evolution bearing fruit to affect the tone of the coming
age."*

Commentary

JOAN ARNOLD: This reading took place on a hot summer evening almost exactly two years since my first meeting with Joan
Pancoe. Over that time we had both made fundamental
changes in our personal and work lives and had shifted our relationship from psychic therapist and client to that of author
and editor. Though the process was long and sometimes tedi-
ous, it was marked by an ease, reciprocity, and mutual respect
constantly refreshed by the book's contents and its affirming
principles. This final reading has within it optimism, ecumeni-
cal generosity, and a clear warning that it is well applied to our
ongoing explorations in this realm, or in any other.

July 14, 1994
Joan Arnold present

"I'm going to count from 1 to 10, where you will please focus on
the highest available channels optimal for this reading to give
closure to the first book, *Openings,* and a sense of completion for
the entities present."

▼

As implied in the title that the channel gave to this closing chapter, in each ending there is always the seed of a new beginning. While rereading and editing this book, the channel has many times questioned the validity and the point of it all. But just as there are cycles and seasons in nature, so too are there cycles and seasons, much longer in duration, in the evolution of the race.

And just as in winter, during the dark and cold nights when the feelings say it will always be dark and cold and one can sometimes forget how blissful it is when spring arrives, just so, in the seasons and cycles of man, does there need to be reminders and pointers—such as this book and many others like it that are coming through—to guide, to ignite the memory, to challenge and catalyze as the race moves into the next great cycle of its evolution.

Not all seeds receive enough nourishment, enough light, enough raindrops to burst forth from the ground, grow, and bear fruit. But the more sun, the more light, the more rain, the more nourishment spread upon the earth to nourish each being's seed of conscious evolution, the more energy each soul puts out in its own unique way to light and nourish these seeds, the more hope there will be of conscious evolution bearing fruit to affect the tone of the coming age.

It is for the channel to know that not only has the channeling and processing of this material nourished the seeds in her, but however many readers get one small drop of nourishment or ray of light from one sentence that they can use and pass on, that is how incrementally the race evolves, how change on the deepest levels of soul evolution occurs.

Through time, there have been many spiritual messages on the path of truth up the mountain—all equally valid in their own way, with their own tone, in their own time. This will always be so. To those who receive the message, watch out for becoming attached—positively or negatively—to the messenger, to the labeling or semantics or the packaging of the message. This is true for all spiritual messages at the core of all the major religions, and it will continue to be as a falling stone to watch out for in the coming age, in all channeled material such as this. We supply our own warning label on this package.

Partake of the message, if it suits you and strikes a chord in you. Unwrap the package and eat and drink of the nourishment within. Do not become entangled with the messenger or label or name, as it is and has always been a ruse of the ego to have a say and control its territory.

We send blessings to all those who are hungry enough or thirsty enough to partake of this or any other nourishment that can feed them, as all roads eventually lead to the top of the mountain. The messages in this book are just guideposts along one path that is certainly less circuitous than many others—straightforward, wide, and deep enough to contain and be accessible to a variety of tones and soul developments, with enough scenic charm so that the journey can be experienced fully—with joy and, we hope, with some humor.

▲ ▲ ▲

Afterword

There are two primary types of evolution of consciousness: one is of the individual soul and the other is of the race en masse. Anyone who thinks that they can affect true change en masse without first dealing with their own spiritual growth is fooling themselves. Conversely, once one is fully awake to their eternal nature, there is a natural impulse to spread this light around.

Many ancient spiritual traditions view life as a game, a dance, a school, or a flow. From the limitations of the ego perspective, the rules of the game of life appear to be that the nature of physical reality is ephemeral and insecure and that there is always a price to pay. It is only from the eternal perspective of the soul that these rules are seen as lower levels of the truth. For on the higher levels, these rules have great depth, meaning, and purpose. As one experiences life more as a learning process for soul growth, the laws of karma become the underlying structure of the game, and grace becomes available in the dance as one attunes and surrenders to the divine plan. This surrender to the flow of life is a vehicle that is both empowering and liberating.

Once I began to see through the illusion of control of the little self and surrendered myself fully to the flow of life, the shift to the soul perspective became much sweeter. As the illusionary boundary between my personality and my soul dissolved, my experience of separateness from others also began to dissolve. As I began to see all others in my life as mirrors of other parts of my greater self, the artificial divisions between sexes, cultures, religions, and nations all began to fall away as well.

Many of my therapy clients, after reviewing their primary reincarnational cycles in depth, reach a point where they ask me, "What's the point of it all anyway?" And all I can say to them is that once one is hooked up to the pulse of the Creative Forces, the energy compels and inspires one to evolve spiritually, return to Source (that's home in the game), and assist others in this process.

I have assured them, as I assure you, dear Readers, that learning how to play the game of life skillfully from the soul perspective increases enjoyment immeasurably as you watch the flow and are both in it and one with it simultaneously. And, besides, ultimately it is the only game in town.

I send each and every one of you energy, love, and joy on your journeys home.

Joan Pancoe

APPENDIX

Joan's Natal Astrology Chart

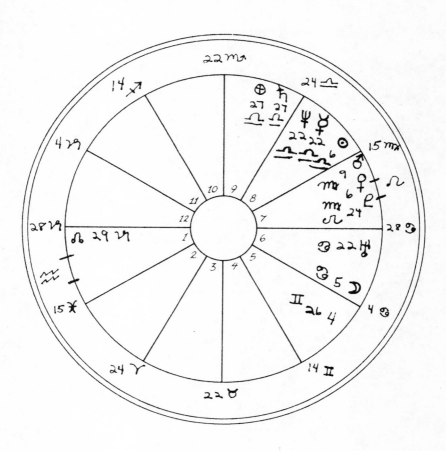

Equations for the Evolution of Consciousness

1. Time and Space

To the degree that one is willing to accept fully the moment in physical form = to this degree then will one's perceptions flower and live in the eternal moment.

2. Clear Vision

To the degree that one sees clearly one's own growth process = to this degree then will one clearly see the layers of depth in physical reality.

3. Choices

The distance of a choice from one in terms of responsibility for creating it = the distance of one's physical focus from the inner light of the soul.

4. External ``Baggage''

To the degree that one is willing to let go of external "baggage" = to this degree then will the vision clear and widen and the being become lighter, freer, and more mobile.

5. Openness and Freedom

The degree of openness, both inner and outer = to this degree then will one have feelings of freedom.

6. Comfortability

To the degree that one feels comfortable with the self on the conscious level = to this degree then will one allow others to get close to one vibrationally.

7. Making Love

The degree of openness on all levels = the degree of wholeness felt through the love act.

8. Wealth

The resources of the physical plane are available to be utilized = to the same degree one utilizes the inner resources.

9. Humor

The degree to which an entity has developed his repertoire of emotional depth through the reincarnational cycle = one of the keys as to how much humor is allowed in.

10. Responsibility

To the degree one takes responsibility for personal reality in physical form = to this degree then can the personal reality be changed.

11. The Key to the Akashic Records

All excess poundage of psychic baggage = in inverse proportion to the amount of information available.

12. The Third Eye

To the degree that the sense of sight is activated on the psychic levels through the third eye = to this degree then will the being have the capacity to view physical reality on multifaceted levels of vibration and purpose within the dance.

13. Fulfillment of Potentials

To the degree that the personality is able to maintain balance from the core vibration = to this degree will the talents and potentials for fulfillment on all levels be possible.

14. Helping Others

On the deepest levels of soul connections, helping others = exactly equivalent to helping one's self.

15. Karmic Debts

The weight accumulated through karmic debts in the dance = the weight carried when not incarnate in terms of potentials for expansion.

16. Openings

The lighter the load of the belief structure = the more available space there is to allow energy, events, and connections to flow in.

17. Evolution of Consciousness

To the degree that one evolves individually = the tone of the mass evolution effected.

Glossary of Terms
Used in the Readings

affirmation—positive thought implanted in the belief system to create a desired result

Akashic Records—the eternal history of all souls written within the ethers of time-space.

alien—a soul whose primary development is not involved with the reincarnational cycles of the earth plane

All That Is—God; Creative Forces; Divine Mind; Universal Mind; Higher Power

altered state of consciousness—a shift of primary focus to levels of reality other than the physical plane; trance or hypnotic state

Aquarian Age—the two-thousand-year astrological world age beginning around 2000 A.D., in which humanity, if aligned with optimal probabilities, will evolve toward peace, spiritual enlightenment, global community, and renewal of the earth

Atlantis—a lost, legendary island civilization in the Atlantic Ocean between Europe and America, said to have sunk beneath the sea in ancient times belief system—primary ideas or attitudes about life that shape one's relationship to reality

catalyst—a guide or teacher who functions as a facilitator to speed one's psychic or spiritual growth

chakra system—the seven energy centers of the physical body through which life-force energy flows

channeling—receiving energy and/or information from other levels of reality, ranging from discarnate beings to the Divine Mind or the collective unconscious

Compassionate Hot Wire—a circuitry that runs through the heart of all souls, fueled with the vibration of compassion

core belief—an idea or attitude ingrained in one's mental patterns as the truth; karmic belief

core tone—a vibrational essence of the individual soul carried within each incarnation

discarnate being—an incorporeal being or spirit that is involved with the reincarnational process

earth plane—the physical world of external reality

ego—the tool that the soul uses to focus and function in the physical plane

emotional body—the octave or level of the body that vibrates with all unresolved emotions from any incarnation

energy body—the level of the body composed of life-force energy (*chi*) that links the soul with the physical body through the chakra system

enlightenment—the state of being at one with the universe; immersion in the Divine with no disconnection or desire

entity—the personalized higher power of each personality; the mediator between each personality and their original creative source energy—their soul; the part of the soul focused on the reincarnational process experiment now in progress—the evolution of the human race along the line of the present probabilities

feeling tone—the vibration of being, emanating from the emotional body, that resonates with the core tone

Hall of Records—the place where the Akashic Records are stored

hands-on healing—channeling life-force energy through the hands to remove blocks and negative energy, to restore balance, and to recharge the being

healer—a person who is a channel for the life force with intent to be of service to others

higher mind—the level of mind fueled by the soul rather than the ego and capable of accessing a broader perspective

higher self—one's essence or eternal nature; soul

incarnate—to be in a physical body

inner child—part of the emotional body that holds unresolved childhood business as well as the capacity to be eternally childlike

inner guide—spiritual guide; inner voice; part of the greater being that is not presently incarnate

karma—the divine law of cause and effect; unfinished business that the entity carries from previous incarnations

karmic bond—a deep connection of two or more souls from past incarnations that is carried into the present lifetimes

karmic debt—what is owed in a present life to balance or complete a past incarnation

Lemuria—a pre-Atlantean civilization located on a lost subcontinent in the Pacific Ocean

mindfulness—a meditation technique in which full awareness is focused in the present moment

New Age—the evolution of human consciousness toward the light in the Aquarian Age

octave—a harmonic interval of vibration; a level of consciousness

peak experience—a glimpse of enlightenment; the realization of ultimate universal truths

personality—the focused part of the entity in an incarnation

personal power—the ability to access one's creative energy, tune it with the core tone, and use it to take action in the physical plane

primal body—the level of the body that contains the cellular memory of all earthly incarnations in any form

psychic living—living from the soul perspective as the normal operating mode

psychic therapy—spiritually based therapy that uses altered states to clear energy, emotional, primal, and karmic blocks and integrate the soul level of consciousness

Quantos—an early Saturnian channel whose function is to keep track

reincarnation—the process through which souls evolve in cycles of development, using the earth plane as a school for growth

Santos—the channel whose vibration is the spirit of joy

soul—the personalized God energy of each entity; the connecting link with All That Is; eternal being; energy essence; higher self

soul consciousness—the eternal perspective and link between the mind/ego and the Divine Mind

soul mates—two or more souls originally split off from the same soul or larger oversoul

soul purpose—a spiritual lesson a soul is working on mastering in an incarnation

Sympathetic Bridge Recorder—the channel in the Hall of Records whose function is to record soul development and karmic gains and losses

synestry—a term from astrology, meaning to compare two or more charts

third eye—the sixth chakra between and slightly above the eyebrows, through which the soul sees into the physical plane; the energy center through which the psychic sense of vision operates

vibration—the velocity of movement of energy or life force through a body that one senses intuitively from an individual

vibratory tone—the essential spiritual feeling one senses emanating from an individual

For more information about Joan Pancoe's work, please write to her care of:

Modern Mystic
P.O. Box 1748
New York, N.Y. 10009

For additional copies of *Openings,* place an order with your local bookstore or order directly by calling (800) 345-6665 or faxing (603) 357-2073.